COMMUNICATOR
STYLE

Theory, Applications, and Measures

Robert Norton

Sage Series in Interpersonal Communication
Volume 1

SAGE PUBLICATIONS
Beverly Hills / London / New Delhi

For information address:

SAGE Publications, Inc.
275 South Beverly Drive
Beverly Hills, California 90212

SAGE Publications India Pvt. Ltd.
C-236 Defence Colony
New Delhi 110 024, India

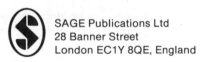

SAGE Publications Ltd
28 Banner Street
London EC1Y 8QE, England

Printed in the United States of America

Library of Congress Cataloging in Publication Data

Main entry under title:

Norton, Robert.
    Communicator style.

    (Sage series in interpersonal communication ; v. 1)
    Includes bibliographical references.
    1. Interpersonal communication. I. Title. II. Series.
BF637.C45N67   1983   158'.2   83-13720
ISBN 0-8039-2118-7
ISBN 0-8039-2119-5 (pbk.)

FIRST PRINTING

COMMUNICATOR STYLE

Sage's *Series in Interpersonal Communication* is designed to capture the breadth and depth of knowledge emanating from scientific examinations of face-to-face interaction. As such, the volumes in this series address the cognitive and overt behavior manifested by communicators as they pursue various conversational outcomes. The application of research findings to specific types of interpersonal relationships (e.g., marital, managerial) is also an important dimension of this series.

SAGE SERIES IN INTERPERSONAL COMMUNICATION

Volume 1: Robert Norton, *Communicator Style: Theory, Applications, and Measures*

Volume 2: Robert T. Craig and Karen Tracy (editors), *Conversational Coherence: Form, Structure, and Strategy.*

Volume 3: Margaret L. McLaughlin, *Conversation: How Talk Is Organized*

Volume 4: Howard E. Sypher and James L. Applegate (editors), *Interpersonal Communication of Children and Adults: Cognitive and Social Processes*

Future Volumes:

Brian H. Spitzberg and William P. Cupach, *Communication Competence*

Mark L. Knapp and Gerald R. Miller (editors), *Handbook of Interpersonal Communication*

CONTENTS

SERIES EDITOR'S FOREWORD

Our efforts to understand communicator style have a long history indeed. In ancient Greece, the Sophists discussed style as an important part of practical speechmaking. Style was one of the "five canons of rhetoric" formulated during Roman times, and it has occupied a prominent role in rhetorical theory ever since. Aristotle's observations on style are still included in contemporary textbooks. The study of style during the twentieth century has been largely a matter of quantifying various linguistic indices (such as word and sentence length, grammatical conventions, word choice, and verbal devices such as parallelism, alliteration, and metaphors) in an effort to understand their relationship to such measures as comprehension and perception of interest.

Why has the study of style in human communication fascinated scholars for so long? It may be the belief that it is a communicator's style that reveals his or her uniqueness and individuality. In that sense, then, questions about communicator style are questions about identity — questions about who we are most of the time, who we are with specific communication partners, who we want to be, or who we are pretending to be. This book, unlike most treatments of style, squarely addresses such matters.

The perspective put forth in this book, which brings together nearly a decade of work, gives a centrality to style that others have not. Traditionally, style has been associated with the manner of communicating, not the matter; with how communication occurs, not with what communication occurs. Norton points out that content also emerges from one's style in daily discourse. It may be in the form of instructions about how to interpret spoken words or it may be in the message emanating from what we believe to be a person's usual behavior. Viewed in this way, style has obvious and important implications for understanding the nature of metacommunication and the nature of persons. In the past, it was useful arbitrarily to separate style and content in order to scrutinize each concept more closely. Now, it is equally important to examine the dynamics of such concepts as they occur in everyday interaction.

This book differs from previous treatments of style in other ways as well. Style is treated as a specific part of interpersonal communication and as a nerve center around which other key parts attach themselves. Thus, while this book is about communicator style, it is also about listening and feedback, openness and disclosure, attraction and perception, metacommunication, nonverbal communication, and communication between teachers and students. Rather than parts of speech, this book is concerned with patterns of communication; rather than limiting style to the more apparent or explicit message units, this book also examines the subtleties of message delivery and the role of expectations and perceptions associated with human encounters. And, unlike previous treatments of style, this book recognizes that only through the application of both quantitative and qualitative analyses will we be able to understand fully how style affects and is affected by human interaction.

Teachers interested in helping others understand interpersonal communication and researchers interested in expanding our knowledge of interpersonal communication should profit from reading this book. It is provocative, practical, and pedagogical. Norton's departure from prevailing approaches to the study of style will surely be provocative. That is, his explicitly stated postulates about communicator style should invite testing and further inquiry. Throughout the book, Norton emphasizes the utility and practical applications of his ideas. Finally, the book is pedagogical. When Norton's own research has not yet provided a basis for answering an important question, he is not hesitant to ask readers to help him find answers — often guiding readers to specific quarries to be mined (such as further observational and longitudinal studies of actual dialogue or nonverbal signals associated with communicator style). The style of the book, like the author's own interpersonal style, is one based on inquiry rather than the assuredness of having "right" answers. Thus my own belief is that Norton is less interested in having his sophisticated research methods and years of theoretical development accepted as "the last word" than he is concerned that his book will serve as a foundation for innovative ideas and approaches to studying the nature and function of style in interpersonal communication. I think that this will indeed be the case.

–Mark L. Knapp

ACKNOWLEDGMENTS

Jerry Kline . . . for a first perspective.
Gerry Miller . . . for timely encouragement.
Jim McCroskey . . . who needed feedback.
Natlie Teethers . . . who never understood.
Loyd Pettegrew, Larry Miller, and
Barbara Montgomery . . . for sweat and dialogue.
Mark Knapp . . . who knows how to talk to me.

Introduction

the intimate union of style and content

When I was at the
University of Wisconsin
working on my doctorate, I
developed, along with David
Mortensen, a self-report instrument
measuring what we labeled "intensity" in
communication. Over the course of the project, I
took a job at the University of Michigan. I did not lose
interest in the intensity research, but a larger puzzle beck-
oned. Intensity seemed but one aspect of the way a person com
municates.

During this time, the work of Watzlawick, Beavin, and Jackson
(1967) both influenced and frustrated me. I preferred to make a
distinction between "relational" and "relationship." All style elements in communication have a *relational* consequence for content. The message gestalt, in turn, contributes to relationships
between people. With this distinction, I began to develop the
notion of communicator style, or, as I wrote in 1978, "the way one
verbally, nonverbally, and paraverbally interacts to signal how literal meaning should be taken, interpreted, filtered, or understood."

It was an adventitious definition. I did not have to back away from it repeatedly. It was defensible and understandable. The fortuitous elements of the broad definition include the following:

(1) The focus is on communicative interactions. This means that the phenomenon is observable.

(2) It is behavior that signals.

(3) It is a special kind of signal because it frames a message; as such, it is a metamessage.

(4) It is always a potentially powerful metamessage because it can change the primary, literal meaning. The change can range from complete negation to total reinforcement. It also can work along another continuum that does not range from negation to reinforcement; it can disconfirm, ambiguate, transcend, or obscure meaning.

(5) It always has pervasive and pragmatic consequences, depending upon how the receiver processes the intimate union of style and content.

Over the years, I did dozens of studies, each of which could be defended in a narrow framework, but the larger theoretical context took shape slowly. In fact, the empirical messiness of the studies tended to stimulate my creativity. Salvaging nonsignificant findings continually stretched my thinking. The sense of style as "form giving" developed after many years of reporting style work in a theoretical vacuum. As a result, inappropriate ideologies did not have to be defended and preserved.

Eventually, the works of three quite different scholars influenced me to commit myself to a perspective. In an ineffable way, the three people shaped my thoughts about communication. The combination of Gregory Bateson's roaming curiosity, G. Spencer Brown's precision and rigor, and Milton Erickson's deep pragmatism helped me to understand.

If one assumes that every message is a multiplex, then style research is compelling. The style element — that is, the way content is communicated — is inextricably part of any message. As a result, style is studied to gain insight concerning both purposes and values that stand behind expressions (Paisley, n.d.).

THE THEORETICAL PERSPECTIVE

The first three chapters in this volume present the theoretical statement, including the essential perspective about style, definitions, axioms, postulates, and hypotheses. In Chapter 1, the notion of the form-giving function of communicator style is introduced via an axiomatic framework. This is the "micro" sense of style. Two definitions, two assumptions, three axioms, and four postulates establish the theoretical perspective.

Chapter 2 builds on the form-giving functions in a "macro" sense. Style is treated as consistently recurring associations. A definition, three axioms, and three hypotheses are presented. The "micro" and "macro" senses of style are intrinsically related.

Chapter 3 presents the structural relationship among nine specific style variables that have emerged from the social science literature.[1] The structural relationships organize the variable set and heuristically point to theoretical underpinnings. Appendix B reports the long version of the Communicator Style Measure. A short form of the CSM can be found in Chapter 9.

SUBCONSTRUCT DEVELOPMENT

Chapters 4-6 show the development of three selective subconstructs of the communicator style domain: (1) open style, (2) dramatic style, and (3) attentive style. These subconstructs were chosen because of the wide-ranging issues each one raises.

Chapter 4 introduces the open style subconstruct.[2] The subconstruct was chosen because it makes a distinction between content and style — that is, information disclosed represents content, and the way it is disclosed represents style. In the Open Style Measure (Appendix B), the questionnaire asks respondents to make the distinction. Three definitions, one axiom, and one postulate anchor the domain.

Chapter 5 addresses the dramatic style subconstruct.[3] This subconstruct traces the elements of commonality across wide-ranging dramatic behaviors that may not be directly related to each other at one level of abstraction. It illustrates the development of essential characteristics of a form-giving component. The Dramatic Style Measure is in Appendix B.

Chapter 6 presents the attentive style.[4] It was chosen because it highlights a powerful interactive function of a style component manifested when a person is receiving another's message. In short, communicator style is not manifested only while a person is talking. A short form of the Attentive Style Measure appears in Appendix B.

APPLICATIONS OF STYLE WORK

The final three chapters report applications of specific communicator style elements. In Chapter 7, it is demonstrated that style impinges upon perception of social interaction.[5] This means that a person's style influences how he or she perceives the communicative reality. The suggestion is that individuals with a low dominant style tend to misperceive the degree of dominant style shown both by the self and by the other.

Chapter 8 relates style to attraction in a series of three studies.[6] A way to analyze style profiles is provided, and the conclusion is clear: Style affects perceived attraction. As such, the consequences are far reaching.

Chapter 9 shows the style impact on effective teaching.[7] Again, the conclusion is clear: Style influences the perception of effective teaching. This means that ineffective teaching probably can be partially alleviated through stylistic interventions.

Finally, an overview summarizes the form-giving functions of the open, dramatic, and attentive styles, points to eight areas to extend style work, and discusses twelve recurring issues in style work.

The appendices do two things. Appendix A summarizes the respective parts of the communicator style theory. Appendix B reports four measures referenced in this book. In particular, it reproduces the long form of the Communicator Style Measure, the long version of the Dramatic Style Measure, and the shortened versions of the Open Style and the Attentive Style measures.

In some ways this work escalates the complexity of analyzing the communicative process by its focus on the ever-present stylistic impact on content. On the other hand, it simplifies the analysis of the communicative process by allowing for explanations to be distributed across a hierarchical model. This work provides a framework within which to explore. It also offers a touchstone for further style work. Although this book is the first theoretical statement about communicator style, it is hoped that it will stimulate more insightful, exciting, and satisfying understanding about the interactions that bind and separate humans.

NOTES

1. The initial statement for this chapter appeared in Norton (1978). This chapter presents a more precise and integrated version of the initial article.

2. This work represents a collaborative effort with Barbara Montgomery (see Norton & Montgomery, 1982). This chapter is an extension and amplification of that work; it is my hope that the changes made here reflect the spirit of the original work.

3. This chapter emerged from the synthesis of two convention papers: Norton, Sypher, and Bradey (1978) and Norton, Baker, Bednar, Salyer, and McGough (1978).

4. The initial statement for this chapter appeared in Norton and Pettegrew (1976). This chapter extends and amplifies the original work.

5. The initial statement for this chapter appears in Norton and Miller (1975). Miller (1977) then replicated and extended the original work, and then extended it still further (Miller, 1980). This chapter represents a synthesis of these works.

6. This chapter synthesizes the initial work by Norton and Pettegrew (1977).

7. This chapter synthesizes a series of style works focusing on effective teaching, including the following: Norton (1977), Norton and Nussbaum (1980), Norton, Andersen, and Nussbaum (1981), Norton (1980b), and Norton and Holladay (1983).

I

THEORETICAL
PERSPECTIVE

1 / Monitoring Content

the form-giving function of communicator style

Two concepts of style emerge from the social science literature. Both perspectives (which are interdependent) have been used to develop the communicator style domain. Both perspectives lead to conclusions such as the following. The *way* a person communicates to a large extent determines self-identity and affects others' perceptions of the individual. The person's communicator style contributes to and reflects whether the person likes the self. It influences both the amount and kinds of rewards and punishments the person perceives from others.

In the first sense, style is seen as a function that *gives form to content.* In this sense, communicator style is broadly conceived to mean "the way one verbally, nonverbally, and paraverbally interacts to signal how literal meaning should be taken, interpreted, filtered, or understood." Style is a message about content.

In the second sense, style is seen as a function of *consistently recurring communicative associations.* Here style not only entails the first function, but is the relatively enduring pattern of human interaction associated with the individual. Observed behavior triggers the associations. This does not mean that the pattern is invariant across situation, context, or time. It does mean that the pattern is sufficiently recurring and consistent that at least one person reliably associates it with the individual.

In this chapter, an initial theoretical statement is presented regarding the first sense of style — namely, the form-giving function. Style as a recurring association will be explored in the next chapter. The organization of this chapter begins inductively. Divergent, informal examples are introduced from which a concept of style as form giving emerges in a suggestive, rather than a rigorous, way. In the second part of this chapter, formal characteristics of style functions will be presented.

STYLE AS FORM GIVING

Style gives form to content. This means that signals create expectations or provide instructions about what to do with literal meaning. The signals are, in effect, metamessages relating to information processing. Some examples from the animal world, from music, and from computer technology provide instances of wide-ranging types of message systems in which style gives form to the final message — that is, the gestalt.

Social Interaction of Rats

Rats exhibit a curious combination of primitive social mechanisms coupled with a repertory of social abilities normally expected only of higher mammals (Lore & Flannelly, 1978). Surprisingly, the social interaction entails form-giving components. In a series of carefully controlled experiments, the same male intruder rat was put into the cage of an established resident rat on two occasions. On the first occasion, the resident fought the intruder *even though the intruder signaled submission.* Both rats typically lost a considerable amount of weight (18 grams) during the 24-hour test. When the now experienced intruder rat was put into the cage of a second resident rat a week later, however, no serious fighting ensued and both animals maintained their body weights.

Visually, the intruder rat sniffed, followed, approached, paid attention, and again signaled submission no differently than the first time. Yet the experience of a single defeat taught the intruder something. He learned how to inhibit the attack of the resident rat.

On the second encounter, the intruder rat emitted long trains of ultrasonic cries (in the range of 20 to 25 kilohertz). He cried ultrasonically early and often. He cried out three times as often with nine times the duration of the first encounter. Sometimes the calls fell within the audible range. To the human ear they sounded remarkably like the whimpering of an injured dog (Lore & Flannelly, 1978).

Both rats lost only about five grams in the second encounter. It was as though the submissive posturing *in conjunction with* a certain kind of cry eliminated enough ambiguity for the resident rat that he interpreted the visual behavior in a qualitatively different manner.

The way the intruder signaled the second time shaped critical information for the resident such that something important happened. The ultrasonic cries sufficiently validated the submissive posturing. The cries functioned at a meta level, essentially communicating the message, "Take this submissive posturing seriously!" Two information systems were used. The audio system impinged upon the visual. It gave form or framed the necessary, although not sufficient, but expected visual information (see Model 1.1). The intruder rat avoided negative consequences only when the gestalt was the interaction of unambiguous information from both the visual and the audio.

A Theory of Play

Form-giving messages have many intriguing functions. Bateson (1972b) argues that they are needed to identify the notion of play. The idea was suggested to Bateson when he saw two young monkeys playing. They were "engaged in an interactive sequence of which the unit actions or signals were similar to, but not the same as those of combat." Bateson maintains that the phenomenon, play, could happen only if the monkeys metacommunicated, that is, they had to signal at some level that "this is play." Bateson (1972b) explains that the statement "this is play" looks something like this: "These actions in which we now engage do not denote what those actions for which they stand would denote." In a loose sense, the gestalt says that something is "true" and "not true" almost simultaneously — namely, "this is combat" and "this is not combat." The two messages, both unambiguous by themselves, *interactively create an ambiguous gestalt momentarily.*

The physical actions that look like combat roughly correspond to the literal message. The almost simultaneous, implicit, negative metastatement — these actions that look like combat, but are not

	VISUAL INFORMATION	
	AMBIGUOUS INFORMATION Fails to Signal Visual Submissiveness	UNAMBIGUOUS INFORMATION Signals Visual Submissiveness
AMBIGUOUS INFORMATION Weak Ultrasonic Cries	uncertain must defend territory fight for dominance	submissive signals not sufficient fighting weight loss
UNAMBIGUOUS INFORMATION Strong Ultrasonic Cries	nonsensical message necessary visual missing	submissive signals sufficient no fighting no weight loss

AUDITORY INFORMATION (row-axis label)

Model 1.1

having the immediate consequences of combat — gives form to the first message. The second message signals how to take the first message.

In watching my daughter learn about play I observed parallels to some of Bateson's observations. When I first tossed Sarah into the air, her eyes got big, her smile disappeared, and her body reacted involuntarily, probably signaling a message such as "this is danger" to the brain. It was no longer a simple gestalt. There were confounding messages. The body says, "This looks like danger." The mind says, "But it does not have the same consequences." "So what is this sequence that looks like danger with its accompanying theatrics/thrills/rushes, but is not?" "It is play." Of course, this projected series of linguistic connections probably did not happen formally, but something like it may have occurred.

The "but-it-is-not" gives form over the physical toss entailing the "it-is-danger" message. The dual messages composed of an unambiguous physiological reaction followed immediately by an unambiguous metastatement momentarily creates an ambiguous gestalt, which is processed at a more complex level and has more complex consequences for human relationships, such as, "Daddy is playing with me because he loves me."

Establishing Trust with Porpoises

Watzlawick et al. (1967) report a similar phenomenon with porpoises in establishing trust between these animals and humans:

> The animals had obviously concluded that the hand is one of the most important and vulnerable parts of the human body. Each would seek to establish contact with a stranger by taking the human's hand into his mouth and gently squeezing it between his jaws, which have sharp teeth and are powerful enough to bite the hand off cleanly.

As in the example with the monkeys, the gestalt contains dual messages. The analogical message, namely, the pressure from the teeth, works like a literal message — "I can bite off this hand." The second message, embedded in the *absence* of physical injury, frames the first message. This is another instance in which the form-giving element is not simultaneous with, but subsequent to the first message.

Within the boundaries of the communicative act, an "X" and a "not X" occur. The indication of an unfulfilled possibility that could easily be executed but is not provides the basis for trust. Watzlawick et al. (1967) offer the following evidence that the complex gestalt strongly affects the relationship:

> If the human would submit to this, the dolphin seemed to accept it as a message of complete trust. His next move was to reciprocate by placing the forward ventral position of his body (*his* most vulnerable part, roughly equivalent in location to the human throat) upon the human's hand, leg, or foot, thereby signaling his trust in the friendly intentions of the human. The authors admit that the above description is obviously fraught with possible misinterpretation at every step, and, in fact, may be a ritual developed "privately" by only the two animals they saw. Even as a ritual, the examples illustrate a metamessage shaping an initial message.

Improvising Jazz

Form giving happens in music, also. The difference between a jazz and a classical version of "White Christmas" is stylistic. So is the difference between one jazz rendition and another. Even within a particular musician's performance, stylistic components pervade the presentation.

Jazz improvisation is an interesting example. Sudnow (1978) describes how he learned improvisation in the *Ways of the Hand*. The melody-producing reaches of the right hand function something like a literal message. The left hand, which provides the "jazz sound," accents the melody. The form-giving capacity of the left hand is a difficult talent to develop. Sudnow (1978) explains:

> Only after years of play do beginners attain full-fledged competence at place finding that the jazz pianist's left hand displays in chord execution. Reaching the point where, with eyes closed, I can sit down at the piano, gain an initial orientation with the merest touch "anywhere" on the field, then reach out and bring my finger precisely into a spot "two feet" off to my left, where a half inch off is a mistake, come back up "seventeen inches" and get there at a fast clip took a course of gradual incorporation.

When he was having trouble, left-hand reaches were often less than solid in their accentually aimed grabs. The chord would be reached for with the left hand, while the right hand reached for melodies that would start out and end the best they could during the interims.

Clearly, Sudnow thinks of one hand, usually the left, as giving form to the gestalt. He reports that when he "saw" a spate of improvised jazz, he "would see a configurating hand, in a certain arrangement with respect to the keys, whose shaping was now being watched, whose shaping and movings became gradually instructable" (Sudnow, 1978).

Again, a two-dimensional model can represent the learning of jazz improvisation. The right hand provides information for one system and the left hand provides information for the other. In the model, four gestalts are possible, given ambiguous-unambiguous dichotomies (see Model 1.2).

When the right hand generates ambiguous information, it gets enormously tired and quickly becomes stiff to the point of almost freezing up; there would be moments that it was simply immobilized and nothing would come out (Sudnow, 1978). The left hand operated similarly in gathering either ambiguous or unambiguous information.

Even with this example, in which no message is exactly equivalent to literal meaning, one message system tends to give form to the second system. The "jazz" pacing of the left hand frames the melody of the right hand to create the final gestalt of improvised jazz.

		RIGHT-HAND INFORMATION	
		AMBIGUOUS INFORMATION Right Hand *Not* Working	UNAMBIGUOUS INFORMATION Right Hand Working
LEFT-HAND INFORMATION	**AMBIGUOUS INFORMATION** Left Hand *Not* Working	no improvisation mechanical playing music was "out of hand"	right hand independent right hand does whatever it wants before next chord
	UNAMBIGUOUS INFORMATION Left Hand Working	left hand independent left hand doing preset moves that obligated things the right hand had to do	improvisation "jazz hands" optimally spontaneous and creative

Model 1.2

Computer Programs

The computer program, operating in a broad communicative sense, depends upon content and style components. First, the computer program needs something like a literal message. In most instances, numbers or symbols are the content. Second, it needs to be told what to do with the numbers or symbols; it needs a metamessage for the content. Usually, the form-giving messages at the metalevel are operators that tell the computer to multiply, add, divide, subtract, execute do-loops, execute if-then statements, and make other logical connections for the information designated as content.

In computer programs, operators transform numbers to other numbers (for example, $3 \times 7 = 21$) and transform other operators to something different through a logical connector, such as an if-then statement. In short, the stylistic component affects both content and style elements.

But the converse is not possible. The content of the system never contaminates the form-giving operators. For example, the sevens in the system never transform the addition operator to a division operator. The sevens only affect other numbers when operated upon by metamessages in the system. This is one of the reasons the computer analogy of communication breaks down for human communication, where content can contaminate stylistic elements and vice versa.

Summary

In the previous pages, examples have been given to illustrate stylistic functions that give form. The commonality throughout the illustrations is that the gestalt depends upon the way the stipulated content is framed. It is obvious that there are many ways to give form to literal meaning, melodies, numbers and symbols, expectations, and realities. The next section formally presents the framework for a communicator style theory in the sense that style works as a metamessage for content.

THEORETICAL BEGINNINGS

The following statements for the form-giving aspect of style mark the formal starting point for a theory. These remarks are designed for public consumption to stimulate dialogue, criticism, and, as an ongoing process, refinement.

The organization of the theoretical statements builds first on definitions, then on axioms, then on postulates, which, in turn, lead to hypotheses. The definitions require no proof because they stipulate parameters of a concept. As such, they are neither right nor wrong, but have persuasive consequences that lead to evaluations relating to pragmatic usefulness.

The axioms function close to the definitional level. They are statements of connections inferred from both defined and undefined elements. They are not testable per se, but indirectly lay the groundwork for notions that are testable. The postulates can be tested, but tend to be obvious, almost like truisms. More importantly, they directly provide a basis for hypothesis testing that often entails surprising connections.

DEFINITIONS

Two definitions broadly identify the first parameters:

Definition 1:   A message system provides information.

Definition 2:   A communication "gestalt" is the interaction of information from the respective message systems.

| | MESSAGE SYSTEM 1 | |
	AMBIGUOUS INFORMATION	UNAMBIGUOUS INFORMATION
MESSAGE SYSTEM 2 — AMBIGUOUS INFORMATION	nonsynchronous gestalt vagueness fragmentation confusion high entropy	partially synchronous gestalt "best" information must be distinguished
UNAMBIGUOUS INFORMATION	partially synchronous gestalt "best" information must be distinguished	synchronous gestalt isomorphic match between message systems low entropy, redundancy likely

Model 1.3

In each previous example, at least two message systems contributed to the gestalt. The two models relating to animal territoriality and jazz improvisation can be represented as illustrated in Model 1.3.

When either system provides too little information, overloads, or contradicts in some way, vagueness, fragmentation, confusion, or entropy may result for the gestalt at the first level of meaning. For example, if the first system indicates that "X is true" and the second system indicates that "X is not true," then the gestalt does not contain in itself enough information to be resolved unequivocally. Only random decisions are possible, unless one of the systems is valued more.

When both systems provide adequate or appropriate information, then precision and accuracy result. Usually the gestalt contains at least some redundancy, although not necessarily. Most often, however, the information from both systems overlaps, does not deviate from normal expectations, and contains a lot of redundancy.

There can be instances in which the information from the first system must be joined with the information from the second system for the gestalt to be meaningful. For instance, the "fail-safe" system for the nuclear defense of this country requires two independent keys to activate the whole system. In human interaction, this type of communication is approached when a mother says to her child, "Look me in the eye and tell me that." The mother wants bits of information simultaneously from the verbal and the nonverbal to help her decision process concerning the quality of the final message.

The model need not be an either/or representation. It can be, and probably is, in most human communication, a product of continuous information. For example, if Model 1.3 were increased in complexity by adding a neutral point along the ambiguous-unambiguous continuum for each system, then nine gestalts would result. If the dimensions are thought of as continua, then the product of the probabilities associated with the dimensions determine the weights for the interactions — namely, the gestalts.

The idea of "interaction" entails the notion of "form giving." At this point, it is useful to highlight some characteristics of "form giving." In geometry, a "point" is undefined. In like manner, here "form" will remain undefined, except to identify its function; that is, **form draws a distinction** (Brown, 1973).

Topologically, a boundary, which may be a political agreement, a physical barrier, or a gerrymandered line on a map, draws a distinction by separating sides so that a point on one side cannot reach the other side without crossing the boundary. *In the communicative process, the boundary is not physical, but analogical and/or digital information.*

Assumptions

Before introducing the initial axioms, two critical assumptions must be presented:

Assumption 1:   There can be no distinction without motive.

Assumption 2:   There can be no motive unless contents
are seen to differ in value.

Some Japanese artists practice a nice art using nature. A person walking through a forest, for example, might see a ribbon tied around a rock left there by an artist who wanted to call attention to and set off the rock from all the other rocks in the forest. In essence, the artist draws a nonrandom distinction because he or she prefers the "value" of this rock and, furthermore, commends this preference to others.

The above assumptions provide an ongoing guideline in the task of establishing style theory. Throughout, two questions help focus on the pragmatic consequences embedded in the theory: (1) What is the motivation? (2) What are the value differences?

Axioms

The first axiom relates the notion of a distinction to a communicative process.

Axiom 1:   Any message can draw a distinction either by literal meaning or by stylistic means.

A person can negate literal meaning through nonverbal messages. In this case, style components draw the distinction. Also, a person can negate literal meaning by directly saying that "it is not true." In this instance, additional content, subsequent to the first message, draws the distinction.

It is easy to see that human communication is more complicated than the computer program example, where "content" never contaminates "style" — where the numbers never change the operators. In human communication, *content can function stylistically.* If somebody says, for instance, "I cry very easily," the literal meaning is a metamessage about another metamessage, namely, the crying. Content gives form to the nonverbal message by signaling the laconic characteristic.

The second axiom identifies the function of the stylistic components:

Axiom 2:   One message system gives form to another when the literal meaning of one system is reinforced or changed.

The reinforcement is a matter of redundancy. If the person says yes and vigorously nods "yes," then the nonverbal message reinforces and is redundant to the initial affirmation. Changes manifest themselves in many ways, including contradiction, negation, exaggeration, dilution, and disconfirmation. The literal message often is changed in intensity by the form-giving aspect of the second message.

In short, the stylistic distinctions do communicative work in general and specific ways. In general, form-giving messages become part of the gestalt by furnishing premises that provide the receiver instructions about the way to interpret the whole message. Sometimes the premises are inferred; sometimes they are established by convention.

Form-giving messages draw two kinds of distinctions. First, they *exclude* certain messages from the gestalt. In the territoriality example, the visual signals of submission by the rat excluded visual signals of dominance. To the degree that metamessages exlude conflicting information, the gestalt is less ambiguous.

The information from one system does not necessarily exclude information from a second system. A person may indicate calmness with verbal assurances, but the nonverbal information may be different. Information about nervousness is excluded in the verbal system with the assurances of calmness. The assurances, however, do not exclude conflicting information from the nonverbal system. The interaction of information at a higher level, in this instance, excludes information that says the verbal and nonverbal messages are redundant.

The second kind of distinction of form-giving messages is that they *include* information. As such, they can play an important function in highlighting what is, rather than what is not. The frame around a picture, for instance, does not organize the perception of the viewer concerning what is outside; it organizes the visual information inside. Messages signaling trust, for example, indicate that some primary information, at minimum, centers on vulnerability.

Inclusion and exclusion are simultaneous and inextricable functions. They work in the gestalt in an enthymematic way. The example given above of the monkeys at play illustrates the point. The initial distinction or frame functions as a working premise in the interactive sequence. The enthymematic process looks like this:

Framing Premise: *"This is something that looks like combat."*

Bites that are not harmful, scratches that are not painful, and shoves that are not injurious determine the framing premise, which gives form to the following primary message.

Primary Message: *"It is not combat."*

Both the simple and complex conclusions have the same consequence in that violence, pain, and injury are absent. The complex conclusion, however, forces the receiver to *react actively, to supply premises interactively.*

The enriched message invites the receiver to attend to the intracacies of the gestalt, to the nuances and subtleties, to the possible motivations, and to the value of the content. In the example, a reasonable conclusion is that "this is play." Such a conclusion has strong consequences for the relationship between two participants.

In addition to each form-giving component working to include and exclude information, the components also have impact in uniquely particular ways. In Chapter 3 the core influences of nine style variables and their structural relationships to each other are identified. For example, an attentive style essentially *signals a willingness* to engage in or continue an interaction.

In summary, every stylistic message gives form that may affect the content in a conventionally simple, normative, and tightly rule-governed way. Punctuation marks in a printed message, for instance, give form to information. At a more complex level, mythologically obscure and complicated signals embedded in the professional role, such as a psychiatrist, teacher, or policeman, give form to information.

Every stylistic message functions enthymematically to signal how a literal (primary) message is to be taken, filtered, interpreted, or understood. Sometimes the stylistic message merely generates redundancy; at other times it encourages the receiver to consider a message that is greater than the sum of its immediate parts.

A third axiom that lays the groundwork for some surprising postulates allows for independence of message systems:

Axiom 3:   Form-giving messages can be antecedent to, simultaneous with, or subsequent to another message.

This means that all form-giving messages do not have to be simultaneous with the literal meaning, although every communication entails at least one form-giving element that is inextricable from and simultaneous to the literal meaning.

POSTULATES

Given the above axioms, the following postulate is introduced:

Postulate 1:   Stylistic components function with a hierarchical impact.

Because the gestalt depends upon the interaction of all form-giving elements, the thrust of this postulate is important. Consider some examples.

The conversation between a husband and wife at a cocktail party can be analyzed in terms of the content and style:

Husband: What do you think of this party?

Wife: It's great!

However, if the couple agreed before the party to let this interaction be the signal to leave in ten minutes, the precoding gives form at a higher level. Here, the hierarchical impact negates the essence of the style component at the literal level. In this instance, the form-giving message was antecedent to the other message systems.

Or, consider the hierarchy of messages in visiting a doctor. The form-giving messages physically begin in the doctor's office, with its concomitant props that signal that the doctor's message should be trusted. This is not the office's message; it is the doctor's message structured in terms of appropriate and symbolic inanimate objects.

At a more obvious communicative level, the metamessage of a doctor's hesitancy in explaining a particular illness signals that his or her message should be listened to very carefully and that it should be listened to for nuances of meaning that will help alleviate ambiguity. The hesitancy has a hierarchical impact.

The corollaries to the first postulate are far reaching and provide important clues to understanding the richer meanings of the communication gestalt.

Postulate 2:   Whenever a gestalt is ambiguous, one style component in the hierarchy moves more to the center of attention and is valued more.

Postulate 3:   Whenever the gestalt deviates from normal expectations (it is surprising), one style component in the hierarchy probably commands more attention and operates with greater leverage.

The doctor's hesitancy is an example of Postulate 3.

The hierarchy of form-giving messages provides a critical tool for helping to decide about ambiguity. In many instances the highest form-giving level delimits ambiguity in the gestalt, although in some instances it may exacerbate it. Most of the time, the form-giving levels are redundant to the literal meaning and help anchor conventional understanding. It gets interesting when style components interact with literal meaning in such a way that the gestalt is ambiguous.

At least two decisions have to be made. Both address the question, "Why is ambiguous information being sent?" **To answer this question is to inferentially and interactively begin the communicative process.**

First, a competency issue must be addressed. Is the person who is communicating ambiguously in touch with reality? If so, the receiver is put into a one-down position. To use a rough analogy, it is like a person saying, "Yes, I know this match will burn you and I am going to do it anyway." In this case, the person is saying, "Yes, I know the message is ambiguous and I am going to give it to you anyway."

The immediate consequence for the relationship is that the receiver is being communicated to as though he or she were in a submissive position. Perhaps the receiver is being rejected, disconfirmed, challenged, or tested. If the communicator is not in touch with reality, then the receiver probably should not accept or acquiesce in the submissive role; rather, the receiver should strive for a one-up position. In the most extreme case, the receiver should not yield to perceived ineptness, incompetency, or even "madness" and should not allow a symmetrical relationship.

Second, an intentionality issue must be addressed. If the person who is communicating ambiguously is doing so intentionally, then the consequent for the relationship manifests itself in terms of teasing, teaching, playing, or manipulating. If the sender is not communicating ambiguity intentionally, then he or she is disinterested, disconfirming, and probably oblivious to the communicative impact.

Whatever the case, when two message systems conflict because of competence or incompetence or with intentionality or without it, the gestalt entails a hybrid message that points to "extra" information. Extra information typically includes signals that tacitly say:

(1) Disconfirm all or part of the primary message.

(2) Interpret the primary message ironically, metaphorically, irrationally, or extraordinarily.

(3) Weight the primary message even more than the literal content suggests.

The final postulate of this section states:

Postulate 4:   An ambiguous gestalt motivates the receiver to interactively and inferentially supply premises that alleviate ambiguity.

The implication of this postulate is that the receiver is motivated to reduce ambiguity actively. Of course, this does not guarantee that it will happen. In effect, this postulate parallels a critical assumption in Festinger's (1957) dissonance theory — namely, a person will move to eliminate a state of imbalance or remain psychologically uncomfortable.

Not only does the postulate suggest motivating dynamics, it also indicates how ambiguity will be reduced — it requires (1) interaction and (2) inference. In short, the main consequent of style components not being completely redundant with content is to change the gestalt in one of two ways. Either the gestalt gets more ambiguous or its intensity changes. In both instances, the interaction of the style and content components creates a final message more informative than the impact of the sum of the separate components.

The far-reaching implication of the postulates is that stylistic components make a pragmatic difference. That is, form-giving messages affect the relationships message systems have to each other and the gestalt, in turn, influences the relationships between communicators. This is a nuance not found in the work of Watzlawick et al. (1967).

SUMMARY

This chapter has addressed style as form giving. In this sense, any stylistic component influences content. For clarification, two definitions, three axioms, and four postulates were introduced to outline the theoretical structure of this thinking. Some concepts are left undefined, including "form," "message system," "communication," and "information." These definitions may be found in other works.[1] This chapter has presented critical connections concerning the impact of communicator style in the sense of giving form to content. There are many issues to explore, many doors to open, and this chapter has partially established the foundation. A summary of the definitions, axioms, and postulates presented here may be found in Appendix A.

NOTE

1. Brown (1973) discusses the notion of form; the style researcher should not ignore this provocative book. For a wide range of readings discussing "information," "message system," and "communication," see Smith (1966); this is an early but richly useful book.

2/ Creating Communicative Identity

norm-defining patterns of style

Many television
and movie stars are
tagged with certain styles by
the popular media. Bing Crosby
was usually described as having a relaxed style. Some comedians foster a sarcastic style. Some politicians have a smooth style. It is
a compliment to say, "That person has style!" The opposite is an insult. *The reason that style attributes can be made is
that enough associations have consistently recurred.*

This chapter does three things. First, it examines what style means in the sense of consistently recurring associations. Second, three examples illustrate this use of style: (1) style assessment as a diagnostic, therapeutic tool, (2) style from a linguistic viewpoint, and (3) style as a reflector of personality. Finally, style as a reflector of personality is analyzed for its communicative function.

Together, these three points show the pervasive usefulness of treating style components as consistently recurring associations in human interaction. In addition, it will be shown how style as consistently recurring associations is directly related to style in the sense of its form-giving function.

CONSISTENTLY RECURRING PATTERNS

Consistent association does not directly give form to literal referents, but to a pattern of behaviors, beliefs, or attitudes. As such, it provides information for classifying people or for making accurate predictions. *Such association is known only through repeated observations of a given population.*

For example, the letters O T T F F S S E N T E T do not have an obvious pattern.[1] Hence, it is difficult to identify a consistency and impossible to associate a style, except in a trivial sense. Unless one has special information, the best description of the sequence of letters is that it is a random pattern.

The letters TTT AAA TTT CCC SSS have at least one pattern that is predictable, but not determined. Because there is a consistency within the sequences and because one expects the sample to be drawn from English letters, a style can be defined as a function of "threeness" and letters. That is, groups of three letters are an apparent, consistent, and recurring association. This example is but one of an infinite number of ways to display a sequence of letters such that a multiplicity of style focuses can be generated.

Consider Bing Crosby again. The media and the public perceived him as having a relaxed style because they consistently associated a cool, calm, and collected demeanor with his public persona. This is not to say that he never manifested other communicative behaviors; it simply means that these associations generated a sufficient pattern for one to feel comfortable or confident in thus describing Crosby's general style.

Thus, **referencing style in this way depends upon two keys: (1) What constitutes consistency? (2) What constitutes enough of it?** That is, when does it recur enough? A person's interaction is seen as consistent when it reminds one of the same form, manner, or degree; when it is does not vary too much. The interaction is seen as consistent when it is in agreement or congruent with what has gone before, when it corresponds to similar earlier behaviors.

A population issue is embedded in the problem of consistency. To have a sense of consistency, the individual needs two things: first, sufficient knowledge of the objects of the population domain; second, sufficient knowledge of the frequency with which the respective objects occur.

For example, in the English alphabet 26 letters are expected. In a typical text, the letter "e" is expected more often than any other letter; "u" is expected to follow "q." Cryptographers, crossword puzzle fans, and linguists can testify to more extensive and complex expectations.

To the extent that an individual has a sense of what is in the population, the expectation concerning consistency is shaped. If the person has a perfect idea of the variables and the respective frequencies, then the expectations are shaped accordingly.

In the above example concerning the letters clustered in batches of three, one would expect that the next batch might be BBB, CCC, DDD, or some other group of three English letters. Because of this expectation, almost any three letters would be consistent with the suggested pattern, even though the larger pattern is not known.

It would be inconsistent if $\Delta\Delta\Delta$ formed the next batch. At this point, one might expand the population domain to include both English and Greek alphabets, which, in turn, would reshape what constitutes consistency. Consistency is not statistically determined; it often evolves developmentally. This is especially true when processing communicative behavior.

With communicative phenomena, consistency can be attributed to an individual even though the target behavior is not invariant, even though it does not occur in monotonic intervals, and even when it is not free from apparent contradictions. For instance, a person can be described as having a humorous style even though there are many examples in which he or she is serious, even though he or she is not cyclically predictable, and even though he or she is frequently not humorous, which does not necessarily mean "serious" — a person can be serious and humorous at the same time. In effect, the person can be designated as consistently humorous. This pragmatic association is not alien to the notion of consistency when addressing communicative processes. In contrast, such slippage would be tolerated to a lesser degree in the physical sciences.

The second point is "How many times must a behavior be perceived before consistent associations are related to a person?" There is no answer to this question. The process is ongoing and complex; it is developmental.

A person feels increasingly confident and comfortable in predicting another's interaction pattern as a function of having more knowledge of that person. Of course, some people classify, type, and make predictions about others early and offhandedly based upon slight, illusory, or superfluous behaviors that may have been spontaneous, carefully crafted, context or situation determined, random, or authentic.

Whatever the case, **it is an accumulation of "microbehaviors" giving form to literal content that add up to a "macrojudgment" about a person's style of communicating. Style as a consistently recurring pattern of association is form giving at the macro level.** Style components function with a hierarchical impact.[2]

DEFINITION AND AXIOMS

The following definition and axioms establish the framework:

Definition 3:   A consistently recurring pattern occurs when any set of behaviors is likely to occur again within a predictable time period.[3]

The definition does not depend upon the behavior occurring within an equal interval of time. For example, a researcher studying expressions of affection in a marriage need not find such behavior every two hours to claim that there is a consistently recurring pattern. If he or she finds a normative pattern and no critical deviations from the norm within a designated period, then the researcher can maintain that a pattern consistently recurs.

Such patterns do the type of communicative work suggested in the following axiom:

Axiom 4:   A consistently recurring pattern gives form to an interaction by creating anticipations or expectations about the way one communicates.

The pattern functions as a metamessage in the sense that it frames interaction, not in an inviolate or in an intractable way, but in an anticipatory way. This is what Bateson (1972a) talks about when he discusses psychological frames.

The expectations draw distinctions by probable exclusion. To the extent that a person is viewed as a "nice guy," expectations about conflicting information are excluded. The "macrojudgment" provides a norm that excludes competing norms. This does not mean that once a person is judged to be a "nice guy" that the judgment is necessarily permanent. It only suggests that the judgment entails a kind of inertia — once it is made, it tends to remain unchanged, but it is not guaranteed to remain unchanged.

Quantity is a critical element, as identified by Axiom 6:

Axiom 5:   A consistently recurring pattern of style behaviors depends upon enough behaviors to establish at least one norm.

The consistently recurring pattern not only excludes information, but it simultaneously frames behavioral sets by shaping expectations about *what is being framed.*

The frame around a picture, for example, does not organize the perception of the viewer concerning what is outside; it organizes visual information inside. Messages signaling trust indicate that some primary information centers around vulnerability. If enough messages have accumulated, the norm organizes the appropriate expectations.

In short, a consistently recurring pattern helps the individual interpret, filter, or understand literal meaning and social interaction. Because style has a hierarchical impact, the pattern can be historically or developmentally emergent; it can be culturally impinged, idiosyncratically generated, or created in an impromptu fashion. Some brief examples illustrate each point.

Historical or Developmental Pattern

The historical or developmental pattern is made up of the accumulated behavior sets. Whenever an individual responds to the question, "What is that person like?" the list tends to summarize modal behaviors — that is, behaviors that have occurred most often with the greatest consistency.

In *Abel Sanchez,* by Miguel de Unamuno y Jugo (1958, p. 278), the developmental pattern is described:

All during their secondary school studies, which they pursued together, Joaquin was the incubator and hatcher, hotly in pursuit of prizes. Joaquin was first in the classroom; Abel was first outside class, in the patio of the Institute, and among his comrades, in the street, in the country, and whenever they played hooky. It was Abel who made everyone laugh with his natural cleverness; he was especially applauded for his caricature of the professors.

Cultural Expectations

Cultures impinge upon judgments of style. In our culture, a presidential candidate is expected to act presidential. Deviance from the norm is punished. When Edmund Muskie cried because a New Hampshire newspaper attacked his wife, the tears were deemed "unpresidential." The charge, "Act like a gentleman," entails another culturally impinged expectation. In essence, anticipations can be derived from a larger social group rather than accumulating from experience.

Idiosyncratic Expectations

Some style associations emerge idiosyncratically. For example, James Cagney never said, "You dirty rat!" Yet this line is used by impressionists to trigger the Cagney image. Paralleling the process of rumor transmissions, sometimes idiosyncratic expectations are generated by the omission of some details and the addition of others. Gossipmongers occasionally create behavioral associations that stick with an individual and become an inextricable part of that person's social profile.

Impromptu Expectations

This pattern is established in a relatively short period of time. First encounters, extraordinary events, and memorable or impression-leaving situations often mark the occasion. For example, humor capitalizes upon such a pattern by first establishing it and then violating it. W. C. Fields, for instance, in one of his movies, teaches the audience the pattern to expect within seconds. He is trying to break a set of billiard balls. The cue repeatedly falls out of his left hand. Each time he tries to get the stick through the left fingers, he fails. The tip of the cue, seemingly with a life of its own, "chases" the fingers, parallels their every movement, but never matches the target. After establishing the pattern, the comic frame is set for the unexpected.

In each example, enough consistent associations are established to generate a norm, which, in turn, determines expectations. The norm is important for two reasons: First, it provides a useful summary descriptor of a central tendency; second, it provides an anchor from which to measure deviance. The following axiom relates the function of a norm to style:

Axiom 6:   Style in the sense of consistently recurring associations manifests itself only as the function of a central tendency or a deviation from the central tendency.

The central tendency can be operationally stipulated as a norm, mean, median, modal effect, or phenomenon within a range of summary descriptors. If the person is thinking of a style that has occurred developmentally within his or her experience, then it is probably expressed in terms of a central tendency. "Joe is a funny person — always has been." "Lester never is careful in what he says; if he said something negative, he probably didn't mean it."

If style is expressed as a deviation from a central tendency, it is likely connected to a larger social group or a culture. "It takes a really sick mind to talk that way constantly." "She's weird and very spacey." In these instances, the judgments of "sick" or "weird and spacey" entail a tacit notion of what is "healthy" or "not weird and not spacey." The latter attributes are determined by the larger reference group.

The deviations need not be only negative and, as a result, punishable, but may also be positive. To say that somebody is an absolute genius, gifted, or saintly is to express a deviation from a central tendency. In short, any deviation far enough beyond the criterion level tends to mark a very visible style. What constitutes "far enough" is, of course, an open question. Sometimes it is formally stipulated by law; sometimes a researcher sufficiently operationalizes it appropriate to the phenomenon being studied; sometimes the individual simply intuits it. Sometimes it is whatever it takes to motivate talk about it.

In the following sections, brief examples illustrate both uses of style — that is, as a norm and as a deviation from a norm. The first example from the therapeutic literature looks at hybrid categories of "neurotic styles." Then, two examples of "linguistic styles" are considered in which both norm and deviation are incorporated. Finally, style is examined in a normative perspective as a function of personality variables. The examples demonstrate the multifaceted ways to ascribe style.

NEUROTIC STYLES

The practical gain of being able to describe a particular neurotic style is found in parsimonious diagnoses, quick and better treatment, and a more sensitive understanding of the problem. If the person is correctly classified, then the expectations concerning how the person will reduce tension, feel emotion, perceive reality, and react to interventions will be more accurate.

With neurotic style, the recurring and consistent associations entail large variability and a wider range of synthesized information. Shapiro (1965) identifies four neurotic styles: (1) obsessive-compulsive, (2) paranoid, (3) hysterical, and (4) impulsive. Multiple variables determine the four style categories.

A neurotic style is seen as a mode of functioning that is identifiable in an individual through a range of specific acts that recur consistently. With each style, the person thinks, perceives, and experiences emotions in a sufficiently enduring pattern. With each style, idiosyncratic, subjective experiences and behavioral activities are strongly associated with the person.

Shapiro (1965) claims, for instance, that the following characterizes part of the hysterical style:

> When one asks a question of a hysterical person, . . . one is likely to get an answer not fact, but impressions. These impressions may be interesting and communicative, and very often vivid, but they remain impressions — not detailed, not quite sharply defined, and certainly not technical. *Once, for example, in taking a case history from an exceedingly hysterical patient, I made repeated efforts to obtain a description of her father from her. She seemed, however, hardly to understand the sort of data I was interested in, and the best she should provide was "My father? He was wham-bang! That's all – just wham-bang!"*

Shapiro uses both perspectives of style. He emphasizes style as a deviation from a norm by isolating a particular neurotic style. The normal person, he says, has a directed sense of work, but the obsessive-compulsive person has an extraordinarily intense and extremely directed sense of work. The contrast can only be made if Shapiro has a sufficiently stable idea of a "directed sense of work" from a person typifying a central tendency given the population.

Shapiro cannot know the extreme without understanding the moderate; he cannot know the "extraordinary" without appreciating the ordinary. Thus the style category labeled "neurotic" and its concomitant value judgments represents *a contrast between a norm and a deviation* from the norm.

Shapiro also uses style in a sense to describe a norm within a particular classification. By focusing on typical behaviors, responses to external influences, affective experiences, and abilities to handle pressure, he provides a style norm within a category. For example, the norm for a paranoid in responding to external influence is to be touchy, guarded, and suspicious.

In summary, Shapiro's work represents a typical strategy to classify the way "abnormal" people behave and interact. It is a necessary move for therapists to make. Intervention for improvement implies a healthy state. To understand the ways one can deviate from the healthy state is of critical importance. Thus it makes sense to isolate consistently recurring patterns that define the essence of a considerable departure from health.

LINGUISTIC STYLES

There are two comprehensive treatments that are organized around linguistic style, one by Sandell (1977) and one by Giles and Powesland (1975). Both the norm and deviation from the norm perspectives are used.

Sandell (1977) talks about a linguistic style that shows a consistent pattern of variation among populations using language. The recurring associations are typically found in vocabulary variability; the use of exceptional words; the use of key words; word type frequencies; parts of speech; structural organization relating to clauses, sentences, or paragraphs; measures of periodicity; frequency of rhetorical devices; and measures of subjective impressions.

Linguistic style relates to all kinds of language phenomena. Sandell, for instance, has attempted to demonstrate that style variables affect components of persuasion such as comprehension, acceptance, and retention. The questions have pragmatic import. Research questions often focus on memory, learning, and social interaction. Some representative questions would include: Do unusual words in advertisements cause greater retention of the persuasive message? Can children learn to read faster with optimal vocabulary variability? Do different rhythms of dialogue affect social interaction?

Linguistic work also emphasizes styles that deviate from the central tendency. The farther away from a norm a particular unit of analysis is, the more visible the style variable. Unusual copy in advertising can be identified because certain words in the message are rare, idiosyncratic, or unique.

Sandell points out the fallacy of using style only in the sense of a deviation. He says that some researchers see style only as a way of using language that is unconventional, that deviates from what is normal. For example, for these researchers, using adjectives is stylistic only if done in excess. Sandell concludes that the researchers, by implication, must maintain that those who express themselves in a perfectly normal way, and thereby define the "encoding norm," do not exhibit any style in their use of language. Sandell rejects this view.

Style as a deviation is frequently an easy and visible referent, but it distorts the overall picture if used by itself. All "normals," who make up about 70 percent of the population by virtue of being within a standard deviation of the mean, are omitted using this approach unless the definition of deviation is increasingly relaxed, at which point it becomes a rhetorical exercise to justify where the line of demarcation should be drawn.

Clearly, neither perspective is right or wrong. It is a matter of focus and sometimes a matter of taste. By deduction, the emphases are the opposite sides of the same coin. *The researcher cannot stipulate a deviant score without identifying, either implicitly or explicitly, a norm from which to deviate.* Conversely, a norm represents the central tendency score between some upper and lower deviant scores.

Giles and Powesland (1975) talk about style in a linguistic framework also, but they highlight different chunks of information than does Sandell. They stipulate two "speech styles": (1) context related and (2) class related. According to Giles and Powesland, "A context-related 'standard' often appears in cultures where speakers have two or more varieties of the same language at their disposal. Cultural norms prescribe the use of a standard variety in formal, public situations, and 'nonstandard' varieties appear in less formal contexts."

Within context-related standards, many substyles can be stipulated, such as vernacular (speech used within the home and with peers) versus superposed (speech used in formal situations) or dialect versus standard speech. The style focus, in turn, influences research questions. Typical questions include: When is the speaker unconcerned about culturally prescribed verbal usage and the demands of code loyalty? Which well-established patterns of verbal behavior characterize a relationship? Which style works best in a given situation?

"Class-related standard speech occurs where a particular language variety is generally accepted as the most socially desirable, regardless of context," according to Giles and Powesland (1975). The consequences of class-related speech tagging an individual are far reaching. The authors claim that speech style affects employ-ment, cooperation, medical and legal contexts, and education. Their work supports the relationship suggested in Axiom 1 — namely, a perceived speech style gives form to an interaction by generating expectations.

In short, in linguistics, style refers to the manner in which language works as either a norm or a norm deviation. Sometimes qualitative features distinguish a style (for example, "Shake-speare's *Midsummer Night's Dream* is sublime"). Sometimes a quantitative aspect categorizes a style (for example, "The prose was too wordy").

STYLE AND PERSONALITY

If style is broadly thought of as the "way" one behaves, thinks, perceives, remembers, images, or experiences, then it is relatively easy to identify perspectives in personality research that phrase their explanations in terms of style. Whenever style is referenced in personality research, the common assumption is that there is at least one enduring or habitual pattern that defines a norm or norm deviation.

The purpose here is not to present an exhaustive review of the major personality theories. Wiggins (1973) does an excellent job of identifying and evaluating this research. Rather, this section fo-cuses upon an exemplar in the personality literature in which there are style and personality relationships expressed both as norm and norm deviation based on consistently recurring patterns.

The example is from the Interpersonal System of Personality Diagnosis developed by Leary and his associates during the early 1950s (see Leary, 1957). The overall model representing Leary's work is depicted in Figure 2.1, which shows an eight-variable cir-cumplex of interpersonal behavior generated by two dimensions. The first dimension represents power ranging from dominance to submission; the second dimension represents affiliation ranging from love to hate. Managerial variables and modest variables an-chor the respective ends of the power dimension. Cooperative variables and aggressive variables anchor the respective ends of the affiliation dimension.

Leary (1957) maintains that all other variables are "blends" of the power and affiliation dimensions. For example, skeptical behavior

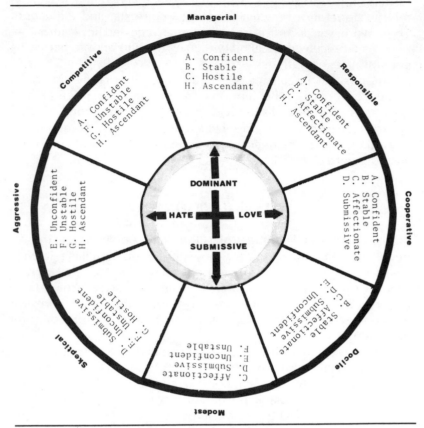

Figure 2.1   Eight-Variable Circumplex of Interpersonal Behaviors Adapted from Leary's Model of Personality

is a blend of submission and hate; docile behavior is a blend of submission and love. The evidence of a habitual pattern is provided by self-report, ratings from significant others, peers, or experts. So, if a person is consistently characterized by the self and others as manifesting managerial, interpersonal behavior, it is easy to think of that profile as the individual's style of interaction. In this sense, style is treated as a convergent norm.

In addition, the model incorporates a way to interpret the degree of intensity relating to each dimension. Behaviors of mild intensity fall near the center of the circle and behaviors of extreme intensity fall near the perimeter of the circle. Wiggins (1973) provides the following example:

Within the cooperative octant, for example, behaviors of mild intensity would fall near the center of the circle and be described by such terms as "cooperative" and "friendly." Behaviors farther from the center of the circle would be described as "always pleasant and agreeable" and "sociable and neighborly." At the perimeter of the circle, intense forms of the behavior would be described as "too easily influenced by friends" and "friendly all the time."

Consequently, style of interaction can be examined in terms of norm deviation also.

COMMUNICATOR STYLE

Style in the context of interpersonal communication is the *way one communicates*. It can be defined broadly as "the signals that are provided to help process, interpret, filter, or understand literal meaning." As such, communicator *style gives form* to literal meaning. Communicator style is marked by the following characteristics: It is (1) observable, (2) multifaceted, (3) multicollinear, and (4) variable, but sufficiently patterned.

Observable

Communicator style is not a "black box" phenomenon — that is, it can be observed. If one is said to have an animated style of communicating, then it is expected that certain kinds of liveliness can be observed that might be operationalized as a function of frequency of gestures, body movement, and actively expressive eye and facial behavior.

Everybody has a style of communicating. One cannot *not* have a style. With every communicative interaction, the way one gives form to literal content can be observed. Sometimes what is to be observed is relatively easy to stipulate. The level of abstraction corresponds closely to the overt behaviors. For instance, physical activity will be seen as an animated style. The units of evidence can be recorded visually and then coded without too many decision rules regarding what properly determines a classification.

Sometimes what is to be observed is relatively more difficult to operationalize. The level of abstraction requires more inferential steps and more training to recognize. For example, an open style of communicating might not necessarily be seen through physical evidence. It might be inferred from a pattern found in both the nonverbal behaviors and the content. An open style may be manifested by a quick or frequent expression of either positive or negative emotions. Also, an open communicator may reveal personally private, risky information more readily. Delineating what counts as manifestations of emotion and what makes up risky information to define units of analysis for an open style demands more inductive steps than a style variable at a lower level of abstraction. Whatever the case, whether the style variable is at a lower level of abstraction (as with an animated style) or at a higher level of abstraction (as with an open style), observable data can be determined.

Multifaceted

An individual's communicator style has many facets. An individual does not have one style, but aspects of many styles. A person can simultaneously communicate in a friendly, attentive, relaxed, and serious style, to name but a few combinations. From Leary's model (Figure 2.1), a cooperative person should communicate in a confident, stable, affectionate, and submissive way.

Deethardt and McLaughlin (1976) have identified 90 communicator style traits or variables. Figure 2.2 shows the relationship among them in a two-dimensional space. Only a subset of the variables are shown to provide an idea of the domain with which Deethardt et al. are concerned. The variables closest to each other in the space are the ones most highly related.

In short, there are as many style variables and combinations as there are attribution combinations in a language. The task is to develop a parsimonious way to talk about and use the wide-ranging facets.

Multicollinear

A style profile is multicollinear. This means that many style variables are not independent from each other; variance is shared. For example, to say that a person has a dramatic and dominant style allows for the possibility that essential elements of a dominant style overlap essential elements of a dramatic style. If a dominant style entails talking a lot and a dramatic style entails frequent joking, then it is easy to see that sometimes both activities can be identical. On the other hand, a person can have a dominant style without being dramatic, and vice versa.

The combination of styles can have a synergistic impact. A person with a dominant, relaxed style exudes confidence. A person with a nondominant, nonrelaxed style might signal insecurity. Any blend of styles can combine synergistically to signal a unique

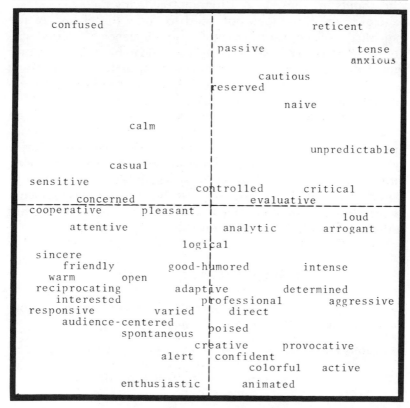

confused   reticent

                                    passive   tense
                                                              anxious

                                              cautious
                                    reserved

                                                    naive

                    calm

                                                            unpredictable

            casual
sensitive
                                    controlled   critical
            concerned   evaluative
cooperative   pleasant
                                                            loud
        attentive   analytic   arrogant

                        logical
    sincere
            friendly   good-humored   intense
        warm   open
    reciprocating   adaptive   determined
        interested   professional   aggressive
    responsive   varied   direct
        audience-centered
            spontaneous   poised

                        creative   provocative
            alert   confident
                                colorful   active
        enthusiastic   animated

NOTE: Only 50 of the 90 style traits that Deethardt et al. used are represented
in this figure. The traits are only approximately placed. The exact placement
can be found in Deethardt et al. (1976).

Figure 2.2   Two-Dimensional Representation of Subset of Style Traits

metamessage. The communicator has an incredibly high number
of stylistic combinations that can give form to literal meaning.

Variable, but Sufficiently Patterned

A style profile is not an absolute portrayal of the way a person
communicates. For any given interaction, a person can deviate
from his or her own habitual style pattern. It is not surprising that
the person can not only adapt communicatively, but can adapt
radically.

At least one norm — but probably multiple norms — is implicit
in any recognition that a person has deviated stylistically. A person

who shouts in a library, at a funeral, or during a play violates a cultural norm. One does not need to know the history of the individual to claim that the behavior is an instance of norm deviation. In contrast, a man expressing affection to his wife may represent a deviation from his normal reluctance to show positive feelings overtly. In this instance, only the wife may recognize a norm deviation.

Every communicative interaction contributes to determining a style profile. As such, norms are constantly shaped, usually reinforced, and ever present as implicit criteria. Hence a deviation in light of an established norm adds intensity to the form-giving function of style. The absence of an established norm violates expectations and, in the process, sets the stage for a message out of the ordinary. In short, most style profiles are variable, but sufficiently patterned to create resistent expectations.

RESEARCHABLE POSTULATES

In light of Definition 3, Axioms 4-6, and the above discussion, the following postulates are suggested:

Postulate 5:   Expectations about consistently recurring patterns in style become.increasingly stable as a function of more association with the communicator.

Postulate 6:   Style expectations can influence the literal message more powerfully than the immediate style exhibited.

Postulate 7:   If the style expectations are different for various receivers, then the immediate style that is exhibited can be differentially interpreted by the various interactants.

Each of these postulates highlights a critical function of style as a consistently recurring association. For each postulate, an empirical test can be generated to provide evidence that would support or refute the claim.

Increasing Stability

The more one knows another person, the better chance one has of accurately predicting that person's behavior. Long association with a person should generally result in knowing very well the way the person communicates. This generalization, however, is mitigated by two factors: (1) the context and (2) the amount of intentional masking.

A spouse should be able to predict his or her partner's communicator style more accurately than an acquaintance or a boss because of the relative exposure. If the person's style is affected by the context, however, then different expectations are functioning. The style that the boss sees may not coincide with the style that the spouse sees. A husband, for example, may be relatively mild and unassuming at home, but extremely aggressive and dominant at the office. It would be a mistake to say that the person's style profile is an average of the two different patterns. It would be better to talk about context-specific styles of a person. If the person's style is relatively homogeneous across context, then similar expectations are functioning.

The second factor that confounds generalizations is the degree to which an individual deliberately masks the way he or she usually communicates. It is for this reason that a characterization by one person of another is sometimes surprising. The immediate style may be accurately portrayed, but it may not be representative of the person's usual style in that context. The person may intentionally suppress communicative information that would add to the literal message. For example, a person may check his or her anger to the point that the literal message sounds like mere irritation. In this case, the receiver might report that the communicator was not angry. The intriguing question is, does the masking of styles result in any pragmatic consequences? Is the person more believable, likable, or trustworthy?

Powerful Impact

Consistently recurring styles that create expectations can sometimes influence a literal message more than immediate style. The enthymematic process is an inherent part of communicative interaction. Almost every communicative sequence entails at least one incomplete syllogism. Both interactants continually supply unspoken premises. Consider some trivial dialogue:

Husband: What's for dinner?

Wife: Should we do what we did last night?

Husband: Sure, but let's get a babysitter.

Neither person has to articulate what the couple did last night, nor does the wife need to specify the referent regarding dinner.

Neither person has to say why they should get a babysitter; both supply unstated premises. The history of interaction that each person accumulates from a culture or another person serves to provide a pool of usable and appropriate premises. **The pool of premises, furthermore, is not random; the premises organize themselves into patterns and norms, which, in turn, create expectations, which, in turn, frame every communicative interaction. The remembered pattern monitors the interaction and helps the person to make attributions and evaluations about another. The remembered pattern gives form to the interaction. Because of this, it is a powerful factor in communication.**

Multiple and Differential Impact

The consistently recurring patterns that relate to style can be remembered differently by different people. Thus, in a given group of friends, much of the shared pattern may be the same, but some people have had more exposure or more intimate exposure. An individual may communicate in such a way that one friend interprets the literal message one way and another friend interprets it a second, more complex way.

Erickson and Rossi (1981) epitomize this kind of communication phenomenon. They record more than one instance in which members of a group audience were selectively hypnotized. Every person in the audience heard the same literal message, but Erickson and Rossi could give form to the literal message in different ways for different people.

This is why a private joke works. Some members of the audience can supply meaningful premises because they have a larger understanding of the culture or person. This is how coded messages work. Some information is piggybacked on a literal message and the receiver knows how the added information either gives form or is given form.

PRAGMATIC CONSEQUENCES

The consistently recurring patterns that determine a style profile have important consequences. The way one communicates over time and also at the given moment probably affects the perception of interactional competence. The following sections point to researchable questions related to competence.

• **Do certain style profiles help in task competence?** It might be expected that a friendly, dominant style would move a group toward task resolution faster than any other style combination of friendly or dominant. For example, a friendly but not dominant style might aid in social facilitation, but do nothing to move the group toward completion of the task.

• **Do certain style profiles contribute to intervention competence?** Is there a set of optimal styles that will help the therapist move the client toward a qualitative change? The answer probably depends upon the school of therapy. The style profiles used in "provocative" therapy should differ radically from the style profiles used in a Rogerian orientation (Farrelly & Brandsma, 1974). Some therapies would suggest that the therapist mirror the client's style to gain leverage (Bandler & Grinder, 1975a). Style can be used to set up a paradox. For example, the therapist could tell the client what he or she thinks is accurate, but say it in such a way that the patient must consider whether the therapist really thinks that or thinks the opposite. The therapeutic benefit is derived from the patient dwelling on the analysis.

• **Do certain style profiles help in instructional competence?** The person in the role of teacher is charged with leading students to knowledge. The way one communicates when teaching is characteristically different from the way one communicates in a dialogue with a peer, although some of the best teaching has the form of dialogue, as exemplified in Plato's *Republic*.

Often the teacher's task is to balance between being entertaining enough to secure the students' attention and didactic enough to get the material across. Of course, there are teachers devoid of wit, humor, anecdotes, and metaphors who command attention partially through the formal nature of education and partially through an authoritarian style. Regardless of the style type, the best teachers force students to supply critical, unstated premises, force them to be optimally interactive with the teaching process.

Style probably not only affects feelings toward the teacher and the class, but also influences learning. Style affects the *way* the teacher emphasizes material, organizes ideas, provides crucial focus, and sorts the trivial from the critical.

• **Do certain style profiles facilitate relationship competence?** The way one communicates can enhance the quality of a marriage or a friendship. In some instances, style profiles that are complementary work well. George and Lenny in Steinbeck's *Of Mice and Men* illustrate such an interaction. In other instances, style profiles that are symmetrical work well for a couple. Most of the Hepburn and Tracy movies are examples of this type of interaction.

On the other side of the coin, there are probably combinations of style that especially alienate people within a relationship; there are patterns of style that contribute to spouses' feeling "bad" or "mad." If the dysfunctional pattern can be broken through intervention, then perhaps the relationship quality can be enhanced.

In brief, focusing on style as a consistently recurring pattern holds the promise of increasing the understanding of communicative competence. In particular, task, intervention, instructional, and relationship competence are fertile areas in which style should be studied.

SUMMARY

This chapter has examined what style means in the sense of consistently recurring associations. One definition, three axioms, and three postulates were introduced, and four areas for future research have been suggested.

Also presented were three illustrations of style being used in the sense of consistently recurring associations: one from the therapeutic literature, one from linguistics, and one from personality research.

Finally, style in this sense has been analyzed here in terms of its communicative function. The relationship between style as an immediate microbehavior that gives form to literal content and style as a macrobehavior that is the consistently recurring pattern was established. Style in the latter sense is the accumulated pattern of styles determined by microbehaviors. As such, the macrostyle gives form to interaction by creating expectations dependent upon norms. Although both senses of style are frequently used in the literature, in essence, the macrostyle is inherently dependent upon multiple instances of the microstyle.

NOTES

1. If a person spelled out the numbers 1 through 12, these would be the first letters of each word. The next sequence of twelve letters would be T F F S S E N T T T T T.

2. This is one of the axioms outlined in Chapter 1.

3. This does not mean that the pattern occurs in a symmetrical fashion. If any interaction can be divided into k equal intervals and each interval subdivided into j parts, a pattern may be labeled consistently recurring if it happens again in any jth part. In other words, a set of behaviors does not have to happen every three minutes, for example, for it to be considered consistently recurring.

3 / Boundaries and Blueprints

the foundation of a communicator style construct

This chapter, as its title suggests, identifies the domain content by *defining* the relevant variables that determine subcontructs. The respective style variables are derived from the literature. *The structural relationship* among the subcontructs establishes a foundation, an anchoring point with which to reference theoretical connections.

Each subconstruct provides a way to summarize a particular consistently recurring pattern. In short, each subconstruct is a general synthesis of a style behavior. The items that reflect the subconstructs are used to determine the makeup of a self-report questionnaire. As such, *each item asks the respondent to assess communicative behaviors.* In short, the "macro" sense of style as identified in the previous chapter is addressed.

SOURCE OF ITEMS

The items were derived from two sources. First, major, comprehensive works relating to interpersonal communication were examined. Works were considered major and comprehensive only if the research represented a long-term productive endeavor and reflected a holistic framework. Only five studies, briefly reviewed below, met the criteria.

Second, the psychological and social science literature relating to communicator style was studied. Both senses of style were found — that is, style as form giving and style as a consistently recurring patern. Nobody to date has distinguished or related the two senses of style.

RESEARCH BIAS

The bias in this research favors a pragmatic perspective. Consequently, each item in the self-report questionnaire asks about a behavior, namely, something that can be observed. The questionnaire does not attempt to measure "black box" phenomena. For example, if a person claims to have a dominant style, then it is expected that another person could see the individual speaking very frequently, coming on strong in social situations, taking charge of things, and controlling informal conversations, *assuming that a representative sample of that person's behavior is taken.* This does not mean that the person will manifest a dominant style in every situation or context. It only means that the person is reporting that *in general* he or she perceives him or herself to have a dominant style. That is, the person will manifest dominant style behaviors both consistent and recurring enough across interactions that this particular pattern is associated with the individual. It is for this reason that Axioms 4 and 5 (Chapter 2) are part of the theoretical system. Accordingly, the more an individual *knows* another, the better he or she can accurately characterize the other's style profile.

STRUCTURAL RELATIONSHIPS

The structural relationships established in this chapter are important for two reasons. They show both the conceptual and statistical connections among variables. For instance, if a dominant style is conceptually different from a relaxed style, but relatively close to a dramatic style, then it can be said that both dominant and dramatic styles share at lease one characteristic — perhaps both are very active ways of communicating.

If this connection is valid, certain statistical properties are expected. In the example, the degree of association, represented by correlations, should be higher for the dominant and dramatic variables than either the dominant-relaxed or dramatic-relaxed variables. **To know the structural relationship among variables is to begin to understand an organizing principle.** Such an organizing principle cuts across disciplines. When the history of the chemistry discipline is examined, for example, many critical events can be identified that helped the field to mature. The introduction of the periodic table of elements is especially interesting because it organized the way chemists think about the variable set and provided a way to shape expectations and generate innovations. When the table of elements was undeveloped, there were "holes" in it. That is, there were vacant spots indicating that particular elements had yet to be discovered and analyzed. It must have been an exciting time when hypotheses were later confirmed exactly as anticipated.

By analogy, it is entirely reasonable to expect that communication variables interrelate in some organized way. As a result, it is helpful to focus on the structural relationships of communication variables. This chapter identifies such a structure.

FUZZY BEGINNINGS

Whenever a new contract is being established, the beginnings tend to be fuzzy or imprecise. It seems as though researchers know where to go intellectually, but need to "get their hands dirty" with the operationalizations, definitions, and procedures before the focus becomes sharp. The development of the communicator style domain is no exception.

Initially, the study reported in this chapter was a partial replication of a pilot study. The product of this work is the Communicator Style Measure (CSM), which is the tool used to gather self-reported and observer-reported data about consistently recurring style behaviors.[1] A copy of both long and short forms of the CSM are reproduced in Appendix B.

What should be included in a communicator style construct? The problem is aggravated because there is no established domain of communicator style similar to such heavily validated constructs as attraction, credibility, or empathy. Fragments of assorted variables focusing on styles of reacting, negotiating, and talking are found in the literature, but no researcher has pulled together sets of variables to be identified and justified as "communicator style," a construct in its own right.[2]

Periodically, researchers have alluded to "style of communication," but the explications have never matured to create a construct emphasizing style.[3] In this chapter, **"communicator style" is operationally defined to measure "the way one verbally, nonverbally, and paraverbally interacts to signal how literal meaning should be taken, interpreted, filtered, or understood"** in terms of nine independent variables and one dependent variable. The independent variables (subconstructs) are dominant, dramatic, contentious, animated, impression leaving, relaxed, attentive, open, and friendly. The dependent variable — also a subconstruct — is communicator image, which represents an evaluative consequence, for example, "I am a good communicator."

STRUCTURE OF INTERRELATIONSHIPS AMONG STYLE VARIABLES

This chapter presents a partial theory for the *structure* of intercorrelations among the variables defining communicator style. This means that some style variables are expected to be closely related to one another and some are expected to be unrelated. In essence, the empirical observations presented in this chapter focus upon the correlations among style variables from self-report data for a sample of people at a single point in time.

In keeping with Gratch's (1973) notion of theory,[4] the following steps are taken: First, broad parameters of the communicator style construct are identified. Second, each style subsconstruct is defined. Third, expected relationships are posited. Fourth, empirical data are analyzed.

Broad Parameters of Communicator Style

Five major contemporary studies either approach describing a communicator style construct per se or parallel similar concerns of such a construct, but with fundamental differences in perspective; these studies were conducted by Leary (1957), Schutz (1958), Mann, Gibbard, and Hartman (1967), Bales (1970), and Lieberman, Yalom, and Miles (1973). The following sections briefly delineate the main concerns of these researchers. These studies help situate the variables of the style domain. Each orientation directly or indirectly deals with style-related communicative behavior. No attempt is made to critique each perspective systematically. That is not the purpose here; rather, the purpose is to identify style-related elements of commonality across the approaches.

In addition, the five studies point to practical implications for a variety of communication situations, especially along problem-solving or therapeutic lines. As such, the studies have generated additional research that amplifies the initial concepts.

LEARY'S ORIENTATION

The two critical dimensions, dominance-submission and love-hate, embedded in Leary's (1957) system could be rephrased to develop limited communicator style construct. The original system classified interpersonal behaviors into sixteen categories that represent various nuances among the dimensions (see Figure 2.1, Chapter 2). The system requires diagnosing five levels of personality for the respective categories.

Only the first three levels address types of communication:

(1) Public communication of the individual is assessed in terms of the social impact that one human being has on another. It is *overt* behavior of the individual as rated by others along the sixteen-point circular continuum.

(2) Conscious communication is the perception of oneself and one's world. It is the verbal content of all statements the person makes about the interpersonal behavior of the self or others derived from diagnostic interviews, therapy interviews, scores from the Interpersonal Adjective Checklist, and autobiographies written by the patients.

(3) Private communicaion comprises the expressions an individual makes about an imagined self in the preconscious or symbolic world.

Level 1 concerns what is communicated to the other. It is measured in terms of effect. Levels 2 and 3 concern what is communicated by the self to the self. Although Leary's system formally ignores the way something is communicated, throughout his system, style of communication, implicitly defined by his coding procedure, provides the best guide to score interactions at the first two levels. That is, the way a person communicates yields useful information.

If the researcher chose to use Leary's system to analyze the way an individual communicates, the transition could work. For example, dominant style in Leary's model would be characterized by personal strength, assertion, and confidence; a submissive style would be characterized by weakness, immobilization, and lack of confidence. An affiliative style is marked by friendliness, helpfulness, and outgoingness; a hostile style is marked by alienation, disaffiliation, rebellion, and unfriendliness.

SCHUTZ'S ORIENTATION

Schutz's (1958) FIRO (Fundamental Interpersonal Relations Orientations) presents a less complex framework than Leary's system. Schutz (1958, p. 1) argues that an individual needs three kinds of relations:

> "I've called them *Inclusion* ("No, Laurie, you can't come down and join the company.");
>
> *Control* ("I said, 'Go to bed!' "); and
>
> *Affection* ("Yes, I still love you; I was just angry at what you did.").

Any manifestation of wanting to be attended to, wanting to attract attention or interest, or wanting people to associate with falls into the domain of inclusion. The desire for power and authority to manipulate decision-making processes between people belongs in the domain of control. Any behavior reflecting the need to be emotionally and personally close to other people pertains to the domain of affection.

It is reasonable to assume that one's communicator style moves the individual toward satisfying these needs. With some careful refocusing, two of the FIRO dimensions could be used as a part of a style construct. An "affectionate" or "controlling" style of communication could be defined. The inclusion dimension, however, does not easily fit into the construct. Of course, some style behaviors might be effective in securing inclusion. In short, the dimensions of control and affection that are similar to Leary's dominance-submission and love-hate dimensions suggest pertinent themes that a style construct could incorporate.

MANN, GIBBARD, AND HARTMAN'S ORIENTATION

Mann, Gibbard, and Hartman (1967) classify style (via five categories) in terms of verbalized effects on a group. The first two categories, impulse hostility and impulse affection, define a dimension similar to Leary's love-hate continuum and Schutz's affection continuum.

The hostility end of the dimension includes effects that move against, resist, withdraw, or induce guilt in a group. For example, "I am tired of all this crap" would score as a hostile act moving against the group. The affection end of the dimension includes making reparation, identifying, accepting, and moving toward.

The third category entails any effect that shows dependence, independence, or counterdependence. Mann et al. label it the "authority relations" category. The statements, "You're the expert here. We don't know this stuff" would be scored in this category. It resembles Schutz's control category and Leary's dominance-submission dimension.

The last two categories reflect the ego state of anxiety and depression. Mann et al. (1967, p. 56) define anxiety as "an affective state which accompanies a person's recognition that he is approaching or is already in a dangerous situation." Expressions of anxiety ("I feel threatened"), denials of anxiety ("I have been rather amused by this"), and expressions of self-esteem ("I'm beginning to feel comfortable in this group") fall into this category. The second ego state encompasses depression, which is defined as a function of guilt or powerlessness.

The style of communicating the verbalizations provides relational information about how intense or how serious particular content is — in essence, **it is form giving.** Again, with adjustments, this orientation could lend itself to the development of a style construct. A hostile, counterdependent, anxious style or an affectionate, dependent, depressing style or any one of the other combinations could be addressed.

BALES'S ORIENTATION

Bales (1970) developed one of the best and most researched systems for analyzing interpersonal interactions. His six dimensions — (1) seems friendly-seems unfriendly, (2) dramatizes-shows tension, (3) agrees-disagrees, (4) gives suggestion-asks for suggestion, (5) gives opinion-asks for opinion, and (6) gives information-asks for information — in the Interactional Process Analysis (IPA) system can be used to classify how a person communicates.

As with the Mann et al. model, the functional effect of the content determines the scoring in the respective categories. Three of the dimensions, excluding the giving and asking behaviors, could be construed to establish a style construct.

As it stands, the system favors style-related scoring because of priority rules in the IPA system. To illustrate, if a hypertense person screamed, "The phone is out of order!" the communicative act would be scored in the "shows tension" category rather than the "gives information" category according to the hierarchical decisions that preserve mutual exclusivity in the system. Still, two components operate simultaneously. First, functional content is provided — information is given. Second, an emotional valence is signaled by the way the communicative act is expressed.

Elements of the IPA system also could be adopted for a style construct. It would be easy to talk about a friendly, dramatic, or agreeable style. Likewise, it would be easy to talk about the respective counterparts — namely, an unfriendly, tense, or disagreeable style. Chapter 10 provides a modified model of the IPA system that is oriented more directly to style and content considerations simultaneously.

LIEBERMAN, YALOM, AND MILES'S ORIENTATION

Lieberman, Yalom, and Miles (1973) present the most ambitious study examining style components. At Stanford University, 210 students were randomly assigned to 18 different kinds of encounter groups for a semester-long therapeutic experience. One of the major research questions was "Which leader style best predicts positive growth?"

Six styles emerged from the extensive factor-analytic work: (1) energizers, (2) providers, (3) social engineers, (4) impersonals, (5) laissez-faires, and (6) managers. The styles were determined by the frequency and kind of communicative behavior from four categories.

First, in the *emotional stimulation* category, the style is characterized by challenging, confronting, exhorting, revealing personal feelings, and expressing emotions. The energizers and the impersonals scored high in this category. That is, they were very dramatic, extremely open, contentious, and somewhat tense in the interactions.

Second, in the *caring* category, the style is reflected by acts that protect, offer friendship, support, praise, encourage, love, and show affection. The providers scored high in this category. The dimension embedded in this category is analogous to Leary's love-hate continuum, Schutz's affection component, Bales's friendliness-unfriendliness dimension, and Mann et al.'s impulse affection classification.

Third, in the *meaning attribution* category, the style is related to understanding, explaining, clarifying, interpreting, and providing frameworks for change. The providers, the social engineers, and to some extent the laissez-faires scored high in this category.

TABLE 3.1   Style-Related Components in the Five Studies

Cluster 1

(1) dominance-submission, (2) control, (3) authority relations, (4) executive function

Cluster 2

(5) love-hate, (6) affection, (7) impulse hostility-impulse affection, (8) friendliness-unfriendliness, (9) caring

Cluster 3

(10) emotional stimulation, (7) impulse hostility-impulse affection, (11) dramatizes-shows tension

Cluster 4

(12) inclusion

Cluster 5

(13) anxiety, (11) dramatizes-show tension, (10) emotional stimulation

Cluster 6

(14) depression

Cluster 7

(15) agrees-disagrees, (8) friendliness-unfriendliness

Cluster 8

(16) meaning attribution

Fourth, in the *executive function* category, the style is related to limit setting, suggesting or setting rules, limits, and norms, pointing to goals, managing time, interceding, stopping, and pacing. Dominance best marks the style. The managers typified the essence of the category. Obviously, the verbal behaviors used to designate leader styles in the therapeutic context could be borrowed to identify aspects of a style construct.

Synthesis

In this research, most of the communicator style variables are adopted from the five studies cited above and supplemented by the literature. Table 3.1 shows the summary of the style-related components in the five studies with the analogous components indicated for the interrelated concepts.

Some clusters have more than one component listed. For example, clusters 3 and 5 have the Bales category (11) dramatizes-

TABLE 3.2   Analogous Style Relationships to the Five Studies

Communicator Style Subconstructs	Probable Relationships with Style-Related Components from Table 3.1
(a) Dominant	Cluster 1 and (c) contentious
(b) Dramatic	Cluster 5, Cluster 3, (d) animated, and (h) open
(c) Contentious	Cluster 1, Cluster 5, (a) dominant, and (b) dramatic
(d) Animated	Cluster 3, Cluster 5, and (b) dramatic
(e) Impression leaving	Cluster 3 and (j) communicator image
(f) Relaxed	Cluster 5, Cluster 6, and (12) dramatizes-show tension
(g) Attentive	Cluster 2, Cluster 7, and (i) friendly
(h) Open	Cluster 2, Cluster 5, (i) friendly, and (b) dramatic
(i) Friendly	Cluster 2, (g) attentive, and (i) open
(j) Communicator image	(e) impression leaving

NOTE: Refer to Table 3.1 for components making up clusters.

shows tension. This suggests, of course, that aspects of the component satisfy multiple functions. A person could show emotional stimulation by dramatizing. Also, a person could show anxiety by dramatizing.

Clusters 4, 6, and 8 stand alone. This is because the level of abstraction seems different for these components. For instance, it is awkward to talk about an inclusive style. However, one can do things stylistically to foster inclusion, such as manifesting a friendly, agreeing style.

Table 3.2 shows the probable connections to the style components in Table 3.1. The analogous components are meant only to be suggestive. Some theorists talk about whole dimensions; others break them up. Only the style-related behaviors from the respective studies are shown in Table 3.2.

DOMAIN OF THE
COMMUNICATOR STYLE CONSTRUCT

For some of the selected variables, there is an abundance of literature; for other variables, the literature is sparse or nonexistent. In the following sections, each communicator style variable is discussed briefly. Tentative relationships to other subconstructs are indicated. In each instance, the subconstruct for the respective style variable will be operationally defined by a series of five self-report items.[5]

Dominant

Dominant, as a style variable, pervades the communication literature and encompasses a wide range of semantic and operational meaning. It is found in one form or another in each of the five studies cited. The literature tends to focus upon the following three things.

First, physical manifestations of dominance are reported. The assumption is that "might makes right." The stronger someone is the more dominant that person is.

Second, nonverbal and psychological correlates of dominance are reported. Dominance is manipulated by eye contact, congruent body movements, voice loudness, voice modulation, rate of information, and undue hesitations (see Eisler, Miller, & Hersen, 1973; Goldstein, Martens, Hubben, Van Belle, Shaaf, Weirsman, & Goedhart, 1973; Kazdin, 1974). Third, dominance as a predictor of behaviors, attitudes, or perceptions is reported. In general, the more dominant person responds longer and louder with shorter latencies, less compliance, and more requests for the other to change his or her behavior (see Hersen, Eisler, Miller, Johnson, & Pinkston, 1973; McFall & Lillesland, 1971; Serber, 1972; Jakubowski-Spector, 1973).

A sex difference is suggested. Males nonverbally signal dominance differently than females. Dominant males use personal space and rate of approach to indicate dominance; dominant females use reciprocal eye contact (Fromme & Beam, 1974).

In addition, dominant communication relates to assertiveness.[6] The person who communicates in a dominant way appears to be more confident, enthusiastic, forceful, active, competitive, self-confident, self-assured, conceited, and businesslike (Schereer, London, & Wolf, 1973), and also tends to feel more understood in communicating with another (Mortensen & Arntson, 1974).

Dramatic

The dramatic communicator manipulates exaggerations, fantasies, stories, metaphors, rhythm, voice, and other stylistic devices to highlight or understate content. Dramatizing, which is probably the most visible style component, serves a profound, complex, often unconscious, often intentional, interactional communicative function.

What this means is that when a person communicates in a dramatic way, the simple literal meaning of the message is transformed. Postulate 3 (see Chapter 1) is operative here. To repeat that postulate:

Whenever the gestalt deviates from normal expectations (it is surprising), one style component in the hierarchy probably commands more attention and is operating with greater leverage.

Hence the dramatic signal takes on a greater importance. Attention is being called to the message in an extraordinary way.

Sometimes the person does not realize that extra information is provided by the dramatic way of communicating. The dramatic style often gives away true feelings. Sometimes the person deliberately dramatizes to satirize, devalue, disown, deflate, or ruin the literal meaning. In most instances, dramatic communication works because the receiver knows how to process the underlying or double meaning suggested by the sender. Both people interactively share premises that give form to the message.

Freud (1905) was the first to analyze dramatic behavior systematically in the psychotherapeutic framework. He argues, for instance, that hostile, obscene, and tendentious jokes yield two kinds of information: First, important clues about the communicative self are provided; second, the need to interact is revealed. The joke psychologically mandates seeking social contact with another. The joke must be told to someone else!

As seen earlier, Bales (1970) anchors one end of a major dimension in the IPA system with the dramatizing concept. He sees the dramatizer as the communicator who plays with tension. Also, fantasy underlies dramatization in the system. Schutz (1958) relates dramatizing to the inclusion dimension; he labels the joke teller a "prominence seeker." In fact, Goffman (1974) urges the researcher to uncover dramatizations as a routine procedure in examining interpersonal encounters because the communicator often must resort to an intrinsically theatrical means to relate what he or she experiences.

As a style variable, communicating in a dramatic way relates to many phenomena. Hospital patients dramatize to cope with anxiety (Coser, 1959). A witty person is perceived by him- or herself and others as having a positive self-image (Goodchilds & Smith, 1964). Joking behavior relates to one's status within certain groups (Lundbert, 1969). Dramatizing relates to popularity (O'Connel, 1969). A person who tolerates ambiguity more tends to dramatize more (Norton, 1975). Dramatizing in groups helps reduce group tension, develop a group history, and create cohesiveness (Bormann, 1975).

Communicating in a dramatic way is a key concept to investigate as a style variable because it functions in the communicative process in two ways: First, it provides the individual or group a way to cope, relieve anxiety, or resolve tensions; second, it allows the communicator a way to make a metastatement about the literal content — that is, it clues the listener in on how to interpet the intensity, truth, or quality of the context — in short, it is form giving. In addition, dramatizing influences popularity, status, self-esteem, and attraction. Chapter 4 explores the dramatic style in much greater detail.

Contentious

The contentious communicator is argumentative. No psychological literature specifically addresses itself to the domain encompassed by this variable. The variable emerges as one closely associated with the dominant style, but potentially entailing negative components. Contentious is included here because it can provide a greater understanding of the dominant style variable. Also, it is found in various forms in each of the five studies (see Table 3.1).

Animated

Physical, nonverbal cues define the domain of the animated subconstruct. The literature is replete with this research. By definition, an animated communicator provides frequent and sustained eye contact, uses many facial expressions, and gestures often.

Generalizing from recent literature, animated eye contact, with some exceptions, characterizes the powerful, the attractive, and the truth teller (see Exline, 1971; Thayer, 1969; Argyle & Dean, 1965; Kendon, 1967; Kleinke, 1972; Kleinke, Bustos, Meeker, & Staneski, 1973; Thayer & Schiff, 1974; Kleinke, Staneski, & Berger, 1975; Knapp, Hart, & Dennis, 1974). This component even impinges in exotic ways during interaction. In a dyadic situation, animated eye contact influences the experiencing of time (see Thayer & Schiff, 1974). It usually punctuates certain kinds of verbal content (see Ellsworth & Carlsmith, 1968; Scherwitz & Helmrich, 1973; Naiman & Breed, 1974). Also, it relates to specific biological manifestations (see Nichols & Champness, 1971; Ellsworth, Carlsmith, & Henson, 1972).

Emotions are readily identified on the face of the animated communicator. The research dealing with facial expressions is underdeveloped, even in light of early speculations by Darwin (1872), Wundt (1877), Piderit (1925), Huber (1931), and Lorenz (1935). Today, much of the nonverbal research continues to develop and test the earlier speculations.[7]

Finally, an animated communicator actively uses gestures, postures, and body movements to exaggerate or understate the content. High degrees of emotional arousal directly relate to body movement (Sainesbury, 1955; Dittman, 1962). Status affects an animated style, and partially determines postures and body movements (Goffman, 1961). A highly expressive communicator solicits approval by smiles, head nodding, and a high level of gestural activity (Rosenfeld, 1966). Animated behavior such as preening, positioning, and readying oneself relates to courtship behavior (Scheflen, 1965).

In brief, the three distinct emphases in the nonverbal literature are eye behavior, facial expressions, and gestures, body movement, and posture. The headings are not mutually exclusive, but it is easy to classify the research using them. Animated activity clearly is form giving as a style variable across all contexts. It punctuates literal meaning, signals moods, indicates theatrical emphases, increases or decreases intensity, and filters qualitative content.

Impression Leaving

Impression leaving, as a style variable, is relatively unresearched. The concept centers around whether a person is remembered because of the communicative stimuli he or she projects.

Impression leaving is a complex process dependent on both the sender and the receiver. The communicator controls cues, but the receiver must process them; this is dependent upon the perceiver's propensity to process information concretely or abstractly and the perceiver's tolerance for inconsistent information (Ware & Harvey, 1967).

Much of the impression leaving research deals with initial encounters (see Lalljee & Cook, 1973; Newcomb, 1961). Berger and Calabrese (1975), for example, frame a series of developmental axioms about initial impression leaving in terms of uncertainty, amount of verbal communication, affiliative expressiveness, information seeking, intimacy levels, rates of reciprocity, similarities between persons, and liking.

A person who leaves an impression should manifest a visible or memorable style of communicating. The variable probably represents a general indicator of particular components of communicative activity. As such, it should relate closely to the dependent variable, communicator image, if the positive components outweigh the negative.

Relaxed

Relaxed, as a style variable, opens the door to rich and complex analyses. Sullivan (1953, 1972), who defined psychiatry as the study of interpersonal relations, points to the anxious-not anxious, relaxed-not relaxed, tense-not tense dimension as a key to personality.

Sullivan provocatively and unequivocally relates anxiety to experiencing and to energy transformations to explain interpersonal dynamics. An assumption is that to the degree the person manifests anxiety, a relaxed style will not be manifested. Influenced by Sullivan, Reusch (1957) includes a relaxed-tense dimension as part of the interpersonal process (see also Reusch, 1961). It is also found in Bales's (1970) IPA system in the shows tension category and Mann et al.'s (1967) system in the anxiety category.

In recent literature, the validity development of anxiety as a construct is undergoing a critical examination (see, for example, Cattell & Scheier, 1958; Speilberger, 1972; Endler & Okada, 1974). The data should be of particular interest to communication researchers because the disputants usually include interpersonal situations as the major stimulus with which to test hypotheses concerning anxiety. For example, Endler and Okada (1975), in a seminal investigation, posited that situational anxiety (state anxiety) differs from anxiety proneness (trait anxiety). To support the claim, they tested individuals in three situations: (1) interpersonal communication, (2) physical danger, and (3) ambiguous contexts. In like manner, Strahan (1974) used interpersonal situations, such as being introduced or being threatened with a fight, to examine anxiety. In short, the relaxed style can signal multiple messages. On one hand it suggests calmness/peace/serenity; on the other, it suggests confidence/comfortableness. The lack of tension in each signal may give form to the message in markedly different ways.

Attentive

There is not much empirical research describing attentiveness per se as a style variable. As a broader concept, it is frequently embedded in interpersonal and therapeutic literature under the label "empathy" or "listening" (see, for example, Iannotti, 1975; Jamison & Johnson, 1975; O'Connor & Alderson, 1974; Rogers, 1975). In general, the attentive communicator makes sure that the other person knows that he or she is being listened to.

Rogers (1951), with his client-centered therapy, introduced listening as an *active* communicative component. Since then, many researchers have addressed themselves to listening, attentiveness, and empathy as therapeutic tools (see Kelly, 1975; Wells, 1975; Shantz, 1975; Hogan, 1975).

The arguments are enticing. For example, Shave (1974), in his book *The Therapeutic Listener*, maintains that nonmedical persons can and, in many instances, should interact with emotionally uncomfortable persons attentively. He argues that *listening* can be curative. The claims focusing on listening, being attentive, and being empathic have profound, challenging, and far-reaching implications for people in interpersonal communication.

What little empirical research there is under the heading of "attentiveness" is related to nonverbal covariates (see Kendon, 1967; Duncan, 1972). Naiman and Breed (1974), for example, found that gaze duration was a sufficient factor to signal attentiveness, which, in turn, influenced the other's perception of valuative aspects (good-bad, honest-dishonest, nice-awful).

Attentiveness should relate inversely to such concepts as dominant and dramatic. To the extent that activity of a particular behavior (such as talking) marks the dominant communicator, inactivity of the same behavior (not talking) may, although not necessarily, mark the attentive communicator.

This is not to say that the attentive communicator is inactive, passive, or indifferent; it merely implies that a different behavioral activity is operating. In essence, this style variable introduces an important counterpart to some of the previous subcontracts, including dominant, dramatic, contentious, and animated.

Open

Behavior associated with the open subconstruct probably includes communicative activity that is characterized by styles that are conversational, expansive, affable, convivial, gregarious, unreserved, unsecretive, somewhat frank, possibly outspoken, definitely extroverted, and obviously approachable.

Stylistically, the open communicator readily reveals personal information about the self in communicative interactions. The counterpart of this notion is manifested in the poker-faced individual who is hard to read. Research about openness is abundant.

The open communicator tends to be perceived as attractive and trustworthy (Brown, 1976; Carkhuff, 1966; Giffin, 1967). The literature suggests that an openness threshold is determined by the nature of the target person, the verbal and nonverbal behavior of the target person, the type of information disclosed, and the strategies used to elicit disclosure by the other (Levinger & Senn, 1967; Pedersen & Higbee, 1969; Shapiro, Krauss, & Truax, 1969; Worthy, Gary, & Kahn, 1969; Jourard & Lasakow, 1958; Taylor & Altman, 1966; Norton, Mulligan, & Petronio, 1975; Bundza & Simonson, 1973). Openness is a pertinent style variable to examine in the communicative process because it relates to trust, reciprocity, para-verbal cues, and liking (see Ellison & Firestone, 1974; Becker & Munz, 1975; Chaikin, Derlega, & Shaw, 1975; Ehrentheil, Chase, & Hyde, 1973; Pedersen, 1973; Lomranz & Shapira, 1974; Fisher & Apostal, 1975; Cash & Soloway, 1975; Kohen, 1975). The open style subconstruct is explored in greater detail in Chapter 4.

Friendly

Friendly, as a style variable, ranges in meaning from simple lack of hostility to deep intimacy. Like dominance, it is found in one form or another in each of the five major studies. In Leary's (1957) system, it is embedded in the love-hate dimension. In Schutz's (1958) system, it falls into the affection category. Mann et al. (1967) call it impulse affection. Bales (1970) defines it as one of his extreme categories in the IPA system. Lieberman et al. (1973) include it in their caring category

Friendliness is an integral part of other major perspectives. Buber (1957, pp. 101-102) expresses the notion in terms of confirmation:

> The basis of man's life with man is twofold, and it is one — the wish of every man to be confirmed as what he is, even as what he can become, by men; and the innate capacity of man to confirm his fellowmen in this way. That this capacity lies so immeasurably fallow constitutes the real weakness and questionableness of the human race: actual humanity exists only where this capacity unfolds.

Watzlawick et al. (1967, p. 84) also analyzed friendliness in terms of confirmation, which they claim "is probably the greatest single factor ensuring mental development and stability that has so far emerged from our study of communication."

The transactionalists treat friendliness as a stroking function. Steiner (1974), for instance, instructs his group members to give loving strokes, to ask for strokes when needed, to reject strokes if not wanted, to accept strokes when wanted, and to stroke the self.

In brief, the friendly communicator confirms, strokes, and positively recognizes the other. As such, the friendly style should be a solid predictor of attraction, sociability, leadership, and possible social status.

Communicator Image

The communicator image subconstruct represents the dependent variable in this research. The items that define it tap the person's image of the self's communicative ability. It is assumed that a person who has a "good" communicator image finds it easy to interact with others whether they are intimates, friends, acquaintances, or strangers.

As such, this subconstruct represents an overall evaluation of the person's perception of whether the self is a good communicator. It is left to the person to testify about this ability. Consequently, the person's tacit criteria are invoked. The person may not even be able to articulate the specifics of why the self is perceived to be a "good" communicator. It is enough that the overall perception is present. Without delving into the specifics, it is easy to see that different people may use differing criteria.

EXPECTED RELATIONSHIPS AMONG VARIABLES

Two general relationships can be anticipated given the themes of the variables. First, the style variables should cluster according to a certain pattern. Those style behaviors that are similar should group more closely together than those that are not. Second, some style behaviors should be better predictors of communicator image than others.

Clustering

In light of the literature, two groups should cluster together both mathematically and thematically. It is expected that dominant, dramatic, animated, contentious, open, and impressive leaving will group together. These subconstructs entail *"active" communicative behaviors that emphasize doing and entail being talkative.*

In the second cluster, attentive, friendly, and relaxed are expected to group together. *These subconstructs tend to be more passive, receiver oriented, and other oriented.*

Two assumptions should be noted. First, *overall,* this study assumes a nonadditive model. This means that *it is inappropriate to assign a person a single, total communicator style score.* Second, the variables *within* each subconstruct are additive *to the extent that they cluster together,* and scores from clusters are additive *to the extent that the clusters are correlated.*

The most crucial test in the clustering analyses will be whether the items defining the domain of each subconstruct will cluster together in the same region — in other words, whether they will be "close neighbors" of each other. Dominance items, for instance, should group with all other dominance items. Items that do not group accordingly will be considered "bad" questions. The following study provides evidence for the expectations.[8]

Predictors of Communicator Image

In certain respects, best predictors are merely the function of redundancy. That is, if the independent variable is very close, say, in phrasing, to the dependent variable, then it becomes an uninteresting and foregone conclusion that one can predict the other with a lot of explained variance. On the other hand, the researcher does not want a set of unrelated predictors. Consequently, the researcher often is in the position of hoping that the predictors are good, but not too good. To say it another way, the researcher hopes for predictor variables that are more than semantic truisms.

In this study, dominant and impression leaving are expected to be strongly associated with communicator image. Impression leaving also seems to tap behaviors similar to the dependent variable. It differs from communicator image in a distinct way, however.

The communicator image variable suggests affirmative nuances *only* if the person perceives the self to be a good communicator. The impression leaving variable suggests positive perceptions as long as the person perceives the self as creating a memorable or visible image that generally is approved by society. On the other hand, it suggests negative perceptions if the person sees the self as creating memorable images that are disapproved by society.

The single most pervasive predictor of communicator image is dominant in one form or another. The premise is that the dominant communicator has proficient abilities to control conversations interactively, although the assumption may be weakened if dominance contains interactive effects caused by components such as status, authority, or wealth. Nevertheless, this study treats dominance as though it were a unidimensional variable.

METHOD

This study does three things: (1) It establishes the structural relationship among the communicator style variables; (2) it shows a set of predictors of a "good" communicator; and (3) it provides the basis for a tentative model.

Subjects

Subjects were students in introductory communication classes at the University of Michigan and Western Michigan University. In total, 1086 Communicator Style Measures (CSM) were completely filled out by volunteers. Feedback about the CSM was given if the subject put a name on the questionnaire.[9]

Measure

Each subconstruct consists of five items. A four-point scale was used, ranging from "very strong agreement" with the statement to "very strong disagreement" with the statement. A sixth item relating to communicator image was added that asked the subject to rank order himself or herself in terms of typical communicators. A copy of the CSM may be found in Appendix B.[10]

Procedure

The questionnaires were administered by faculty members and teaching assistants in their respective classes at the beginning of the semester. Completion of questionnaires took about eight minutes.

RESULTS

Two analyses are used to identify the internal structure of the CSM. In the first analysis, all 51 items are examined using smallest space analysis. In the second analysis, the items are standardized and summed for the respective subconstructs. The subconstructs, in turn, are analyzed using smallest space analysis.

Smallest Space Analysis
of 51 items

Smallest space analysis (SSA) is a form of nonmetric multidimensional scaling.[11] It maps a set of variables into a set of points
in a metric space such that variables that are similar by some
empirical standard are close neighbors in the space, and variables
that are dissimilar are distant from each other in the space.

Figure 3.1 shows a two-dimensional solution for the 51 items.
Since it is impractical to report the original and derived coefficients, which include 1275 distances, the coordinates for the two-
dimensional solution are reported in Table 3.3 along with the
wording for each item.[12]

The subconstructs are graphically located very well even in light
of the large number of items. Six of the subconstructs ended up
with all the original items located in approximately the same region. The impression leaving item only lost item 18, resulting in a
four-item cluster. Also, the open subconstruct ended up with three
of the original items, losing items 3 and 35. Finally, the contentious
subconstruct ended up with three items, losing items 10 and 13,
which formed a separate cluster.[13]

Smallest Space Analysis
of the Subconstructs

Table 3.4 shows the original (correlations) and derived distances
for the subconstructs. As before, the items for each subconstruct
were standardized and summed. Figure 3.2 shows the three-
dimensional solution for the ten subconstructs.[14]

CLUSTERING

Six clusters are suggested in light of the configuration and the
conceptual considerations that emerged in the literature review:

(1)   communicator image and impression leaving

(2)   dramatic and animated

(3)   attentive and friendly

(4)   dominant and contentious

(5)   relaxed

(6)   open

Table 3.5 shows the averaged correlations among the clusters.[15]

TABLE 3.3   Coordinates for Two-Dimensional Solution and Items Used

Dominant

    5. In most social situations I generally speak very frequently. **7, 48**

    7. In most social situations I tend to come on strong. **−6, 46**

    9. I have a tendency to dominate informal conversations with other people. **−23, 62**

  20. I try to take charge of things when I am with people. **−7, 60**

  44. I am dominant in social situations. **−6, 48**

Dramatic

  22. My speech tends to be very picturesque. **−11, 9**

  28. I *very frequently* verbally exaggerate to emphasize a point. **−77, 38**

  30. Often I physically and vocally act out what I want to communicate. **−30, 17**

  32. *Regularly* I tell jokes, anecdotes, and stories when I communicate. **−33, 41**

  39. I dramatize a lot. **−34, 34**

Contentious

    2. Once I get wound up in a heated discussion I have a hard time stopping myself. **−65, 56**

  10. Very often I insist that other people document or present some kind of proof for what they are arguing. **−48, −36**

  13. In arguments I insist upon very precise definitions. **−36, −40**

  37. When I disagree with somebody I am very quick to challenge them. **−24, 50**

  41. I am very argumentative. **−39, 63**

Animated

    6. I actively use facial expression when I communicate. **−5, 19**

  21. I am *very expressive* nonverbally in social situations. **−13, −8**

  24. I tend to constantly gesture when I communicate. **−49, 0**

  34. People generally know my emotional state, even if I do not say anything. **−63, 13**

  42. My eyes tend to reflect to a very great degree what I am felling when I communicate. **−2, −28**

Impression Leaving

  11. *What* I say usually leaves an impression on people. **38, 9**

  14. I leave people with an impression of me which they tend to remember. **29, 20**

TABLE 3.3   Continued

18. The *first* impression I make on people causes them to react to me.
    −12, 85 (bad item)

31. The *way* I say something usually leaves an impression on people. **−19, 12**

40. I leave a definite impression on people. **16, 25**

Relaxed

4. I am conscious of nervous mannerisms in my speech. **89, 86**

12. As a rule, I am very calm and collected when I talk. **100, 17**

16. Under pressure I come across as a relaxed speaker. **65, 42**

17. The rhythm or flow of my speech is affected by my nervousness. **88, 57**

36. I am a very relaxed communicator. **46, 44**

Attentive

15. I can always repeat back to a person *exactly* what was said. **−2, −38**

23. I always show that I am very empathetic with people. **25, −47**

27. I am an *extremely* attentive communicator. **69, −42**

29. I really like to listen *very carefully* to people. **59, −66**

45. I *deliberately* react in such a way that people know that I am listening
    to them. **20, −31**

Open

1. I readily reveal personal things about myself. **7, 70**

25. I am an *extremely* open communicator. **16, 39**

26. Usually I do not tell people very much about myself until I get to know
    them *quite* well. **22, 93**

33. As a rule, I *openly* express my feelings or emotions. **2, 35**

38. I would rather be open and honest with a person rather than closed and
    dishonest, *even if it is painful for that person*. **65, −3** (bad item)

Friendly

3. I always prefer to be tactful. **48, −100** (bad item)

19. Most of the time I tend to be *very* encouraging to people. **49, −23**

35. Often I express admiration to a person even if I do not strongly feel it.
    −100, −42 (bad item)

8. I am an extremely friendly communicator. **25, 15**

43. I habitually acknowledge verbally other's contributions. **5, −20**

(continued)

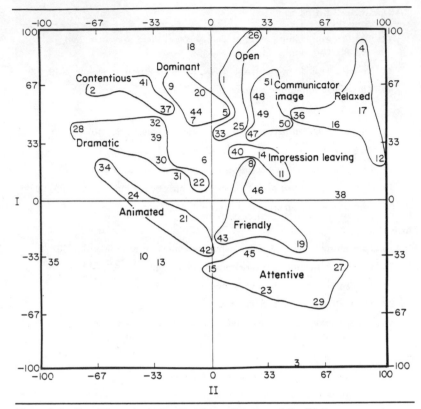

Figure 3.1   Two-Dimensional Smallest Space Solution of the 51 Items

TABLE 3.3   Continued

Communicator Image

46. The *way* I communicate influences my life *both positively and dramatically*. **25, 34**

47. I am a *very* good communicator. **25, 34**

48. I find it *very easy* to communicate on a one-to-one basis with strangers. **28, 52**

49. In a small group of strangers I am a *very good* communicator. **30, 46**

50. I find it extremely easy to maintain a conversation with a member of the opposite sex whom I have just met. **39, 38**

51. Out of a random group of five people, including myself, I would probably have a better communicator style than 1, 2, 3, or 4 of them. **37, 63**

NOTE: The pair of numbers at the end of each item are the respective coordinates for the two-dimensional solution in Figure 3.1.

TABLE 3.4 Correlations and Derived Coefficients Among Communicator Style Subconstructs (N = 1086)

	(1)	(2)	(3)	(4)	(5)	(6)	(7)	(8)	(9)	(10)
(1) Dominant	—	60	102	107	88	142	178	76	156	72
(2) Dramatic	.51	—	97	65	100	194	175	94	148	106
(3) Contentious	.48	.41	—	143	102	193	187	166	190	140
(4) Animated	.39	.54	.32	—	106	211	142	92	101	111
(5) Impression leaving	.48	.45	.41	.42	—	129	99	106	101	58
(6) Relaxed	.36	.26	.19	.22	.37	—	180	147	184	101
(7) Attentive	.24	.31	.29	.37	.38	.28	—	160	59	124
(8) Open	.48	.38	.32	.42	.40	.31	.33	—	118	61
(9) Friendly	.35	.35	.25	.40	.39	.25	.50	.37	—	105
(10) Communicator image	.59	.41	.36	.37	.54	.48	.38	.53	.42	—

NOTE: The lower triangular matrix represents the original coefficients for the smallest space analysis; it is a table of correlations using only the good items. The upper triangular matrix represents the derived coefficients for the smallest space analysis for a three-dimensional solution with semistrong monotonicity.

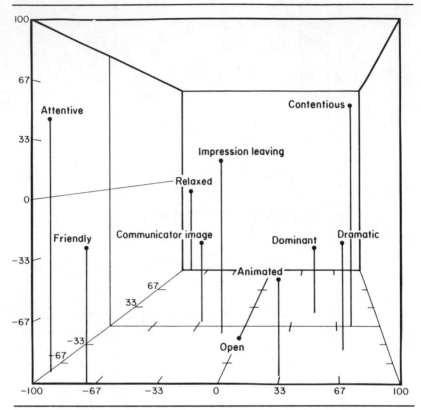

Figure 3.2   Three-Dimensional Smallest Space Solution for the Communicator Style Subconstructs

In the SSA solution, two kinds of continua are suggested. The first continuum is anchored by attentive and friendly style components at one end and by dominant and contentious style components at the other end. The continuum ranges from nondirective communicative activity to directive communicative activity.[16]

The second continuum is anchored at one end by communicative activity that requires energy expenditure and allows tension release, namely, the dramatic and animated components. The other end is anchored by a style component that conserves energy and reflects a state of already-released tension.[17]

Best Predictors:
Smallest Space Analysis

The most likely predictors of communicator image are the closest neighbors in the configuration. Three subconstructs are relatively close to communicator image. Impression leaving is the

TABLE 3.5   Averaged Correlations Among Clusters

				Clusters		
		1	2	3	4	5	6
I	Impression leaving/communicator image	.54					
2	Dramatic/animated	.41	.54				
3	Attentive/friendly	.39	.36	.50			
4	Dominant/contentious	.46	.41	.33	.48		
5	Relaxed	.42	.24	.30	.27	1.00	
6	Open	.46	.40	.42	.40	.31	1.00

NOTE: The correlations shown in boldface represent the average correlations within each cluster.

closest variable in the three-dimensional solution with a derived coefficient of 58 — in other words, it is 58 units away from communicator image.

Open is the second closest neighbor at 61 units away. Dominant is the third closest unit, 72 units away. In short, the three best candidates for strong predictors of communicator image are impression leaving, open, and dominant. The following analyses specifically identify best predictors.

Best Predictors: Regression Analysis

Three regression analyses are reported here: (1) a regression analysis using a binary split algorithm, called THAID (Morgan & Messenger, 1973), (2) standard regression, and (3) stepwise regression.

THAID

This analysis asks which is the single best predictor of communicator image of the nine style variables, which are all recoded on a mean split. That is, a person is either seen as dominant or not dominant, relaxed or not relaxed, and so on. In this analysis, dominant turns out to be the best predictor of communicator image, as shown in Figure 3.3. Out of the 1086 subjects, 569 reported that they were dominant; 517 reported that they were not dominant.

After the first predictor is identified, the question becomes what is the single best predictor from the remaining eight style variables of the 569 dominant respondents and what is the single best predictor from the remaining eight style variables of the 517 nondominant respondents? In the second split, for the dominant group, open is the best predictor. Out of the 569 subjects in the dominant group, 380 reported that they were *both* dominant and open; 189 reported that they were *both* dominant and not open.

For the nondominant group, relaxed is the best predictor. Out of 517 nondominant respondents, 252 reported that they were *both* nondominant and relaxed; 265 reported that they were nondominant and nonrelaxed.

As shown in Figure 3.3, the THAID analysis continues to split the respective groups until a group has less than 25 members or until the explained variance is not improved sufficiently.

Given the THAID model, "petigrees" of communicator style can be identified or "style profiles" can be determined. For example, a person might fall into the style profile of being dominant, open, dramatic, and very attentive in the way he or she communicates. Another person with a closely similar profile might be dominant, open, and dramatic, but less attentive. Yet another person, with a radically different profile, might be nondominant, nonrelaxed, nonopen, and nondramatic in the way he or she communicates. Essentially, the model allows for a complex typing of style profiles.[18]

STANDARD AND STEPWISE REGRESSION ANALYSES

Table 3.6 reports the results of both standard and stepwise regression analyses of the data. Again, dominant turns out to be the single best predictor of communicator image. In the stepwise analysis, dominant by itself explains 34% of the variance. Only three variables do not make it into the regression analyses — animated, contentious, and dramatic. The other six variables account for 53 percent of the explained variance.

DISCUSSION

Context, Situation, and Time

Like any other psychometric construct, the communicator style construct is contingent upon context, situation, and time. Accordingly, Postulate 6 (see Chapter 2) can be modified as follows:

> Style expectations created by context, situation, and time can influence the literal message more powerfully than the immediate style exhibited verbally, nonverbally, or paraverbally.

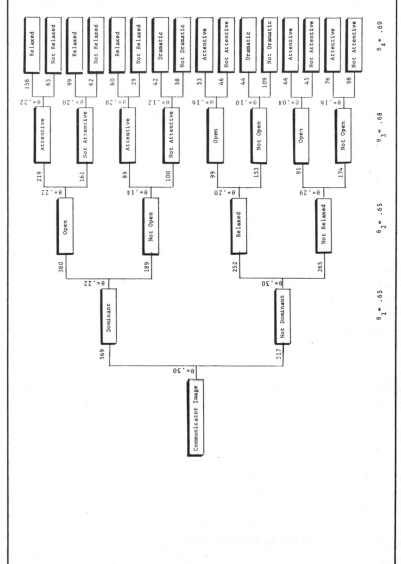

Figure 3.3 THAID Model of Communicator Style Subconstructs

TABLE 3.6   Regression Analyses on Communicator Style Data Set

Variable	Standard Regression		Stepwise Regression	
	Beta	t Statistic	R^2	t Statistic
Dominant	.25	9.7	.34	23.8
Impression leaving	.18	6.6	.43	12.6
Relaxed	.20	8.8	.48	10.2
Open	.19	7.5	.51	9.0
Friendly	.10	3.4	.52	4.9
Attentive	.08	3.0	.53	3.0

NOTE: Animated, contentious, and dramatic did not make it into the equations with $p < .05$. For the standard regression, the variables that entered the regression equation were significant, $F(9, 1076) = 134.1$; $p < .001$. For the stepwise regression, the variables that entered the regression equation were significant, $F(6, 1079) = 201.6$; $p < .001$.

CONTEXT

The context refers to the interactive stage and its setting, including props, rituals, and expectations. A mortuary, a department store, a university, and a restaurant are examples of context.

A person with a normally active style — dramatic, animated, dominant, and contentious — is not as likely to manifest this style of behavior in a funeral home. The context has the capacity to shape style behavior.

SITUATION

The situation refers to what people do within contexts. For instance, processing the dead is expected in a funeral setting, although other interpersonal activities are possible. It is inappropriate in the funeral setting to ask for a loan from the closest relative of the deceased.

TIME

Time is a complex operant that impinges across the microsecond punctuation of a punchline in a joke to different hours in the day to demarcations ranging from youth to old age. For example, my normal style profile may be noticeably different at the end of the day simply because I am tired at that time.

All these components to some extent substantially influence the way one communicates. Exploration of these components will increase our understanding of communicative processes.

"Holes" in the
Structural Solution

One advantage of smallest space analysis, which visually represents the variables, is that the configurations have heuristic impact. For example, "holes" in the construct might be observed. With the SSA solution (Figures 3.1 and 3.2), three areas for further improvement are suggested relating to (1) the relaxed style, (2) the attentive and friendly styles, and (3) the open style.

RELAXED

First, the relaxed subconstruct is isolated. It is likely that there are other subconstructs that naturally belong in this region with the relaxed variable. Another possibility is that the subconstruct of relaxed might be better treated as a multidimensional concept, as suggested earlier, and be broken into distinct types of style variables related to relaxed.

The relaxed subconstruct is complicated. On one hand, a relaxed style may indicate a state of inactivity (nonaction) manifested by appearing listless, unconcerned, lanquid, apathetic, or exhausted. On the other hand, a relaxed style may entail a certain kind of activity, such as focused alertness, that may suggest calmness, inexcitability, or steadiness.

Whatever the case, relaxed is an important variable. It is a relatively good predictor of communicator image. In the regression equations it is the third variable in the equation. In the THAID model, it gets in on the second split for the nondominant group. In the dominant group, it eventually becomes part of six of the eight style types. The task at hand is to discover further the cumulative, form-giving impact that a relaxed style signals.

ATTENTIVE AND FRIENDLY

The attentive and friendly subconstructs are in a region by themselves. Perhaps similar variables focusing on listening, empathy, or comfortableness would explain additional variance in the model.

These style components anchor two of the continua pointed out above. The variables are highly listener oriented. The most attentive communicator not only seems to be listening to the other person, *but often demonstrates that he or she is doing so by "deliberately reacting in such a way that the person" gets feedback.*

Friendly communicative behavior goes hand in hand with attentiveness. Both components require a degree of alertness to the other and probably a large amount of perspective taking. Both components function to complement what the other is doing or has done — that is, it is an action on the part of the other for the friendly or attentive communicator to signal something.

The friendly communicator, for example, is *reacting* to something; the friendly communicator acknowledges, admires, encourages, and is tactful. In short, the friendly communicator delivers a metamessage about the other's behavior. Similarly, the attentive communicator is *reactive*, responsive, and alert. Both behaviors imply that the other has provided some stimulus to acknowledge, encourage, react to, or be tactful about.

Both components are part of the regression equations. Friendly does not make it into the THAID model, probably because the subconstruct is not as cohesive as the attentive subconstruct. Attentive, however, makes it into the dominant group on the third split and into the nondominant group in six out of the eight possible styles.

Research relating to leadership, teaching, therapy, power, and attraction are directions to explore with these subconstructs. The notion that these style variables are form giving in a *reactive* sense is intriguing and complex.

OPEN

The open style component is partially isolated, even though it is near communicator image. If communicator image and open are projected to dimensions I and II, the two subconstructs are closely related. It is in the third dimension that open differs from communicator image. Because of the closeness on two of the dimensions, it is suggested that "readily revealing personal things about the self" and "*openly* expressing one's feelings or emotions" is associated with being a "good" communicator. But this may not be a necessary association. Research may show that a person may be too open, brutally frank, or insensitive to another's perspective.

The open style component is associated with communicator image in the THAID model. Open gets into all eight style profiles. Consequently, several questions emerge: (1) Why is an open style of communication a strong covariate of communicator image? Does it generate trust? Does it alleviate tension? (2) What are the sufficient components that signal openness? These issues are explored much further in Chapter 4.

Additional Directions

In addition to the directions suggested by the "holes," other questions about style associations are brought into sharper focus. Questions about impression leaving, dominant and contentious, and dramatic and animated are raised.

IMPRESSION LEAVING

Impression leaving clustered with communicator image. Along two dimensions it is closely related; on the third dimension it moves away from communicator image. In one sense, both sub-constructs are consequents to the interactive process. That is, communicator image and impression leaving can be treated as results of the interactive process. The difference is that impression leaving can be either positive or negative. A person's style might be remembered because it was so obnoxious or, by contrast, because it was so classy. The primary work to be done with this construct is to identify the combination of signals, clues, or contents that cause another to remember that communicator.

DOMINANT AND CONTENTIOUS

The dominant style seems to have fewer negative connotations than the contentious style, although both are closely related on at least two dimensions. Dominant predicts communicator image most strongly in all regression analyses. Contentious, on the other hand, does not make it into any of the equations.

The communicative activities that mark the dominant style — coming on strong, taking charge, and talking frequently   are often associated with confidence, self-esteem, and leadership. Thus, these are the directions in which to explore further.

Contentious as a subconstruct (Figure 3.1) split into two clusters. The first cluster centers on being quick to challenge the other and being argumentative. The second cluster seems more closely related to "being precise," but not necessarily contentious. In fact, items 10 and 13 have a close connection to the attentiveness sub-construct. This positioning suggests that preciseness could be a style subconstruct in its own right.

The previous questions apply to these concepts: (1) Why is a dominant style a strong covariate of communicator image? Does it generate respect, fear, or obedience? (2) What are the sufficient components that signal dominance or contentiousness?

DRAMATIC AND ANIMATED

Neither of these style components is closely associated with communicator image. The dramatic, animated communicator probably expends relatively more energy than one who is neither dramatic nor animated. The communicator with this style of communication potentially invites a certain kind of risk into his or her interactions because the form-giving function intensifies, exaggerates, or distorts the messages.

The questions initially raised by Freud still apply to these components. Why do people dramatize in their interactions? Does dramatizing release tension? Does it help a person create or think through the vehicle of extended metaphors, fantasies, and "articulated repressions"? Chapter 4 pursues these issues in greater detail.

SUMMARY

The research reported in this chapter deals solely with self-report data (later chapters address other-reported data). One conclusion is that different people claim to be "good" communicators for different reasons. People report that they are "good" communicators across radically divergent styles. For example, the dominant, open, and relaxed communicator and the nondominant, nonrelaxed, and nonopen communicator might evaluate themselves at the same level of communicative competence.

One of the next phases of this research is to have other people, including significant others, acquaintances, strangers, and trained raters, evaluate the communicator in terms of style components. *The difference between self-report and others' assessments will depend upon* (1) *the degree to which the person knows about his or her style and* (2) *the degree to which the person masks various elements of his or her style as a function of situation, context, and the people involved.* Clearly, it should not be surprising if in many instances the self-report does not match an acquaintance's report, especially with one-shot, idiosyncratic comparisons. The following chapters extend many of the points raised here, including examples of behavioral observation by others.

The process of communicating is so intricate that one is relegated to fragmented pieces of knowledge. Substantive communication theories are rare in our young discipline. A minimally satisfying interpersonal communication theory must include both what is communicated (content) and the way it is communicated (style). In other words, the focus on how form is given to the literal meaning of a message in the interactive process is essential to an interpersonal communication theory. A richer theory assimilates explanations, abstractions, inferences, and conclusions about handling complex learning, dealing with complicated cognitions, coping with social relations, and encountering culturally evolved systems of coding (Scheflen, 1965).

This research lays a foundation for style-related components in communication. Ten subconstructs make up the basic configuration, although these need not be the exclusive components. The intercorrelations among the variables indicate that the basis of the construct is stable (reliable) for two reasons. By itself, the first reason is not fully convincing, but it does satisfy a necessary criterion in the development of the construct — namely, the "goodness of fit" statistics show that the configurations did not happen by chance alone.

The second test is more difficult to satisfy, and, hence, provides substantial evidence if passed — that is, replication of the configurations. Essentially, the data in this study represent a replication of a pilot study. The results confirm the structure found in the pilot. Since this replication, many studies have successfully duplicated the communicator style structure.[19]

No configuration of subconstructs, however stable, is theoretically interesting in its own right without practical implications. In addition to the theory-building rational, the following implications warrant the communicator style foundation:

- **It provides a context in which other style components can be anchored.**
- **It provides a perspective from which to examine perceptual processes intrinsic to the communicative process.**
- **It provides a set of relationships that help explain consequences of interpersonal encounters, especially in terms of attraction and effectiveness covariates.**

Communicator Style Construct as a Context

The communicator style construct, with its multivariate structure, provides a context for other, style-related variables. For example, one of the variables that has been popularized is assertiveness.[20] It may be that assertiveness is another way to talk about a combination of particular communication variables. If it is merely a function of established style components, then it might be more parsimonious to resist naming a "new" construct. On the other hand, assertiveness may be closely akin to contentiousness, dominance, and impression leaving on two dimensions, but interestingly different on a third dimension.

Whatever the case, it is useful to study related constructs within a framework that is already established. The structural solution indicates where an assertive style component probably would fall given its thematic connections to dominance, impression leaving, and contentiousness. In fact, this prediction was later confirmed in another study (Norton & Warnick, 1976).

Communicator Style Construct in Perceptual Processes

The way one communicates may affect perceptual processes of the individual. From an information theory orientation, communicator style contributes to both noise and redundancy during an interaction. To the degree that the way one communicates negates, contradicts, blurs, or fails to confirm, it generates ambiguity, uncertainty, or noise. Postulates 2 and 4 (see Chapters 1 and 2) are appropriate:

Whenever a gestalt is ambiguous, one style component in the hierarchy moves more to the center of attention and is valued more.

An ambiguous gestalt motivates the receiver to interactively and inferentially supply premises that alleviate ambiguity.

Consequent to this is the fact that more information is required to make "good" decisions. On the other hand, to the degree that the way one communicates confirms, validates, complements, or intensifies the content, it creates redundancy. Less information is required to make "good" decisions.

Clearly, perceptual processes are complex. Only recently has evidence been found that relates style components to perceiving. It was found that subjects with low communicator style scores (primarily relating to dominance) do not report perceiving any appreciable difference between their way of communicating and that of subjects with high communicator style scores. In contrast, subjects with high communicator style scores report perceiving a significant difference (Norton & Miller, 1975). Chapter 7 explores this phenomenon further.

The critical issue here is whether the differences can be accounted for as a matter of inference or actual perception. The evidence points to a perceptual difference (Chapter 7 explores this notion further). If this is the case, then it would not be surprising that perceptual covariates of communicator style could include self-esteem problems, empathy abilities, and leadership capacities:

- The person *sees* another as confident because of the way the other communicates.
- The therapist fails to *notice* telling nonverbal cues because of the person's style of communication.
- The leader is *perceived* as charismatic as a result of his or her communicator style.

If any of these hypothetical relationships emerge, then consequents dependent upon perceptual processes should be influenced, such as whether a person is evaluated as being attractive, sensitive, effective, or the like.

Communicator Style Construct and Interpersonal Consequents

The primary assumption is that communication processes influence human behavior, especially interpersonal exchanges. Since style is an inseparable component of communication, it is part of the effect determinant by definition. The biggest consequents will relate broadly to variations of attractiveness and effectiveness.

For example, in group therapy the way a person communicates affects whether the therapist is perceived as attractive (Lieberman et al., 1973). In another study, it was found that a dominant, open style of communicating was seen as significantly more attractive in terms of physical, personality, and pragmatic components than a dominant, nonopen style, a nondominant, relaxed style, or a nondominant, nonrelaxed style (Norton & Pettegrew, 1977). This relationship is examined in greater detail in Chapter 8.

Similarly, certain communicator styles are likely to perceived as more effective in particular interactions. For instance, a contentious and dominant style might be inappropriate for a union negotiator, but might work well for certain provoking therapists. Styles have impact on group processes. It was found that dominance components of communicator style are good predictors of effectiveness in a three-person problem-solving situation (Norton,

Schroeder, & Webb, 1979). Further, it is the friendly, dominant, and talkative person who makes things work in a task-oriented group (Carson, 1969). Throughout the following chapters other interpersonal consequences are discussed.

In summary, the communicator style construct is a useful multivariate domain for the researcher, theorist, and practitioner. Internally, the domain works as expected. That is, the respective variables are in anticipated relationships to each other. To a large extent, this chapter is an extensive examination of content and construct validity. It represents an attempt to establish a foundation of a communicator style construct.

Although some of the initial definitions and focusing were stipulative, the nine independent variables and one dependent variable correspond to an a priori framework. As a result, this variable set establishes a domain anchoring point that contributes to a communication theory centered on style components.

NOTES

1. A shortened version of this chapter, including a detailed examination of the pilot study, first appeared in *Human Communication Research* (Norton, 1978). As reported in that article, a questionnaire entailing 102 items representing 10 subconstructs was given to 80 respondents for the pilot study.

2. There are many methods to organize the variables that legitimately fall into the domain of constructs. As Nunnally (1967, p. 85) indicates, a construct is something that the theorist "puts together from his own imagination, something that does not exist as an isolated, observable dimension of behavior." A construct is willed by the theorist. Of course, after the initial stipulation of the boundaries of the construct, the researcher is obligated to demonstrate stability and conceptual cohesiveness in the internal structure of a data set within the domain. And, more important, pragmatic applications need to be established eventually if the construct is to survive.

3. The following researchers, for example, mention styles very broadly: Reusch (1957), Kendon (1967), Gordon (1970), Leginski and Izzett (1973), O'Brien (1974), and Giffin and Patton (1974).

4. Gratch's (1973) notion of "theory" is adopted here; namely, "theory" means "an hypothesis of correspondence between a definitional system for a universe of observation and an aspect of the empirical structure of those observations, together with a rationale for such an hypothesis."

5. There is no rule regarding which variables should define a domain of any subconstruct. Initially, the best the researcher can do, especially for a multivariate construct, is to stipulate the boundaries of the domain. If the nuances defining what belongs in a domain are subtle or small, then capricious relationships are more likely to be made. If elements of commonality recur across theoretical systems dealing with similar phenomena, then the boundary stipulations can be made with increasing confidence.

6. See such popular works as those by Smith (1975), Fensterheim and Baer (1975), Alberti and Emmons (1974), Bloom and Coburn (1975), and Osborn and Harris (1975).

7. In 1975, Ekman concurred with Darwin's (1872) postulation that some facial expressions connected to nonvoluntary actions are due to the constitution of the nervous system. Ekman and Friesen (1976) found that the management of facial expressions varies within each culture, but that some expressions may be universal across cultures.

8. Dimensions help to organize structures in a data set. If a dimension is contained within a configuration, then a monotonic function can be used to describe an individual's score along that continuum. The activity intrinsic to the dimension defines a general orientation to understand the configuration. A person at one end of the continuum can be said to manifest a high amount of the activity that anchors that extreme, and conversely. If the clustering expectations hold as suggested, there will be at least one underlying dimension in the structure pointing to the following broad hypothesis: If a person communicates in a style that is active and sender oriented, then that person tends not to communicate in a style that is relatively more passive and other oriented. Of course, the hypothesis is simplistic and speculative, but it reflects the heuristic import of locating dimensions.

9. In a pilot study, 80 subjects for the University of Michigan voluntarily filled out a longer version (102 items) of the CSM.

10. In the pilot study, a 7-point scale had been used. Thus the commitment to the smaller scale range and the reduction in the number of items, omitting 52, represents a loss of information. Finer distinctions are disallowed. The smaller scale size and the reduced items commit one to the following conservative, but functionally pragmatic, assumption: *An effect will be considered trivial or too weak to be interesting unless it can be detected by five items per subconstruct using a four-point scale.* In later chapters when individual subconstructs are examined more closely, this assumption is modified.

11. See Norton (1980a). The technique was developed by Guttman (1968) and refined and computerized by Lingoes (1973).

12. The coefficient of alienation with weak monotonicity is .25, which, for the purposes of structural information here, is relatively good. A .15 coefficient is usually preferred.

13. A factor analysis was done with a random sample of 383 cases from the same data set. Ten factors emerged in expected patterns. The open, relaxed, impression leaving, and communicator image subconstructs were defined by the appropriate items. The dominant subconstruct lost only one item. However, the contentious construct defined by three of its original items loaded on the same factor as dominant. Similarly, the dramatic subconstruct (four items) and the animated subconstruct (four items) loaded on the same factor. The attentive subconstruct lost two items. The friendly subconstruct did not hold together as well as the others in the factor analysis. It scattered across factors 5, 7, 8, and 10. Nevertheless, the results from the factor analysis parallel the results from the smallest space analysis.

14. With semistrong monotonicity, the coefficient of alienation is .07. Clearly, a three-dimensional solution is more than adequate for the structural solution with the ten subconstructs.

15. The number and character of the dimensions are suggested with this SSA solution. A one-dimensional solution has a coefficient of alienation of .43; a two-dimensional solution has a cofficient of .17; a three-dimensional solution has a coefficient of .07 (all with semistrong monotonicity).

16. Of course, it is too early to identify the exact nature of the continua at this point in the development of style research. The above continua can be defined formally in terms of simplexes. In brief, if all the variables within a set (space) can be projected without any intransitivities onto a line that does not bend back on itself, then the variables determine a simplex. An easy way to discern a simplex pattern is to arrange the variables in the correlation table such that all the values in both the rows and columns monotonically decrease away from the diagonal.

17. In this data set, there are three five-variable simplexes that reflect the characteristics outlined for the continua.

18. Note that scores are not added together to obtain a single communicator style tally, but style components are grouped to create a single nominal type.

19. Not all of the structural replications of the communicator style domain are reported, but the interested reader is referred to Pettegrew (1977a), Norton (1977), and Norton and Robinson (1980).

20. For example, see Alberti and Emmons (1974), Fensterheim and Baer (1975), and Glassi and Glassi (1974).

II

SUBCONSTRUCT
DEVELOPMENT

4 / Open S...

the accessible and unrestrained communicator

Before marshaling
the formal arguments
about open style, let us in-
dulge in some word play with the
word "open" while holding the following question in mind: What does open style
signal?

Webster's Dictionary provides many definitions for
"open":

(1) **not closed or barred at the time, as a doorway or passageway by the door**

What is capable of being closed or barred interpersonally?

What corresponds to the passageway interactionally?

What constitutes a door or blocking device?

(2) **(of a barrier, as a door) set so as to permit passage through the opening it otherwise closes**

Open cannot be defined without having a notion of "something to get into." Similarly, it cannot be defined without the notion of being "not open," that is, being closed.

Stylistically, what is the concept of being closed?

What are the essential characteristics of a passage or a door being open?

What is the functionally pragmatic import?

- One can see what is inside.
- One can get to the inside.
- Things can be retrieved from the inside.
- One can take things to the outside.
- One can take things to the inside.
- Insides can be changed because the system can "leak" or be "leaked into."
- It can be a transition to another system; it can be a link to another system.
- Options are increased.

(3) having no means of being enclosed

No parameter is possible and/or apparently possible. The great outdoors is "open." Space is "open."

Here is a notion/concept of "open" that is expansive; it is difficult to think of its opposite. Is a closed outdoors a *defined* space? What is a *closed* universe?

Anything goes when something like the universe is "open."

Is being open equivalent to being accepting?

Is being open an "on" condition?

(4) having the interior immediately accessible, as a drawer that is pulled out

What is the communicative interior? One's hopes and fears? One's identity? One's sense of self? Oneself? One's strengths and weaknesses?

"Immediately accessible" implies that little, if any, work is needed to get the "something on the interior."

Does an open style signal little resistance to "core communication processes?" Does it signal a willingness to be drained? Deprived? Ransacked? Destroyed and made void of content?

(5) relatively free of obstructions: an open floor plan

What are the communicative obstructions? Content? Context? Overlapping contexts? Defense mechanisms? Style doors/style barriers? Language filters? Predispositions? Culture?

Physical/spiritual/biological/chemical/legal obstructions?

(6) constructed so as not to be fully enclosed: an open boat

Can social interaction be constructed so as not to be fully enclosed? An open marriage? An open complementary structure?

(7) having relatively large or numerous voids or intervals: open ranks of soldiers

When something is open, NOTHING blocks the way! A void blocks the way; an interval blocks the way. Is "open" nothing? The "instant photocopier inside our head" prevents the drawer from getting empty; 2800 images from the inside get transferred. If one image gets transferred — through an open passage — a change may be triggered. No more energy is lost saying the "content" to one person than saying it to 40 million people.

Can we get a void in the communicative process? Large intervals in the flow of communication could be construed as obstructions in the process. Open has the capacity of being interpreted as "closed."

(8) relatively unoccupied by buildings, fences, trees, etc.: open country

A space. A communication space. A communicant space. Unoccupied by emotion, idea, commitment, etc.

(9) extended or unfolded: an open newspaper

What does it mean to stylistically extend the self? Reach out? Touch the other? What does it mean to unfold oneself stylistically? Signal the complexities, the subtleties, the nuances, the distortions, the turns, the perspectives?

The jackknife is open/extended. It can do more. It is now useful. It can do work. What is the communicative work? What is the stylistic work? Is it also dangerous? What is dangerous about being open?

(10) without restrictions as to who can participate: an open competition

Being open invites unrestricted participation; it invites reciprocal openness, but does not mandate it.

The unrestricted participation comes in using/abusing/dealing with the "something" that has been made available. If I make M available to a person, that person has the freedom/option to make M available to anybody. Unrestricted participation is inherent in my openness; it is the potential intrinsic to the communication.

(11) available; accessible, as for trade: Which job is open? It is an open port.

If my communication is made open, it becomes the coin of the realm for others. Like other money, it is susceptible to inflation, but not necessarily. Like money, it is a "rough promise to pay the bearer upon demand/request" something. Like money, it can be counterfeited. Like money, it may be worthless across somebody else's border.

(12) not restricted as to the hunting of game: open season

Being open, "going public" with something.

There are about 20 more definitions of "open" listed. The above definitions are both informative and suggestive of what might be stipulated as an *open style*. The emergent reflections are woven into the rationale below.

The open communicator invites the other to believe that the perceived information accurately characterizes the self. In its most banal form, the perceived information can be boring, trivial, or irrelevant. The statement "I like pie" can accurately characterize an individual, but it hardly matters in defining a relationship. In the most dynamic form the perceived information is often intense, risky, traumatic, or dangerous. The statement "I have had an abortion" can change the course of a relationship.

The subtlety here revolves around "perceived accuracy." This means that a person may provide inaccurate information about the self and still be perceived as being open. In other words, perceived openness is not dependent upon accuracy.

This chameleon aspect is not intrinsic to other style components. For example, the perceived animated style usually approximates the degree of physical expressiveness; the perceived open style may or may not match the degree of accurate information set about the self. However, for the remaining discussion, unless otherwise specified, it will be assumed that the individual is attempting to transmit real information about the self.

The more abstract term that establishes the context for this discussion is "openness." At this point it is necessary to make a subtle and important distinction: *Being open may be different from being self-disclosive.*

A person may be perceived to be both open and self-disclosive without actually being self-disclosive. That is, the receiver learns very little personal, private, and risky information from the other, but, nevertheless, has the impression that the other was open. In effect, this is a misperception on the receiver's part. The communicator did things that looked and sounded like self-disclosure.

What are some of the cues? Talking extensively about another's illicit behavior is a typical example. The talk has characteristics of frankness, secret knowledge, confidentiality, and privacy. It would be precise to say that the communicator is being open about another's life, but not about his or her own life — that is, the person is not being self-disclosive. Sometimes only careful listening prevents misperception and incorrect attribution.

In addition, other perceptual combination can occur:

- A person may be perceived to be neither open nor self-disclosive.
- A person may be perceived to be both open and self-disclosive.
- A person may be perceived to be open, but not self-disclosive.
- A person may be perceived to be self-disclosive, but not open.

For instance, presenting false information about the self but indicating that it is true causes another person to perceive the communicator as being open when the individual is actually quite the opposite.

In essence, this dynamic is the core of lies and deception on one hand and drama, humor, magician's patter, and tact on the other. Because of the various nuances, it is easy to interchange such phrases as "being open" and "self-disclosure." It is useful, however, in style work to attend to the distinctions.

The content of disclosure, the style (the way the content is communicated), and the target of disclosure impinge upon perceived openness. As a consequent, this chapter builds around these three components by (1) discussing open style in the context of the self-disclosive process, (2) introducing an instrument that integrates the three components, (3) accessing an instrument that measures openness, and (4) resynthesizing the subconstruct of open style.

THE SELF-DISCLOSIVE PROCESS

The self-disclosive process entails revealing something to someone in a particular way. The minimal elements in the process involve content, style, and a target of communication. Even though content, style, and target are often inextricable, it is useful to examine each one separately. The following sections focus on the isolated elements.

Content Component

The content component is verbal and digital. It is the literal meaning of the message; it is the referent in the message. The content component can be infinitely complex. For example, the message "I get extremely emotional talking about cancer" can be mitigated by another content component. If the message about cancer was preceded by the statement "What I am about to say is untrue," then the cancer message is either completely or partially changed.

This dynamic reflects Axioms 1-3 (Chapter 1), which state:

Axiom 1:   Any message system can draw a distinction either by literal meaning or by stylistic means.

Axiom 2:   One message system gives form to another when the literal meaning of one system is reinforced or changed.

Axiom 3:   Form-giving messages can be antecedent to, simultaneous with, or subsequent to another message.

In short, any content *about* a content component functions stylistically because it draws a distinction that at least reinforces the original literal meaning. Most content, however, does not function at the meta level. It informs at a literal level. Soap operas highlight some extreme examples. Statements such as "I am married," "I really am not blind," and "I want you to pull the plug on the life system when I can't function" should have relational impact for the interactants. Of course, there are countless instances in which information from the personal domain of the other does not have such dramatic impact.

Because the content itself is a powerful and important factor in interaction, the following axiom is used to call attention to it:

Axiom 7:   The content component establishes the parameters of the referents in the self-disclosure process.

CONTENT TYPE

The degree of *perceived risk* and the *amount of qualitative information* are the two central concerns in studying content type in the self-disclosure process.

Qualitative Information. In order to talk about open style, the notion of qualitative information is introduced. The following definition connects the individual to self-disclosed information:

Definition 4:   Qualitative information about the self is information that is representational of the self.

> That is, it is information about the self that is isomorphic with what the self knows the self to be. It is information that indicates that the self is what the self appears to be.

This means that all risky information about the self is qualitative, but the converse need not be true. In the self-disclosure process, qualitative information is the "coin of the realm." It ultimately makes a difference in how the relationship between two people will be defined. In the next section, the value of Definition 4 is shown. As always, the style component — discussed in the next section — synergistically affects the message.

Risky Information. The key to identifying risky information is vulnerability. Consequently, the following definition is introduced:

Definition 5:   A message is risky if the self becomes vulnerable to another person because of it.

The paradox is that the other person may never abuse or misuse the information or even think of it, hence the degree of vulnerability may seem minimal. Nevertheless, the *potential* to hurt the other is there. It is for this reason that the people who love us the most have the capacity to hurt us the most.

Postulate 8:   Personal, private, unambiguous, and explanatory information has the greatest potential to be risky.

The personal element of the message links the communicator directly or indirectly to the content. As such, "personalness of messages" is often assessed in studying openness (Weiner & Mehrabian, 1968; McDaniels, Yarbrough, Kuszmaul, & Griffin, 1971). It is expressed as the degree of identity a speaker has with a topic or as the degree of ownership of feelings and opinions suggested by the phrasing, for example:

- I love you.
- I get hurt easily when you attack my friends.
- It is my thought that I need some time alone.

The more personal the content, the more it may indicate the essence or psyche of the individual. As a result, the potential for rejection or confirmation by another is increased.

The private element of the message reflects the degree to which the informant is in one of the best positions because of status, position, or even accident to reveal the information. Sometimes it is difficult to separate the personal and private elements. The following examples help clarify the distinction:

- *Neither private nor personal:* "The governor is dead."
- *Personal, but not necessarily private:* "I was in the 1968 march on Washington."
- *Private, but not personal:* "I know something about Babs Smith that would make your hair stand on end."
- *Both personal and private:* "I can't cope anymore."

The unambiguous element of the message accurately details the specifics and directly affects perceived risk. Because an individual has a complex set of verbal choices that can distort or misdirect the essence of meaning, riskiness depends upon language constraints.

Ambiguity operates in two ways. If it generates vagueness, then perceived risk is probably diluted. On the other hand, if it suggests multiple meanings, then perceived risk may be increased. The statement "I am funny that way" invites the other person to consider a second interpretation of the content that is more risky, more daring, and potentially more informative.

The explanatory element of the message creates a connected pattern of events (a narrative structure) and, as a result, the perceived risk is manipulated. Causal links, contrasts, and time sequences aid the narrative structure.

For example, the following self-disclosure verbally creates a logical, connecting pattern that enhances the intensity:

In 1950, my father committed suicide *because* he could not resolve the contradictions presented by my mother. *As a result* . . .

The connecting pattern can be expressed in terms of contrasts:

I am *not happy;* I am *sad* because Joe died.

It can be expressed in terms of a time referent:

Before I got my degree, I was compulsive. *Now,* I'm obsessive and compulsive.

In addition, the cultural context for the content of a message shapes expectations about the way certain things are discussed. Some content is more risky to talk about in a particular culture than other content. The most typical research rank orders topics in terms of perceived riskiness (see Taylor & Altman, 1971; Jourard, 1971; Deher & Banikotes, 1976; Norton, Feldman, & Tafoya, 1974; Norton, Moore, Williams, & Montgomery, 1978). For example, topics about sex tend to be perceived as more risky than topics about manners.

In brief, the content component is the core of verbal disclosure. To the extent that the information requires strong logical syntax and introduces complex referent patterns, the information about the personal domain needs to be verbalized.

The next sections briefly examine the functions of style, content, and target in the openness construct. Some functions have been strongly established in the literature and others are speculative. The task of this chapter is not to verify which claims are true, but to provide an instrument that sheds light on research questions concerning openness.

Style Component

CHARACTERISTICS OF OPEN STYLE

The communicator has a sophisticated, wide-ranging repertoire of signals to determine the way literal meaning is to be taken, filtered, or understood. If a person says, "I love you," in a sardonic, hateful, or dispassionate way, then the message is changed accordingly. In this instance, the style component negatively changes the literal message. If a person says, "I love you," in a sensuous, loving, or warm way, then the message is reinforced accordingly. In this instance, the style component positively complements the message.

The open style variable strongly relates to dominant and impression leaving as seen in the structural analysis in Chapter 3. Also, it is the best predictor of communicator image. This suggests that having an open style relates to being able to control an interaction socially and partially determines whether one will be remembered and seen as a good communicator.

Axiom 8:   Open style essentially signals that the message is personal, private, unambiguous, and explanatory. The way the person "openly" communicates indicates that the message should be taken, filtered, or understood to be representational of the self and isomorphic with what the self knows the self to be.

Definition 6 summarizes the essentials:

Definition 6:   Open style signals that qualitative information about the self is available.

Again, it is important to remember that open style does not guarantee that the information will be accurate or honest, only representational.

Open style signals can be both verbal and nonverbal, digital and analogical. Nonverbal indicators can signal an open style, such as the cues associated with the emotions dealing with love, hate, security, happiness, or sadness. Also, an open style can be signaled verbally. The statement "I will tell you whatever you want to know" is a direct, verbal signal of open style.

REASONS TO STUDY OPEN STYLE

It is important to study open style because it affects social interaction in many critical areas. The postulate that communication scholars need to explore thoroughly is the following:

Postulate 9:   As open style is increasingly signaled, interpersonal options increase.

In short, the potential for unique combinations of information that define real choices increases as information in a communicative system increases. By being open, information is increased. If a person signals that he or she is religious, then the other person has a new set of options to explore if interested. The assumption is that qualitative information makes a difference in how two people will relate.

Intimacy, for example, is affected by open style of communication.[2] The most frequent hypothesis is that as openness increases, intimacy increases. An open style influences marital development, but it has a double edge (see Miller, Corraltes, & Wackman, 1975; Regula, 1975). On the one hand, it can strengthen the bond of the couple. On the other hand, openness might trigger an adverse reevaluation of the marriage if it highlights a previously undiscussed issue.

Also, style variables function as mediational components that explain how interpersonal solidarity is derived (Wheeless, 1978). In other words, the way one communicates may directly affect the degree of psychological, social, and physical closeness between people. If style variables influence solidarity, then trust, liking, and frequency and quality of interaction are affected also.

In addition, dating skills (d'Augelli, 1975; Van Zoost, 1973), group skills (Lonber, 1975), adolescent development (West, 1974), sensitivity (Nel, 1975), and specificity of disclosure (West & Boutillien, 1972) vary as a function of open style.

At minimum, the person with an open style seems to grant permission to explore specified aspects of the personal domain. At maximum, the person with an open style invites radically intense and reciprocal interaction that may entail the boundaries of one's identity, value system, beliefs, idiosyncracies, and core commitments.

Although open style invites exploration, it does not mean that the "invitation" will be accepted. Open style guarantees neither change nor a bilateral process. The flow of information about the self in many instances will only be unilateral. This is especially true when reciprocation is inappropriate, unhealthy, or unwise (Chelune, 1977). Also, no amount of information will change a person who is oblivious to it, sufficiently unreceptive, or functionally inept.

The important research question revolves around those instances in which the person with an open style causes something to happen within the dyad. Two general directions are suggested. First, interpersonal options increase as an open style is increasingly signaled. Second, relational consequences change as an open style is increasingly signaled.

By signaling openness, the other is given the right to choose whether to pursue an avenue of communication. The new interpersonal option may cover a wide-ranging area. If the person says, "No topic of conversation is taboo with me," then the potential for increased, shared, personal information is great. In contrast, the new option may be highly directive and parochial. If a person signals that he or she is religious, then the other person has a fairly limited area to explore initially. The conversation agenda may be set to revolve only around religious topics.

If the person accepts the "invitation" to explore the personal domain, then the defined relationship between the two people may change. There may be information in the personal domain of the open communicator that will affect the relational consequences of the dyad.

A variety of relational consequences is posited by the researchers. Open style has been related either directly or indirectly to (1) repression-sensitization (Chelune, 1977); (2) control, trust, and intimacy (Millar & Rogers, 1976); (3) communication awareness

(Emener & Rye, 1975; (4) self-concept (Shapiro & Swenson, 1977); (5) therapy dropouts (Heilbrun, 1973); (6) attraction (MacDonald, Games, & Mink, 1972); and (7) trust (Johnson & Noonan, 1973).

Target Component

Information is perceived to be risky at various levels ranging from a larger cultural framework to an individual orientation. The statement "I am an ex-con" may be perceived as less risky on the average at a generalized, cultural level than for a person who really did serve time in a prison.

In this research, the focus is upon the individual perspective. That is, the person is asked how risky a particular topic is for him or her. The pattern that connects the risk variable across the levels revolves around the capacity to reward or punish.

The target, the receiver of personal information, can reward the discloser with love, confirmation, understanding, tolerance, and acceptance and, if so desired, can punish the discloser with hate, disconfirmation, rejection, and denial. Consequently, openness is also dependent on who the target of disclosure is.

Trust, as it relates to target, is the most frequently cited variable in the openness literature. Being selected as a target often is a sufficient indicator that one is trusted (see Worthy et al., 1979; Pearce & Sharp, 1973; Millinger, 1956). The amount of depth and the honesty of self-disclosure are strongly associated with the perceived trustworthiness of the target (Wheeless, 1978).

The target in the relationship is often reevaluated and reevaluates as a function of openness covarying with trust (Savicki, 1973; Chaiken & Derlega, 1974), intimacy (Altman & Taylor, 1973), commitment (Gilbert, 1976), responsibility (Culbert, 1967), and solidarity (Wheeless, 1978). This means that open communication produces a constant series of interpersonal adjustments for both the target and disclosure.

Researchers report that personal information increases from the target after the first person discloses (Derlega, Harris, & Chaiken, 1973; Davis & Skinner, 1974; Thase & Page, 1977). This finding has been relatively consistent, but researchers have not agreed on the explanation (Altman & Taylor, 1973; Marlatt, 1977; Thase & Page, 1977). The assumption is that a person with a high degree of openness will more readily disclose personal information to a wide variety of targets than a person with a low degree of openness. The second assumption is that the target necessarily influences the amount and kind of disclosure.

Summary

Openness is a gestalt. It occurs only when style, content, and target components are integrated. The exciting prospect is that openness has the capacity to affect interpersonal relationships significantly and importantly. The remainder of this chapter addresses the *perceived communicative openness of the communicator.* It is expected that the style component will play a large part in determining perceived openness because of its powerful, hierarchical impact (Postulate 1).

METHOD

In this section, a questionnaire is presented that includes sections dealing with the style, content, and target components of openness. The measure was given to a large sample and then was statistically analyzed and interpreted.

SUBJECTS

The subjects were 324 students from communication classes at Purdue University who voluntarily completed the measure. All responses were anonymous and strictly confidential. Subjects were provided feedback about the test if they indicated interest.

MEASURE

The paper-and-pencil measure of openness represents a source-oriented approach. It is the person's testimony about his or her perceptions of communicative behavior relating to openness. As such, it is useful for three reasons. First, it provides an organizing tool to analyze the domain variables that are phrased in terms of communicative activity; second, it provides a baseline to contrast receiver-oriented data; third, it helps establish units of analysis for coders to use when observing behavior. In the short run, the person's self-report of the quantity and quality of information being disclosed provides at least one anchor to understand the interactive dimensions of communication. In the long run, it will be used to study the more complex disclosure process of social interaction.

The measure consisted of three parts. Part one was composed of 27 items focusing on the style component. Table 4.2 reports the exact wording of the items that proved to be the best indicators. Of the 27, 19 items were kept. A 5-point scale was used, ranging from "very strong agreement" to "very strong disagreement" with the item. Close to 1000 articles relating to self-disclosure were examined.[3] A content analysis of 60 articles that directly addressed openness and communication or self-disclosure and communication provided the sources from which items were generated.

Part two of the measure addressed the content component. A list of general topics allowed the subjects to describe their openness in terms of the content component. Of course, there are many levels of abstraction with which to examine the content. Since this study is interested in the more general phenomenon of openness, a consolidated list of topics was employed.

The instructions read: "Topics affect your openness. How open are you — that is, letting people know the 'real' you — in your discussion of each of the following topics?" A 7-point scale, ranging from "not very open" to "very open," was used. There were 17 topics listed. The topics were developed over a series of three studies (Norton et al., 1974; Norton, Petronio, & Leenhouts, 1975; Norton, Moore, Williams, & Montgomery, 1978). The assumption is that if a person claims that he or she can talk about risky topics, that person probably is relatively open.

In part three, six targets of disclosure were specified: (1) close friend of the same sex, (2) stranger, (3) the most dominant parent, (4) somebody in authority, (5) close friend of the opposite sex, and (6) the least dominant parent. The subjects were asked to indicate the amount of openness they would likely show each target. A nine-point scale was used, ranging from "a little" to "a lot."

Finally, four dependent variables were stipulated. The following two dependent variables helped provide a test for criteria-related validity:

(1) Out of a random group of seven people, I probably would have a more open style of communicating than (how many of them?).

(2) Out of random group of seven people, I probably would be willing to disclose personally private information more readily than (how many of them?).

The other two dependent variables helped provide an indication for the consequences of being open. They were:

(1) Are you a good communicator in general?

(2) How long does it generally take for a person to get to know you?

TABLE 4.1   Combinations Signaling Openness and Self-Disclosiveness

	Signals an Open Style	Does Not Signal an Open Style
High Discloser	synchronous gestalt	nonsynchronous gestalt
Low Discloser	nonsynchronous gestalt	synchronous gestalt

NOTE: This table reflects Definitions 1 and 2 (Chapter 1).

The first variable uses the same scale employed in the style section. The second variable used a nine-point scale ranging from "not very long" to "very long."

RESULTS

Results can be overwhelming unless they are synthesized in some way. In this chapter, larger units of analysis are created from the style, content, and target items. Factor analysis provides the methodology.

The larger units of analysis were tested in part two to see whether they behaved as expected when stratified into predetermined subsamples. The four subsamples were constructed according to combinations defined by two of the dependent variables — namely, whether a person signals an open style of communicating and whether a person readily discloses personally private information. Table 4.1 shows the combinations.

The most general expectation is that people who are relatively more open in perceived style and are relatively more disclosive of personally private information will also:

(1) see the self as more willing to discuss risky topics;

(2) see the self as communicating in a way that signals openness;

(3) see the self as more willing to disclose and signal openness across a variety of targets.

In part three, the larger units of analysis — namely, the factors within the respective components — were used as predictors of the four dependent variables: (1) whether a person is willing to disclose, (2) whether a person signals an open style, (3) whether a person is a good communicator, and (4) how long it generally takes to get to know a person.

Units of Analysis

The open style items, the topics of disclosure, and the targets of disclosure were analyzed separately.[4]

FACTOR ANALYSES OF OPEN STYLE ITEMS

The units of analysis were obtained by a 2-step process. First, 27 items relating to open style were factor analyzed. A total of 4 factors made up of 19 items from a 7-factor solution were useful according to 2 criteria: (1) whether the item could be conceptually integrated easily and (2) whether the item was normally distributed. These 19 items were then factor analyzed again to generate the following units.

Five units emerged: (1) negative openness, (2) emotional openness, (3) general assessment of openness, (4) direct indications of openness, and (5) nonverbal indications of openness. The units are reported in Table 4.2. The best items in the analysis loaded at least .5 on the primary factor and no more than .3 on any other factor. Items 8, 12, 14, 17, and 19 are the exceptions. These items were retained for the respective factor, however, because they were conceptually appropriate and because they function as bridge items between the factors.

Negative Openness. Negative openness specifically deals with "showing disagreement," expecially in an adverse or difficult situation. The item "I openly show my disagreement with people" best represents the factor. The average correlation among the four items is .3.

Emotional Openness. Emotional openness generally reflects whether one's emotional state is "easy to read." A person with an open style shows emotion, lets others know the mood, and does not hide particular reactions, such as anger. The average correlation among the four items is .3.

General Assessment of Openness. This factor focuses on an overall evaluation of one's openness. It is a direct assessment of one's open style. This factor is the original version, plus item 10, of the open subconstruct reported in the communicator style construct.[5] The structure of this group of items has been replicated in eight independent studies. The average correlation among the items is .4.

TABLE 4.2   Factor Analysis of Open Style Items

Scale Items[a]	Factor Loadings				
	I	II	III	IV	V
Negative Openness (50% explained variance)					
1. I openly show my disagreement with people.	.7	.2	.1	.1	.0
2. I tell people when I really do not like them.	.5	.0	.1	−.2	.2
3. When I disagree with a person in authority, I express my disagreement.	.5	.0	.0	.2	.0
4. I have no trouble expressing strong negative feelings to people.	.5	.0	.1	.1	.0
Emotional Openness (17% explained variance)					
5. People always seem to know my moods from my nonverbal behavior.	.0	.5	.1	.0	.2
6. People can easily read my emotional state from my facial expressions.	.0	.5	.1	.0	.2
7. When I strongly feel an emotion, I show it.	.2	.5	.2	.2	.1
8. I show my anger when people make me angry.	.3	.4*	.1	.1	−.2
General Assessment of Openness (15% explained variance)					
9. I readily reveal personal things about myself	.0	.2	.7	.1	.2
10. I can talk about any intimate subject about myself with most people.	.2	−.1	.6	.1	.1
11. I am an *extremely* open communicator.	.2	.1	.6	.2	.1
12. As a rule, I *openly* express my feelings or emotions.	.1	.4	.5*	.3	.0
13. Usually I do not tell people very much about myself until I get to know them quite well.**	.1	−.2	−.5	.0	.1
Direct Indications of Openness (12% explained variance)					
14. I usually signal to people that they can openly communicate with me.	.0	.0	.1	.5*	.3

(continued)

TABLE 4.2 Continued

Scale Items[a]	Factor Loadings				
	I	*II*	*III*	*IV*	*V*
15. I have told people that they can talk to me about their personal problems.	.1	.0	.1	.5	.1
16. I have no trouble expressing strong positive feelings to people.	.1	.1	.2	.5	.1
Nonverbal Indications of Openness (6% explained variance)					
17. My facial expression reflects my concern for other people.	.0	.2	.1	.3	.5*
18. My facial expressions reflect that I am interested in getting positive feedback about myself from others.	.1	.1	.1	.2	.4
19. I send a lot of nonverbal signals to show that I am an open communicator.	.1	.2	.3	.3	.4*

NOTE: Underscored numbers represent highest loadings among factors.

a. Most items are positively worded, which might create a response bias. However, I agree with Rorer (1965) about response bias; it is consequential in this type of instrument. In fact, to have half the items worded negatively and half worded positively may provide less reliable information because of the difficulty of dealing with two negatives, one in the item and one in the response scale.

*These items represent "bridge" items in the factor solution. For example, item 12 loads moderately high on both Factors II and III, which is reasonable because the item is a conceptual blend of "emotional openness" and "assessment of openness."
**This item must be reversed (6 minimum score for item) before summing scores for factor.

Direct Indications of Openness. This factor reflects two things: First, the person is open; second, the person is receptive to others being open. The best item in the factor is "I usually signal to people that they can openly communicate with me." The average correlation among the items is .3.

Nonverbal Indications of Openness. This factor refers to nonverbal behavior, especially facial expressions, that signals an open style. Although the key item, "My facial expressions reflect my concern for other people," centers on concern, other emotional reflectors could have been substituted, such as joy, love, hope, or boredom. The second item in the factor signals that being open is also receiver oriented. The average correlation among items is .3.

The general assessment factor is the core of the open style domain. All factors revolve around it in terms of correlations among the five factors. The open style domain is highly cohesive, but not purely unidimensional. For instance, it is feasible that a person could score high on negative openness and general assessment of openness and score only average on direct indications of openness. It would be wise for the researcher to attend to the scores of all five factors in relationship to any covariates of interest.

The researcher can expect that if a person scores high on the general assessment factor, the person will also score high on at least one other factor. A high score on the general assessment factor, in self-report data, represents a claim that the person communicates in an open way, but it does not specify the types of open style manifestations. The remaining factors, however, provide direct clues concerning the way open style is signaled. In short, by collapsing the scores of the items, the five factors determine the larger units of analysis for the style component used in other parts of the report.

FACTOR ANALYSIS OF TOPICS OF DISCLOSURE

From a 17-item pool of topics affecting openness, 4 larger units emerged from the factor analysis. The units — general philosophies, negative behavior, personal physical or social assets, and personal mental concerns — are reported in Table 4.3. Every item has at least a .5 loading on the primary factor. Two items, 6 and 17, have a moderately strong .4 loading on a second factor. Although six items, 2, 10, 12, 14, 15, and 16, have a .3 loading on a second factor, an examination of the raw correlations indicated that the six items were approximately grouped by the primary factor loading.

The following four factors defined the units of analysis for the content component.

General Philosophies. This factor includes mostly attitudes and beliefs toward social, religious, or political issues. The topic, attitudes toward stealing and cheating, typifies the factor. All items in the factor are highly interrelated, with an average correlation among them of .4.

Negative Behavior. In this factor, the topics reflect either directly or indirectly aspects of undesirable behavior, including extreme negative behavior, failures, and bad habits. The average correlation among the items is .6. This suggests that there is a high degree of conceptual overlap among the topics.

Personal Physical or Social Assets. This factor entails personal physical or social assets. Assets are thought of in this report as those possessions a person has that may be converted into inter-

TABLE 4.3   Factor Analysis of Topics of Disclosure

Scale Items	Factor Loadings			
	I	II	III	IV
General Philosophies (63% explained variance)				
1. Attitudes toward stealing or cheating	.7	.1	.0	–.1
2. Attitudes about death and life after death	.6*	.0	.1	.3
3. Religious beliefs	.6	.1	.1	.1
4. Attitudes toward drugs and alcohol	.5	.1	.2	.0
5. "Philosophy of life"	.5	.2	.1	.2
6. Personal goals	.5*	.1	.2	.4
7. Political beliefs	.5	.1	.2	.2
Negative Behavior (16% explained variance)				
8. Extreme negative behaviors	.1	.8	.2	.1
9. Failures	.2	.7	.2	.2
10. Bad habits	.2	.6*	.1	.3
Physical and Social Assets (12% explained variance)				
11. Body	.2	.2	.8	.0
12. Physical health	.3	.1	.5*	.1
13. Sexual behavior	.0	.1	.5	.1
14. Financial worth	.1	.1	.5*	.3
Personal Mental Concerns (9% explained variance)				
15. Personal mental health	.2	.2	.3	.7*
16. Fears	.3	.3	.1	.6*
17. Personal relationships	.0	.2	.4	.5*

NOTE: Underscored numbers represent highest loadings among factors.
*Probable bridge items among factors.

personal power. Some assets are more transient than others. For instance, financial worth may have a more erratic impact than physical health in terms of interpersonal power. The first three topics — body, physical health, and sexual behavior — concern at least one aspect of the person's physical nature. The topic of sexual behavior, not surprisingly, is most related to the body (r = .5), but it is also strongly related to another topic in factor four, namely, personal relationships (r = .4). The most surprising topic to fall into the factor is financial worth. The correlations with the other topics — body, physical health, and sexual behavior — are moderately high, with respective coefficients of .4, .4, and .2. A tentative interpretation is that it is as difficult in general to be open about one's financial worth as it is to be open about one's body or physical health. The average correlation among the topics is .4.

Personal Mental Concerns. This factor revolves around personal mental concerns such as mental health, fears, and relationships. These topics are so interrelated that it is often difficult to talk about one topic without talking about either or both of the other topics. The average correlation among topics is .5.

The general philosophies factor is the easiest group of topics to be open about, with a mean of 5.6 on the 7-point scale. Topics dealing with personal physical or social assets and with personal mental concerns are the next easiest groups to be open about, with respective means of 4.6 and 4.1. Topics relating to negative behavior are the hardest topics to be open about, with a mean of 4.1.

FACTOR ANALYSIS OF TARGETS OF DISCLOSURE

Two larger units emerged from the factor analysis of the targets of disclosure, the people with whom one would be open. Table 4.4 reports the results.

Complementary Targets. This factor entails mostly targets who are in a "one-up" position, either a parent or somebody in authority. Also, the target of stranger is associated with this factor. The stranger, as a target, is something of an anomaly. The target clearly is not in a "one-up" position in the same defined way that a parent or somebody in authority is, but, at the same time, the stranger is not on a peer level in the same defined way that a close friend of either sex is. The analysis indicates that the parents function somewhat as bridge variables.

Symmetrical Targets. This factor is made up of targets who represent "symmetrical" relations, namely, a close friend of the same sex and a close friend of the opposite sex. This is not to say, however, that close friends cannot engage in complementary interaction. The term is being used in a broad sense here to suggest peer-oriented interactions.

The mean degree of openness for the symmetrical factor is 7.6 on a 9-point scale, indicating a high degree of openness. The mean

TABLE 4.4   Factor Analysis of Targets of Disclosure

	Factor Loadings	
Scale Items	I	II
Complementary Targets (69% explained variance)		
1. Somebody in authority	.7	.1
2. A stranger	.6	−.1
3. Your most dominant parent	.5*	.4
4. Your least dominant parent	.5*	.4
Symmetrical Targets (31% explained variance)		
5. A close friend of the same sex	.0	.7
6. A close friend of the opposite sex	.0	.5

NOTE: Underscored numbers represent highest loadings among factors.
*Probable bridge variables. In this instance, the parents function like bridge variables. On one hand, they usually have a "one-up" role; on the other hand, they can operate very much like close friends.

degree of openness for the complementary factor is 5.1, indicating that there is less willingness to be open. The average correlation within the complementary targets is .3; the average correlation within the symmetrical targets is .4.

SUMMARY

Larger units of analysis for style, content, and target components were constructed using factor analyses. In each instance, the summed scores for the respective factors were used to create the larger units of analysis. Based on this procedure, five units emerged for the style component; four units emerged for the content component; two units emerged for the target component.

The larger units of analysis serve three functions. *First, they organize and identify the theoretical building blocks of the self-report, paper-and-pencil measure used to classify subjects.* This is useful in understanding the expectations in stratifying subjects for experiments examining the openness construct. *Second, they provide units with which to code interactions in an actual dyadic process.* The units are genetically derived from a theoretical base rather than stipulated. *Third, the integration of the units can be used to outline the parameters of research problems in self-disclosure.*

DIFFERENCES ACROSS STYLE,
CONTENT, AND TARGET

If the measure of openness has content and construct validity, then the respective units of analysis should behave as expected. The subjects were asked to make a distinction in their communicative behavior regarding two components: (1) whether they signaled an open style and (2) whether they were high disclosers. The distinctions created four stratifications for the sample. Two stratifications suggested consistent communicative behavior: (1) those who signaled an open style and were high disclosers and (2) those who did not signal an open style and were not high disclosers. The remaining stratifications suggested inconsistent communicative behavior: (1) those who signaled an open style but were not high disclosers and (2) those who did not signal an open style but were high disclosers. In these cases, Postulates 2, 3, and 4 are operative. The receiver must determine how the content of disclosure is to be processed in light of the way it is communicated.

The question is: Do the larger units of analysis — namely, style, content, and target factors — reflect the prescribed stratifications? The results indicate an unqualified yes. Table 4.5 reports the standardized residuals across the factors and Figure 4.1 shows the graphed differences.

Style Differences Across Stratifications

The largest differences among the stratifications fall into the general assessment factor. Since Table 4.5 reports standardized residuals, it is easy to obtain a sense of the magnitude of effect. For instance, the difference between the people who say they signal openness and are high disclosers and the people who say they do not signal openness and are not high disclosers is 1.81 standard derivation. The stratifications differ significantly for each remaining style factor as seen in Table 4.5.

If the researcher needs an abbreviated form to classify subjects, the general assessment factor would be the single best measure. In an exploratory study, the general assessment factor was successfully used for this purpose (Norton, Wartman, Gaine, Ellis, & Schuster, 1980). Subjects scoring high on this factor claimed that they revealed more of their "real" selves during a discussion of high-risk topics than subjects who scored low. The self-percep-

TABLE 4.5   Standardized Residuals Across Style, Topic,
and Target Factors

Factors	High Discloser		Low Discloser		F Statistic
	Signals Openness	Does Not Signal Openness	Signals Openness	Does Not Signal Openness	
Style Factors					
General assessment	.92	.22	-.22	-.89	46.80**
Negative openness	.27	-.02	-.01	-.44	4.22**
Emotional openness	.37	.17	-.09	-.40	6.25**
Direct indications	.60	-.21	-.06	-.66	16.58**
Nonverbal indications	.60	-.07	-.05	-.80	18.98**
Topics					
General philosophies	.38	-.18	-.05	-.32	5.32**
Negative behavior	.42	-.09	-.05	-.44	7.06**
Personal physical or social assets	.24	.13	-.04	-.41	3.75**
Personal mental concerns	.44	.18	-.09	-.56	10.02**
Targets					
Complementary	.37	.06	-.04	-.56	7.58**
Symmetrical	.38	-.09	-.07	-.26	4.55**
Number in Each Condition	70	36	181	37	

**p < .01.

tions were significantly different, t(44) = 2.32, p < .02, as measured by a 5-point scale with respective means of 3.6 and 2.9.

Topic Differences Across Stratifications

The personal mental concerns factor shows the biggest differences among stratifications. This suggests that content about one's mental health, fears, and relationships will most likely provide observable differences. The person who signals openness and is a high discloser should more readily talk about personal mental concerns than any other stratification.

Similarly, different communicative behavior can be expected for other topic factors. Since only the larger units are reported here, the researcher, furthermore, might expect even larger magnitudes of effect from specific topics within the factors. For example, the specific topic of sexual behavior might generate even larger observable differences than the general personal physical or social assets factor. Particular sexual topics, such as incest, mastur-

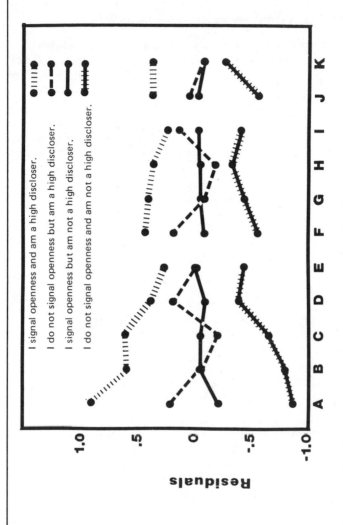

NOTE: **Open Style Items:** A = general assessment of openness; B = negative openness; C = emotional openness; D = direct indications of openness; E = nonverbal indications of openness. **Topics:** F = general philosophies; G = negative behavior; H = personal physical or social assets; I = personal mental concerns. **Target:** J = complementary; K = symmetrical.

Figure 4.1 Graphed Residuals Across Style, Topic, and Target Variables for the Different Types of Disclosers

121

bation, or homosexuality, may highlight communicative differences even further.

Target Differences Across Stratifications

The subsamples also differed in the amount of openness they indicated they would show the various targets. If the targets are of a complementary nature (parent, somebody in authority, and possibly a stranger), then observable behavior is more likely to be manifested differently. There is more at stake in disclosing personally private, and possibly risky, information to somebody in the "one-up" position. Observable differences can be expected for symmetrical targets as well.

Summary

The units of analysis work well across the stratifications. The largest effects in Table 4.5 are in the style factors where the range is as high as 1.81 standard deviations in residual differences. The ranges of the topic and target factors are similar, with respective standard deviations of 1.00 and 1.03.

This analysis suggests that the single best component to classify subjects accurately in terms of openness is the style component, rather than the degree the subject claims to be open concerning any given topic or the degree the subject claims to be open in light of any given target. This is not to say that the topic and target factors are uninformative, however. In the next section, the regression models show the optimal emphasis on style, topic, and target components in predicting variables relating to openness and classifying subjects.

BEST PREDICTORS FOR
FOUR DEPENDENT VARIABLES

Four stepwise regression analyses are reported in Table 4.6. Two regression analyses are designed to check criteria-related validity of the measure. The other two regression analyses are used to see whether the larger units are sufficiently strong to predict less redundant, less semantically related dependent variables.

To the extent that the larger units get into the regression model, there is an indication which factors are the best predictors. Two caveats are in order. First, the nature of the self-report data — an analysis of variables within the closed system of the measure —

**TABLE 4.6   Best Predictors for Four Dependent Variables
Integrating Style, Content, and Target**

Open Style of Communicating is best predicted in a stepwise regression equation by three style variables and one topic variable. The respective weights and variables follow:

(.27) general assessment of openness + (.16) direct indications of openness + (.13) negative openness + (.14) general philosophies + 3.9.

The above equation acounts for 42% of the explained variance (F = 10.2).

- -

Willing to Disclose Personally Private Information is best predicted in a stepwise regression equation by two style variables and one topic variable. The respective weights and variables follow:

(.52) general assessment of openness + (.15) nonverbal indications of openness + (.16) personal mental concerns + 2.9

The above equation accounts for 52% of the explained variance (F = 9.8).

- -

Good Communicator in General is best predicted in a stepwise regression equation by five style variables. The respective weights and variables follow:

(.23) direct indications of openness + (.21) nonverbal indications of openness + (.15) negative openness + (.16) general assessment of openness − (.14) emotional openness + 3.1

The above equation accounts for 45% of the explained variance (F = 5.5).

- -

How Long It Generally Takes for a Person to Get to Know You is best predicted in a stepwise equation by two style variables and one topic variable. The respective weights and variables follow:

(.46) general assessment of openness + (.27) direct indications of openness + (.26) personal mental concerns + 4.3

The above equation accounts for 47% of the explained variance (F = 11.8).

NOTE: Predictors were kept in the regression model only if $p < .05$ for the equation.

preempts making statements about whether the subjects, in fact, will be observed to disclose.[6]

Only further studies will establish the relationship. Until more studies are conducted, the regression analyses shape expectations for controlled studies and replication studies that amplify the openness research. In short, the reader is urged to take the regression analyses in this section cautiously, but to use them as a guide concerning what is expected.

Second, the issue of multicollinearity haunts this kind of research. Thus far, the statisticians have not satisfactorily resolved this issue. Two things were done in this report to increase confidence in the results. First, the raw correlations were carefully analyzed using some of the techniques outlined by Mosteller and Tukey (1977). Second, the order of the predictors (the units of analysis) was controlled such that the five style factors were allowed into the regression model first, then the four topic factors were allowed into the regression model, and, finally, the two target factors were introduced.

The order was determined by examining the individual analyses separately in which only style, topic, and target factors were used, respectively. In the individual analyses, the style factors accounted for the most variance; thus they were entered first in the regression model. The topic factors were entered next because they accounted for the second most variance in the individual analyses. The target factors accounted for the least variance in the individual analyses and, as a result, were entered last into the regression model integrating all openness components. This procedure was used for all predicated variables.

Predicting Willingness to Disclose

There is a lot of redundancy in this and the next regression models. Because the units of analysis were created from instructions to rate variables in terms of openness and disclosiveness, predicting "willingness to disclose" is like asking whether the instructions worked in the instrument. Nevertheless, the regression is useful in identifying the linear combination of variables that is most closely associated with the claim that one is willing to disclose.

Two style factors, two topic factors, and no target factors get into the regression model. The strongest predictor is the general assessment of openness factor from the style component. This is not surprising since the five style items initially used to construct this unit of analysis are semantically and empirically related (see Table 4.2). The respective correlations with "willingness to disclose" and the five items (9, 10, 11, 12, 13) are .4, .3, .3, .4, and .3. Also, the large F statistic (98.8) in the first step of the regression analysis indicates the strong relationship.

The next predictor, also from the style factors, is the nonverbal indication of openness factor. The respective correlations with "willingness to disclose" and the three items (17, 18, 19) of the factor are .2, .2, and .2. The coefficients are not as strong as the previous items, but they still contribute to the regression model.

Two topic factors get into the regression model: (1) personal mental concerns (items 15, 16, 17 in Table 4.3), with respective correlations of .2, .3, .3, and .2; and (2) personal physical or social assets (items 11, 12, 13, 14 in Table 4.3), with respective correlations of .2, .2, .2, and .3.

The target factors did not get into the model. Two reasons are suggested: First, the other factors probably do enough "work" that the target factors can explain very little after the style and topic components are in the equation; second, the target factors by themselves are not strong predictors. In the individual regression analyses, the two target factors accounted for only 4 percent of the variance in predicting willingness to disclose.

Predicting Open Style

Three style factors and one topic factor get into the regression model predicting open style. Again, the general assessment factor is the strongest predictor, with respective correlations (items 9, 10, 11, 12, 13 in Table 4.2) of .2, .2, .4, .3, and .1. The direct indications of openness factor (items 14, 15, 16) is the next best indicator, with respective correlations of .2, .2, and .2. The third best predictor is negative openness (items 1, 2, 3, and 4), with respective correlations of .2, .1, .2, and .1.

One topic factor, general philosophies, gets into the model. The respective correlations for the items (1, 2, 3, 4, 5, 6, and 7, in Table 4.3) with open style are .2, .2, .3, .2, .2, .2, and .3.

Predicting Good Communication in General

One of the useful consequences of developing the components of an openness construct is to see how they relate to other communication phenomenon. In Chapter 3, the construct was seen in the perspective of the communicator style domain. In this perspective, the open style subconstruct was closely associated with the "communicator image" variable (good communicator, in general). Consequently, it is expected that the factors of style, topic, and target would predict whether the person claimed to be a "good communicator, in general."

In the regression analysis, only the style factors make it into the model predicting "good communicator, in general" — all five units of analysis get into the equation. Again, the reader is reminded that this regression model emerged from the closed system of one questionnaire. But it points to a useful direction. If the "good communicator" variable was operationalized in additional ways independent of the measure, such as letting others decide whether the person is a good communicator or allowing experts to evaluate the quality of communication, then the researcher can see whether the person's self-report data about the openness of his or her interaction have the pragmatic consequence of making others evaluate him or her as a good communicator.

Predicting How Long It Takes to Get to Know a Person

Two style factors and one topic factor are the best predictors of the dependent variable concerning how long it generally takes for a person to get to know you. The two strongest predictors are identical to the ones predicting "open style." In addition, the personal mental concerns factor makes it into the regression analysis.

Summary

Four dependent variables were examined. Many different and interesting variables remain to be explored. The regression analyses are useful in two ways. First, they provide partial support for the validity of the openness construct. Second, they shape expectations about areas in which observable behavior is specified and interactions are researched.

CONCLUSION

The measure presented in this chapter looks only at self-report data concerning openness. Three types of questions determined an openness score:

(1) The person was asked how openness was manifested through style behaviors.

(2) The person was asked which topics would be easy to talk about openly.

(3) The person was asked which sets of people it is easier to be open with.

All other things being equal, the person's self-report about style behaviors seems to be the best indicator of openness.

The task now is to observe actual interaction, analyze real consequences, and indicate communication interventions where openness is dysfunctional. Openness research with a special emphasis on open style should be especially fruitful in analyzing the following areas:

• *Marital Situations:* How does openness weaken or strengthen the marriage? Is the lack of openness a contributing factor in unhappy marital situations? How does one partner stylistically influence the other?

- *Therapeutic Situations:* Does openness operate as a curative component in the therapy context? Does it depend upon the type of problem? Can openness be counterproductive?

- *Organizations:* Does an open style help or hinder manager-employee relations? Does the employee need to feel he or she has free access to qualitative information about the job?

- *Teaching Situations:* Does openness affect the quality of classroom interaction or contribute to learning?

- *Interpersonal Bonding:* In terms of interpersonal relationships, does an open style affect such variables as love, security, desire, hate, esteem, humility, admiration, acceptance, and trust?

It is clear that perceived style and perceived self-disclosure mitigate factors relating to communicative openness. When the gestalts are nonsynchronous (Table 4.1), the reported willingness to reveal personally private and risky information changes and the reported ways of openly communicating change. Postulate 4, which states that "an ambiguous gestalt motivates the receiver to interactively and inferentially supply premises that alleviate ambiguity," should become operative for the nonsynchronous gestalts. One of the tasks at hand is to unravel the impact a discrepant style signal has on self-disclosure, and vice versa.

In addition, work needs to be done to develop observational coding schemes tapping open style signals. De Rivera's (1977) *A Structural Theory of the Emotions* will be useful in this regard. De Rivera sees emotions as "instructions" telling the organism how to behave in relation to its stimulus situation; *it is a signal calculated to affect the stimulus situation.* If this is the case, open style that is partially defined as a function of showing emotions represents an *active* intervention in the communication process.

Also, the contrast between how open a person thinks he or she is and how open the person is perceived to be by others highlights the reality-testing capacity of the individual. If a person believes him- or herself to be extremely open when, in fact, everybody else perceives him or her to be relatively closed, then that person is out of touch with a "communicative reality." Such a discrepancy could easily affect other aspects of the social interaction and even the person's mental health. In this kind of research, self-report data are critical.

In conclusion, openness is a fascinating variable to study because it often functions at the core of intense communication. The open communicator allows the possibility of either rejection or disconfirmation, but, at the same time, invites affirmation. *Openness in the self-disclosive process integrates style, content, and target such that qualitative information seems to be communicated freely to another.*

NOTES

1. The notion of openness, while semantically close to "trustworthiness" and "credibility," is distinct in that it always deals with *information about the self* as the individual knows the self to be. If accuracy were introduced, the more precise statement would read "always deals with information about the self as the individual knows the self to be or the image of the self that is presented as 'the self as the individual knows the self to be.'" A person may be a trustworthy and credible communicator, but not an open communicator. The open communicator provides information that influences the other's *image of the individual* by providing personal information. Clearly, open communication has the capacity to affect ethos, especially if the selected information is carefully crafted.

2. Although many of the following authors do not explicitly talk about open style signals per se, it is clear that their conclusions address similar phenomena: L'Abate (1978), Davis (1977), Gilbert (1977), and Bauby (1974).

3. The articles covered the years 1968 to 1978.

4. In each instance, the variables were factor analyzed using a principal-components solution, which was then orthogonally rotated with Kaiser normalization. Oblique rotation yielded redundant conclusions and, consequently, was not reported.

5. Items 1, 25, 26, and 33 from Table 3.2 are the same items that clustered in the general assessment group in the openness measure.

6. Montgomery's (1978) pilot study, reported above, provides some evidence that the self-report will covary with observed behavior. She later addresses some similar issues (Montgomery, 1980).

5 / Dramatic Style

the communicative spotlight

The world loves its clowns, wits, entertainers, comics, great narrators, storytellers, poets, and dramatists of all kinds. They hold up the mirror so that we can see the sense and the nonsense, the comic and the tragic. They are especially effective because they capture our attention through their various devices, gimmicks, and tricks. In many instances, the attention-getting maneuvers arc transparent, but in many more instances the attention-getting moves are seductive, charming, and compelling.

Sometimes the dramatists are too shrill, intense, or negative. Then they are labeled propagandists, charlatans, con men, alarmists, scaremongers, or the like. Whatever the case, the element of the "extra ordinary" — the extraordinary — is intrinsic to the dramatic effect.

Because dramatic style creates the extraordinary, it not only is one of the most noticeable form-giving components, but it also serves a profound, complex, sometimes unconscious, communicative function. In general, the dramatic communicator manipulates messages through exaggerations, fantasies, stories, metaphors, rhythm, voice, and other stylistic devices to highlight, understate, or alter literal meaning.

129

To say it another way, dramatic style signals that literal meaning should be taken vividly, emotionally, intensely, or strikingly. **The dramatic style provides clues that something different and possibly significant is happening in the interaction.** Assumption 1 (Chapter 1) is especially important:

There can be no distinction without motive.

In short, the sensitive communicator assumes that a person dramatizes for a reason. Distinctions are being made nonrandomly by the communicator.

At this point, the following definition, which emphasizes the form-giving function of communicating in a dramatic way, is presented:

Definition 7:   Dramatic communicator style vividly, emotionally, or strikingly signals that literal meaning is being highlighted or emphasized.

It can take the form of overstatement (for example, burlesque), understatement (for example, dry wit), or some other kind of alteration (such as direct contradiction). The style is manifested verbally, nonverbally, or paraverbally. It is noticed, although subtle forms of dramatizing may be muted, suppressed, or selectively controlled.

This chapter does three things to explore the dramatic style variable. First, the theoretical dynamics that underlie dramatic style are suggested. Second, pragmatic applications are discussed. Third, the structure of the dramatic style subconstruct is examined.

DYNAMICS OF DRAMATIC STYLE

The key to understanding dramatic style is to understand the function of tension. **Dramatic style either manipulates tension or is manifested as a result of tension.** It has a dual capacity. If it can be reasonably assumed that tension permeates social interaction, then dramatic style is an essential topic to study in processes.[1]

The dramatic always represents a deviation of some type — from a norm, a routine, the tedious, the painful, and so on.[2] For example, a person can be dramatic simply by talking louder, softer, or differently than whatever the current norm is. Accordingly, the following axiom can be stated in stylistic terms:

Axiom 9:   Dramatic style signals a deviation from some norm.

One of the immediate implications of this axiom for the communication scholar is to identify the norm, its function, and the impact of the deviation. For example, a severely controlled, understated message to a mother from a close friend that the mother should get rid of her daughter's boyfriend should clue the mother to several things. Typical decoding of the dramatic signal might include such messages as the following:

- She is saying this in such a way that she cannot just say what the problem is outright.
- She is indirectly asking me to ask her for more information.
- There must be serious trouble because usually she would not interfere with my daughter's relationships.

In each decoding, potential norms are suggested. In the first two interpretations, directness is the expected norm. In the third interpretation, noninterference is the expected norm. Postulates 2, 3, and 4 (Chapter 1) are operative here.

The deviation can function in dual roles. First, it can lay the groundwork for *tension reduction*. If the tension is too extreme, dysfunctional anxiety results. Second, it can be the impetus for *tension creation*. If the tension is optimal, functional connections, insights, metaphorical processes, and pleasure result. The dramatic style benefits both the self and others. The following sections address the various functions.

Tension Relief for Self

Many anxiety-producing interactions occur in a communicative situation. A particular topic of conversation entailing high-risk components — sexual discussions, for example — can cause tension in an individual. An inadvertent insult can trigger tension. Frustration from a tedious, thankless, or impossible task can create tension.

In each instance, dramatizing relieves tension. A good laugh, a timely joke or pun, a distorted facial expression, or the introduction of a fantasy chain diverts the focus from the cause of tensions and offers a way to lessen emotional strain. The deviation from the source of anxiety provides an emotional safety valve. It is for this reason that dramatic style may directly relate to a person's mental and physical health.

Tension Relief for Others

Similarly, dramatizing works to relieve tensions for others, whether family, strangers, a highly cohesive group, or one other person. Any tense situation, such as waiting for election results, the birth of a child, or the announcement of a winner, includes dramatizing to alleviate the intrinsic strain. For instance, the funeral of a loved one, including the arrangements, wake, and burial, is marked by gentle humor and anecdotal stories about the deceased. The delicate dramatizing in this situation makes the ritual more bearable.

Tension Creation for Self

At first glance, it seems as though a person would not deliberately create tension for the self. Structuring tension for the self, however, can serve a useful function. For example, dramatizing permits reality testing for the person. The person initially creates a tension to see if it will be resolved as expected. Self-ridicule can be an exercise in masochism, but, more importantly, it allows a person to test his or her degree of self-confidence. If a person can hold an audience with a story, a joke, or a metaphor, the process provides feedback about communicative competence, audience analysis, and one's attractiveness.

More than any other form-giving component, dramatic style allows the person a way to stretch and strengthen the communicative "muscles." At its most dynamic, it gives a sense of power and pleasure that is difficult to approach with any other human behavior. At its weakest, it highlights frailty, sense of helplessness, loss of control, lack of health, and unhappiness. In the Christian world, the last utterance of Jesus on the cross epitomizes the latter extreme.

Tension Creation for Others

William Thompson, in his book *At the Edge of History: Speculations on the Transformation of Culture* (1971), presents four archetypes to model society. In their primative forms, the roles are headman, shaman, hunter, and clown. The clown deliberately creates tension for the others; he makes fun of the seriousness of the shaman, the physical beauty of the best hunter, and the authority of the headman. Thompson argues that every society needs the clown to create this dramatic tension to survive.

Although dramatizing provides a way to create tension for a culture, group, or individuals, it can also relieve tension. Dramatizing may be dysfunctional or growth producing. A person who has a malfunctional relationship with another may periodically communicate in a dramatic way to disorient, disturb, disrupt, annoy, or bother that person. Dramatizing in this instance is used to be abusive.

The insidious aspect of dramatizing to affect another negatively is that direct accountability is missing. The abuser can resort to claiming that the literal content is what was meant, not the way it was said. Examples include:

Literal Content	Tension-Creating Move
"Are you going to wear *that* to the party?"	(said with a slight hint of contempt)
"Mrs. Smith always cooks a white sauce with the chicken."	(said with a tone of disappointment)
"I'm glad to see you are looking good today."	(capitalizing on fallacy of emphasis)

On the other hand, dramatic tension could be a springboard for personal insight. Many therapies intentionally dramatize to manipulate tensions that are intended to lead ultimately to catharsis and self-actualization. Much teasing and word play structures tension as a way to enhance social encounters. Many rituals capitalize on dramatic tension to intensify individuals' emotional commitment and ego involvement with groups.

In summary, dramatic style depends on tension, which in turn depends on a manufactured or manipulated deviation. The studied effect caused by dramatic style serves the communicator in complex, sometimes distorted, and many times effective ways. Dramatic behaviors that occur unconsciously provide the receiver significant and rich clues about the individual. The way a person dramatically communicates has the dual power to make the other sad or happy.

PRAGMATIC APPLICATIONS

This section looks at some areas in which dramatic style is pragmatically important. In particular, three areas are examined: (1) physical and mental health, (2) problem-solving situations, and (3) teaching.

Physical and Mental Health

Dramatic style influences both physical and mental health. Formally, it figures heavily in therapeutic processes. It also influences an individual's personal health. The former connection is discussed first, using examples from therapy. The connection to health is discussed next, using an example from people who experience seizures.

THERAPEUTIC COMMUNICATION

Therapeutic communication focuses on the dramatic style in two ways: First, it functions as a diagnostic aid; that is, the dramatic style provides information about psychotherapeutic problems. Second, it functions as a vehicle to alleviate psychotherapeutic problems. In this case, the dramatic style either is used as a communicative strategy by the therapist to provoke "change" or is solicited from the patient as a behavior to trigger insight, ease inhibitions, or tap into the unconscious.

Diagnostic Aid. If dramatic style is seen as a diagnostic aid, an extraordinary amount of information is available. Techniques pioneered by Freud (1933) can be used to discover latent meanings signaled by the way the person communicates. From a Freudian perspective, a person exaggerates, understates, or alters meaning for *nonrandom* reasons. These behaviors reveal the personality of the communicator. They point to the person's conscious or unconscious process of coping or failing to cope with fears, tensions, or anxieties. They identify the focus of the person's conflicts or joys.

On the one hand, dramatic style provides the communicator with the means to disguise critical meanings that are too threatening to manifest in an unequivocal manner. It serves as a buffer in dealing with reality, neurosis, or moral anxiety (Freud, 1965).

Ruesch (1961), for example, maintains that the dramatic style frequently suggests an identity problem. He claims that dramatic style dysfunctionally operates as a deviation of expression in the exhibitionist, who shows off and exaggerates. He also thinks that dramatic style often is triggered by interference with interpersonal feedback circuits. For instance, if a wife ignores a husband's request, he tends to repeat the request in an increasingly dramatic way because he is getting little or no feedback.

On the other hand, dramatic style often signifies intense happiness, joy, or love. It is a way to communicate that displays unusual range and flexibility.

Therapeutic Tool. If dramatic style is used as a tool to effect quality change, an active and intentional intervention is introduced. It typically is seen in one of three functions:

(1) The therapist incorporates it as a direct technique to influence the person.

(2) The therapist uses it as an indirect method to manipulate the person.

(3) The patient is encouraged to be dramatic as part of the therapeutic treatment.

Direct Technique. In Synanon groups, for example, the dramatic style is clearly apparent. The leaders taunt, ridicule, relentlessly attack, verbally fight, scorn, and use a great deal of humor as part of their perspective (Lieberman et al., 1973). Provocative therapy also relies upon the dramatic style as a major technique (Farrelly & Brandsma, 1974).

Lieberman et al. (1973) studied 18 encounter groups over a year representing t-group, gestalt, transactional, Esalen, Synanon, psychodrama, marathon, psychoanalytically oriented, and leaderless approaches. From this research, four styles of leadership emerged, one of which capitalizes on dramatic style — namely, the "energizer." This type of leader prevailed in the gestalt, Synanon, and psychodramatic groups.

The energizer scores high on the following:

• intrusive modeling

• release of emotion by demonstration

• challenging

• charisma

The participants rated the energizer highest across all leader types in four areas: (1) genuineness, (2) acceptance of control, (3) allowing opportunity for open peer communication, and (4) allowing opportunity for expression of anger. Only the energizers were strongly attached to an articulated belief system as well as emotionally tied to the founder of their school of thought. This suggests that the "true believer" probably is going to be more dramatic in proselytizing.

Indirect Method. Probably the most intriguing use of dramatic style is when it is used indirectly to effect change. Milton Erickson was a master at using narratives, fantasies, metaphors, and humor to help people. Erickson seeded indirect, positive suggestions in clients, colleagues, and friends using dramatic vehicles, many of which are outlined by Rosen (1982).

Often a person will press for clarification when he or she first hears a teaching story from the therapist. Many times it seems out of context given the flow of previous conversation. Erickson typically refused to discuss, amplify, or explain such stories because it would constrain the ambiguity and restrict the multidimensional nature and, as a result, defeat the purpose.

The indirect method works because of its capacity to present at least one meaning, usually the literal, while simultaneously presenting at least one other meaning. The other meaning can do communicative work with or without the person's awareness.

This claim should alert the communication scholar to be open, but critical. The implications are far reaching, controversial, provocative, and exciting. One of the central claims is that an individual can communicate in such a way that it can effect change without the other's awareness. The student of communication needs to unravel the interactive dynamics of this phenomenon. The form-giving function of dramatic style points to a beginning for such study.

Part of Treatment. Some therapeutic approaches — gestalt (Perls, Hefferline, & Goodman, 1965), primal (Janov, 1970),[3] and psychodrama — encourage or insist that the participant manifest a dramatic style. Verbatim comments from a gestalt group illustrate the technique:

> Are you crying? . . . I feel you're holding back. Something or somebody . . . I'll come closer. . . . Crying is a woman's second best weapon. . . . All right, close your eyes and imagine you are holding something back. What are you holding back in your past? . . . Okay, stay in that position, exaggerate it [Lieberman et al., 1973].

The assumption is that the dramatic style allows easier free association, permits a means to open up on a different level, or forces the person to function bimodally, that is, as both observer and object of observation.

In short, the variable of dramatic style impinges at every stage in the therapeutic process. However, the variable per se has not been systematically researched, especially from a pragmatic perspective. Nevertheless, because it tends to signal intense discomfort or intense caring, it cannot be ignored by communication scientists developing interpersonal theory.

Personal Health

How one communicates influences one's personal health. In a national survey of people with seizure activity (epilepsy), it was found that those who characterize themselves as having a dramatic style not only perceived their problem as less severe, but also were healthier in related areas.

In this case, the items measuring dramatic style were taken from the Communicator Style Measure (Chapter 3). The measure of health were taken from the Hopkins Symptom Checklist (Derogatis, Lipman, Rickels, Uhlenhuth, & Covi, 1974).[4] Three indicators of health were used:

- *Somatic Variables:* The items constituting this dimension reflect distress arising from perceptions of bodily dysfunction. Complaints focused on cardiovascular, gastrointestinal, respiratory, and other systems with marked autonomic medication are included. Headaches, pain, and discomfort localized in the gross musculature and other somatic equivalents of anxiety are also represented.

- *Depression:* Symptoms of dysphoric mood and affect are represented, as are signs of withdrawal of life interest, lack of motivation, and loss of vital energy. Feelings of hopelessness and futility as well as other cognitive and somatic correlates are also included.

- *Anxiety:* This dimension is made up of a set of symptoms and behaviors associated clinically with high manifest anxiety. General indicators such as restlessness, nervousness, and tension are represented, as are additional somatic signs, such as trembling. Items touching on free-floating activity and panic attacks are also included.

In brief, it was found that the more an individual controls interaction with entertaining, attention-getting, and mood-changing behaviors, the less likely the person is to experience depression, anxiety, or somatic disorders (Norton, Murray, & Arntson, 1982).

The possibilities are endless in making links to physical and mental health and dramatic behaviors. For instance, if a nonmedical intervention would work to prevent a seizure, then the individual with epilepsy would have a better sense of control.[5]

Communicating in a dramatic way may not prevent seizures, but it can effect how the person perceives the difficulty of the problem. This topic promises further real-world applications with a good chance for improving the quality of lives.

PROBLEM-SOLVING SITUATIONS

The dramatic style variable is an important factor in interaction in group problem solving. Bales (1970) has done the most work along this line with his Interactional Process Analysis (IPA) of small groups. The IPA system entails twelve categories that are used to code all behavior in the problem-solving process. Two of the twelve categories relate to dramatic style: (1) dramatizes and (2) shows tension. Generally, if the dramatizing is positive, it is scored in the first category. If it is negative, it is scored in the second category.

Many behaviors fall into these two domains. For the dramatizes category, the following acts would be included:

- presenting images or potential emotional symbols that may be responded to without explicit attention or conscious knowledge
- performing symbolic actions — particularly when they are spontaneous or original — that involve no words
- arousing fantasy
- presenting images in which there are more than one level of symbolic meaning or emotional connotation
- introducing nonserious or nonliteral messages
- reporting the *action* of a person or imaginary being
- telling a story
- shading the voice for effect
- using metaphor or any poetic or literary device
- exaggerating
- using colorful words
- acting out a part physically as well as vocally
- joking or telling a joke
- clowning, bantering, kidding
- expressing good feelings, especially after a period of tension
- expressing joy, happiness, delight, elation, euphoria
- performing or entertaining

The shows tension category in the IPA system includes the negative counterparts to these behaviors.

Across 21 different empirical studies, Bales and Hare (1965) found that dramatizing and shows tension accounted for about 11 percent of the acts scored in the problem-solving groups. Furthermore, in his revision of the system, Bales (1970) weighted these categories even more by giving them scoring priorities, "even for the slightest indication," over all other categories.

Bales (1970, p. 245) argues that the person communicating in a dramatic way fulfills a very special function in the problem-solving group:

> In the group he seems ascendant and expressive, nontask oriented, perhaps unconventional or even deviant. He seems neither clearly friendly nor unfriendly, but entertaining, joking, dramatic, relativistic, free in his associations, taking pleasure in play, activity, novelty, and creativity. In the realization of his own values he seems to be trying to move toward value-relativism and expression of underlying emotions and feelings.

The special function of the dramatizer is that he "tends to express, usually by indirect and symbolic means, underlying tensions of his own, or possibly those of other members of the group — fears, anxieties, hostilities, affections, aspirations, and the like" (Bales, 1970, p. 247).

Bormann (1975, p. 166) corroborates this point of view with his work:

> When group members respond emotionally to a dramatic situation, they publicly proclaim some commitment to an attitude. Indeed, improvising in a spontaneous group dramatization is a powerful force for changing member attitudes. Dramas also imply motive, and, by chaining into the fantasy, members gain motivations. Since some of the characters in the fantasies are presented as sympathetic people doing laudable things, the group collectively identifies, in symbolic terms, proper codes of conduct.

Bormann identifies many functions here. Dramatizing in a problem-solving group allows members to (1) declare not only a public commitment, but reveal its salience, (2) force an attitude change, (3) motivate, (4) identify, and (5) value group norms.

Consider the motivating dynamic of the fantasy chain. Often newcomers in group therapy or self-help groups see others "hitchhike" on a chain of spontaneous testimony about their problems. The spontaneous testimony, usually extremely intense, often causes the newcomer to have renewed hope and to feel that his or her problem is not unique. Both consequences of the fantasy chain are powerful curative components.

The fantasy chain is particularly interesting because it unobtrusively invites group members to participate either consciously or unconsciously in dramatizing. The group member can play out tension by introducing situations removed in time and space from the here and now. Thus he or she is protected and is positioned to get feedback from others reacting to the fantasized situation.

How the group members respond to a fantasy chain provides information about the personal psychodynamics of individuals. Some people eagerly participate; others attempt to control the agenda of topics; still others carefully resist the invitation. In addition, religious, political, and psychological values are tested. Inside jokes are created. Group history and collective memory are established (Bormann, 1975).

In summary, a dramatic style does a lot of work in the communicative process related to problem solving. It helps explain, focus, interpret, and motivate. It represents one of the two major activities in the group problem-solving process. It does not relate directly to moving the group to task fulfillment, but it directly relates to social maintenance in the group.

TEACHING

The better teacher communicates in a dramatic way. An extensive presentation supporting this conclusion is made in Chapter 9. In brief, the teacher who knows how to orchestrate the communicative interaction entailed in the educational process tends to be more effective.

The reasons are multiple. First, the dramatic style more readily commands attention that is a necessary component for learning. Second, it also has the capacity to educate while entertaining. As a result, it is often easier to learn material because surprising connections are made that have mnemonic power, the atmosphere is more conducive to learning because of its relaxed, easygoing nature, and the style itself carries the implicit message that the teacher cares.

Summary

The pragmatic consequences of dramatic style are varied and cut across an extraordinary range of human activity. Although only three areas were briefly discussed here, the prospect of many more applications is unlimited.

STRUCTURE OF THE
DRAMATIC STYLE SUBCONSTRUCT

The structure of this subconstruct begins with the definition of dramatic style introduced earlier, which is used for the basis of a self-report questionnaire. The items within the measure are then analyzed using the same methods outlined in Chapter 3, centering on factor analysis and smallest space analysis. Similarly, the rationale for understanding the structure of the subconstruct is parallel. To reiterate, the structure helps find organizing principles intrinsic to a domain and identifies areas in which more needs to be done.

A 61-item, paper-and-pencil, self-report test was used to define operationally the dramatic communicator style domain. Items were created based on the literature and logical analysis of the concept.

Method

The general method was to give the dramatic style questionnaire to different samples and then to analyze the relationship among the dramatic style variables.

SUBJECTS

A sample of adults and students was used: (1) 139 freshman and sophomore students from introductory communication classes at the University of Michigan voluntarily participated, and (2) 178 adults (nonstudents) from the Detroit area voluntarily participated.

MEASURE

A total of 61 items that tapped the way one manipulated exaggerations, fantasies, stories, metaphors, rhythms, voices, and other stylistic elements to affect literal meaning dramatically were used. A 7-point scale ranging from "very strong agreement" with the item to "very strong disagreement" with the item was employed. The exact wording of the items is found in Table 5.1. Also, two filler items were used.

TABLE 5.1   Factor Analysis of Dramatic Style Variables

Item	Loading
Factor 1: Mood Manipulator (6.8%)	
44 I know how to catch the imagination of others.	.66
48 When I talk to people I know how to catch their attention.	.62
59 I can catch a person up in my stories.	.58
54 I am very good at manipulating the mood of other people by the way I say things.	.56
25 When I am excited about something, I know how to get others excited also.	.45
50 I know how to get people to feel very sympathetic for others.	.41
39 Often I deliberately try to create specific emotional feelings when I communicate.	.38
60 I like to emotionally color what I am saying to create a dramatic effect.	.34
Factor 2: Laugh User (7.3%)	
10 Often I deliberately use my laughter to create a dramatic effect.	.74
45 Often I deliberately use my laughter to create a dramatic effect.*	.73
19 I am *conscious of deliberately* using my laughter for an effect.	.67
47 I have several *different kinds of laughter* that I use to create a dramatic effect.	.56
56 I often use my laughter to indicate that I have negative feelings about what is said.	.50
24 Sometimes I deliberately pretend to be embarrassed to create an effect	.45
46 I like saying things in such a way that people see multiple meanings in my communication.	.39
32 I provide other people with a lot of feedback by my laughter.	.38
35 Frequently I deliberately act silly.	.37
38 My laughter is loud.	.37
11 Very frequently I gently tease my friends.	.35

TABLE 5.1 Continued

Item	Loading
Factor 3: Entertainer (7.0%)	
26 I am very humorous.	.67
5 I am very witty.	.60
28 I have very good timing when I tell jokes or stories.	.60
51 I know how to tell a joke.	.59
14 It is easy for me to make a large group of strangers laugh.	.58
3 I am very good at making puns.	.51
12 I think of myself as entertaining.	.50
22 I know how to tell a good story.	.49
16 I frequently tell jokes to people.	.42
4 I know how to build tension when I am telling a story.	.42
Factor 4: Energizer (4.9%)	
63 I use a lot of energy communicating.	.63
62 I like to get people laughing.	.62
49 I get excited easily.	.50
64 I go to excess to maintain attention.	.44
33 I often exaggerate for emphasis.	.43
61 I am quite an outgoing person.	.42
Factor 5: Voice User (4.7%)	
29 Often I use *different voices* to create a dramatic effect.	.67
31 I often use a *pause* to create a dramatic effect.	.57
34 Sometimes I shade or tone my voice to create a dramatic effect.	.54
27 Sometimes I act out a communication physically as well as vocally.	.47
30 I use a lot of colorful words.	.43
Factor 6: Insulter (4.1%)	
21 I can easily insult a person if I wanted to.	.66
6 I often poke fun at people.	.56
36. Often I am sarcastic.	.53
40 I am very good at responding to an insult when I need to.	.47
18 Often I verbally clown around.	.36
20 I know how to mimic people.	.34

(continued)

TABLE 5.1 Continued

Item	Loading
Factor 7: Performer (3.5%)	
7 I am a good performer.	.63
42 I am quite good at acting when I want to.	.60
8 I am very fast *in reacting* to what others say.	.38
Factor 8: Picturesque Verbalizer (2.4%)	
9 Sometimes I swear to create an effect.	.43
23 My speech tends to be very picturesque.	.40
13 I am a dramatic communicator.	.40
Factor 9: Fantasizer (2.1%)	
57 Frequently I tell people my dreams.	.74
58 I know how to get other people fantasizing.	.48
Factor 10: Story/Joke Teller (2.5%)	
53 I have a set of good stories which I use to create a dramatic effect.	.51
55 I can always think of a story to tell people.	.36
52 I often fantasize to others.	.34
Factor 11: Information Distributor (2.4%)	
37 I often plan the stories or topics I am going to talk about with people.	.46
41 I like to report unusual news events to people.	.41
43 I often use my laughter to get the other person to keep talking.	.38
Factor 12: Gossiper (1.5%)	
15 I often use gossip to keep people entertained.	.54
Factor 13: Dramatizer (1.6%)	
17 I dramatize a lot.	.39

NOTE: Numbers in parentheses report the percentage of explained variance for each factor.
*Item 45 was deliberately included as a duplicate of item 10 so that an indication of error measurement could be obtained.

Results

Two statistical analyses were done to examine the *structure* of the dramatic style domain — factor analysis and smallest space analysis.

FACTOR ANALYSIS

The 61 items were grouped using factor analysis. Table 5.1 reports the results. Below, 11 factors are briefly discussed to show the wide range of behaviors that fall under dramatic style.

Factor 1. Factor 1 is a homogeneous grouping of variables. The items reflect the capacity of the communicator to manipulate moods by creating dramatic effects. All items revolve around the ability to "catch the imagination of others." The items tap an individual's sensitivities to direct emotional feelings by telling stories, generating excitement, and gaining attention. The factor suggests that the dramatic communicator is a good manipulator. The average correlation among the variables in factor 1 is .39.

Factor 2. The items in Factor 2 revolve around what the dramatic communicator does with laughter. The items include qualitative effects of laughter: (1) loud laughter, (2) hostile laughter, and (3) different kinds of laughter.

Also, a quantitative effect is included: "I provide other people with a lot of feedback by my laughter." Three of the items suggest specific functions of laughter. First, laughter is used to signal a teasing situation — item 11. Barbs, criticism, hostilities, and negative strokes can be muted by simultaneously laughing in such a way that teasing is indicated. On the other hand, the laughter itself may be the sole means of teasing the other.

Second, laughter is used to signal silliness. The metamessage of laughter is complex. It may be that if laughter did not accompany "silliness," the behaviors of the person would be perceived as "madness" or "craziness." Third, laughter signals ambiguity. The literal meaning of a message can be diluted, contradicted, or changed by adding laughter. The factor indicates that laughter is a means to create a dramatic effect. The average correlation among the variables in factor 2 is .32.

Factor 3. Factor 3 includes items that provide a general assessment of whether one is entertaining, humorous, and witty. The behavioral indicators of this assessment focus upon knowing how — in terms of timing and building tension — to tell good stories or jokes. The average correlation among the variables is .42. The storyteller is one type of dramatic communicator.

Factor 4. Factor 4 is similar to factor 3 in that it provides an assessment of personality traits that indicate that the individual is outgoing. The dramatic communicator probably expends more energy than average (item 63), gets people laughing often (item 62), and becomes easily excited (item 49). Two behavioral indicators suggested by the factor reflect the dramatic communicator's willingness to go to excess to maintain attention and to exaggerate for emphasis. The average correlation among the variables is .35.

Factor 5. The emphasis in factor 5 is on what the dramatic communicator does with the voice to create an effect. Using more than one voice highlights the message; shading or toning the voice stresses the message; not using the voice (pausing) accentuates the message. All these activities relate to "acting out a communication" (item 27). The average correlation among the variables is .38.

Factor 6. Items revolving around the capacity to insult, poke fun, or be sarcastic constitute factor 6. In this factor, the items fall along a continuum that ranges from the potential ability to manifest the behavior to actually behaving in such a manner. A person who indicates that he or she knows how to mimic or insult, very likely pokes fun, verbally clowns around, and is sarcastic, and, as a consequence, is perceived as a dramatic communicator. The average correlation among the variables is .34.

Factor 7. Factor 7 is similar to factors 3 and 4. It is a three-item factor that focuses on whether a person sees him- or herself as a good performer. Item 8 is a weak item in this factor, although it correlates moderately strongly with items 7 and 42, with coefficients of .38 and .33 respectively. The average correlation among the variables is .41.

Factor 8. Factor 8 is a weak factor. Picturesque language (item 23), which includes swearing (item 9), conceptually defines the factor. However, these two items are correlated moderately with an r of .29. Item 13 has a strong correlation with item 23, but it also has stronger correlations with four other items. The average correlation among the variables is .35.

Factor 9. Factor 9 holds together thematically, but it is only a two-item factor. Both items — r of .43 — concern the use of fantasy in communicating in such a way as to obtain a dramatic effect.

Factor 10. Factor 10 has three items that focus on some of the materials a dramatic communicator uses for effect — namely, stories. The person who can always think of a story to tell tends to be perceived as a dramatic communicator. The average correlation among the items is .44.

Factor 11. Factor 11 seems to be a weaker version of factor 10. Again, stories, including unusual news events, are the materials used to create the dramatic effect. The average correlation among the items is .24.

Remaining Factors. The remaining factors, 12 and 13, had only one item in the factor or no items. Item 15 concerns the use of gossip for dramatic effect and is related to only 5 percent of the items at a level of .30 or greater. Item 17, on the other hand, is related to 50 percent of the items at a level of .30 or greater.

SMALLEST SPACE ANALYSIS OF FACTOR ANALYSIS

Given the wide variety of dramatic behaviors, it is useful to study how factors relate to one another. Smallest space analysis allows such an examination. All the items in a factor were standardized and averaged to create a score for the factor. These scores were correlated to create a distance matrix, which was used as input for the smallest space analysis. Table 5.2 reports the correlations. Figure 5.1 shows the results of a two-dimensional smallest space solution.[7] What emerges is a picture of the dramatic style subconstruct that reflects multiple levels of abstraction. This suggests that the 61-item domain is multivariate in essence.

Two cohesive clusters emerge. First, factors 8, 7, 5, and 3 group. All variables in this cluster have a correlational link of .60 or greater with at least one other variable. The cluster revolves around the "performer" aspect of the communicator. Entertaining, using the voice for effect, and using colorful language characterize the cluster. The cluster coincides with the operational and conceptual expectations of the dramatic construct.

Second, factors 1 and 4 group together. The variables in this cluster have a correlational link of .55 with each other. The cluster reflects the effect of a dramatic style: It manipulates moods and changes energy levels of people.

The remaining factors, 9, 12, 11, 6, 13, and 10, seem to be functionally defined. If the first cluster above (factors 8, 7, 5, and 3) is labeled "performer," then the model in Figure 5.2 is suggested.

The core of the model centers on mood manipulation, energy change, and attention demand. The items that initially make up these factors relate in an increasingly monotonic way to the overall assessment that a person has a dramatic style. This means that as the behaviors increase, the perception of being dramatic becomes increasingly stronger.

The most representative items of factor 1 are the following:

- I know how to catch the imagination of others.
- When I talk to people I know how to catch their attention.

TABLE 5.2 Distances for Two-Dimensional Smallest Space Solution: Relationships Among Factors

	(1)	(2)	(3)	(4)	(5)	(6)	(7)	(8)	(9)	(10)	(11)	(12)	(13)
(1) Mood manipulator	—	.45	.59	.59	.56	.37	.53	.47	.44	.57	.42	.20	.43
(2) Laughter user	66	—	.50	.48	.43	.56	.37	.39	.30	.53	.39	.40	.49
(3) Entertainer	48	48	—	.51	.54	.59	.61	.53	.25	.57	.33	.24	.46
(4) Energizer	19	48	42	—	.44	.38	.49	.48	.28	.50	.35	.30	.45
(5) Voice user	55	106	64	70	—	.36	.66	.54	.23	.43	.28	.10	.43
(6) Insulter	100	45	61	85	125	—	.35	.37	.25	.43	.31	.33	.37
(7) Performer	54	90	44	63	24	103	—	.82	.15	.39	.23	.22	.56
(8) Picturesque verbalizer	61	90	42	68	34	98	10	—	.23	.36	.26	.27	.51
(9) Fantasizer	108	140	152	150	185	159	168	—	—	.24	.45	.37	.40
(10) Story/joke teller	51	40	67	34	104	85	97	100	106	—	.45	.37	.40
(11) Information distributor	145	80	122	126	184	69	165	162	195	106	—	.26	.21
(12) Gossiper	148	110	156	132	202	137	193	195	134	98	98	—	.28
(13) Dramatizer	87	85	44	86	74	73	50	41	195	110	142	195	—

NOTE: The upper triangular matrix represents the original distances (correlations) among the factors. The scores are the standardized and summed raw values. The lower triangular matrix represents the derived distances for the two-dimensional solution. Kruskal's stress with semi-strong monotonicity is .16; the Guttman-Lingoes coefficient of alienation is .09.

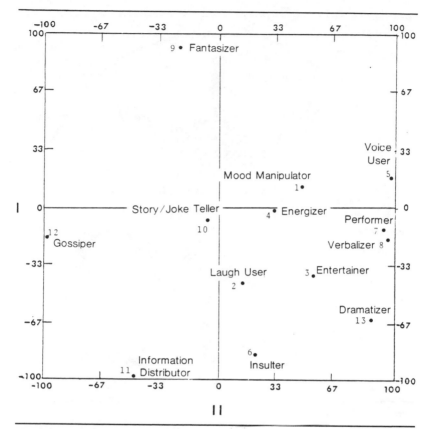

Figure 5.1   Smallest Space Analysis of Dramatic Behaviors

- I can catch a person up in my stories.
- I am very good at manipulating the mood of other people by the way I say things.
- When I am excited about something, I know how to get others excited also.

The five most representative items of factor 4 are the following:

- I use a lot of energy communicating.
- I like to get people laughing.
- I get excited easily.
- I go to excess to maintain attention.
- I often exaggerate for emphasis.

These inferences and perceptions are *necessary* elements of a communicator who is associated with a consistently recurring pattern of dramatic behaviors.

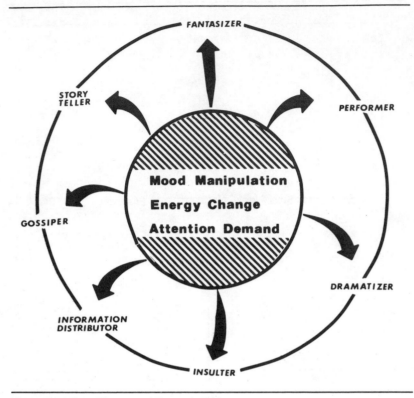

Figure 5.2   Core Elements of Dramatic Style

On the other hand, there are many sufficient ways to communicate such that dramatic style will be connected with the individual. For example, if you perceive a person as an inveterate insulter, that perception is sufficient to characterize the individual as having a dramatic style. If you perceive a person as an incurable gossiper, that perception also is sufficient to characterize the individual as having a dramatic style. However, neither portrayal entails defining characteristics of dramatic style. The person could be dramatic for another reason — he or she may be constantly punning. Whatever the perception, gossiper or insulter, the defining core components relate to mood, energy, and attention; these elements are common to the broad spectrum of essential features of dramatic style. While the insulter, fantasizer, storyteller, gossiper, information distributor, performer, and dramatizer try to manipulate moods, change energy levels, and demand attention, the converse is not true. The mood manipulator, for example, need not be a gossip, but can be.

In short, the dramatic communicator vividly, emotionally, or strikingly signals that literal meaning is being emphasized to manipulate mood, change energy, and/or seek attention. The form-giving function is emphasis; the hoped-for consequent is change of some kind — moods are transformed or shifted, energy is increased or decreased, attention is refocused.

FUTURE WORK

This study represents the first step in extending a dramatic style subconstruct. As such, it attempts to refine and sharpen the focus of a particular component from the larger concept of communicator style. The dramatic subconstruct is the most complex of the domain.

The next task is to distinguish carefully between the necessary and sufficient elements of the dramatic style domain. This entails two things. First, the levels of abstraction for each item must be attended to carefully. For example, "being able to catch the imagination of others by whatever means" is at a different level of abstraction than "telling jokes." The first capacity certainly enhances the talent of a joke teller, but the converse is not necessarily true. Telling jokes does not always — although it has a good chance of doing so — allow the person to catch the imagination of others.

The reason that this is the case is suggested by Postulate 7 (Chapter 2), which states:

> If the style expectations are different for various receivers, then the immediate style that is exhibited can be differentially interpreted by the various interactants.

This means that a joke may catch the imagination of one person but bore, miss, or fail to catch the imagination of another.

Second, antecedents and consequents must be clearly related. The sequence of events is confounded by the fact that the communicator either decides to dramatize to create tension or dramatizes in reaction to tension. Dramatizing is inherently ambiguous because of the dual connection to tension. In one instance, tension is the effect, or consequent and dramatizing is the antecedent. Tension in the second instance is the determinant, or antecedent, and dramatizing is the consequent. In each instance, dramatizing is done by deviating from some norm that may be long standing and enduring or immediate and temporary.

But the most important task is to show that the dramatic communicator style makes a pragmatic difference in interactions across contexts, situations, and time. This step will be the most exciting aspect of this research, and it will be this step that will determine whether the topic is trivial or important.

The dramatic style promises to open useful areas of research. For example, *dramatizing has been identified as a strategy to elicit self disclosure* (Norton, Mulligan, & Petronio, 1975). It works as a probe that often creates pressure to reveal personally private information. Often an individual attempting to elicit self-disclosure from another will present the request in a dramatic frame. For example, one might feign ignorance about a topic. The person might say, "Nobody would deliberately batter his wife" to trigger a reply such as "Oh yeah? My cousin was beat up once a month." By appearing ignorant, the first person put the second person into the position of "teacher." In the process of educating the first person, the second person is likely to disclose.

Using the dramatic style is often a strategy used by those seeking information in situations entailing therapy, intimidation, courtroom testimony, obedience, and idle gossip.

Also, *dramatizing has been identified as a rich source of clues signaling what is on a person's mind, what is unconsciously bothering a person, what a person may be repressing, or what is preoccupying a person.* Freud popularized this thinking in psychoanalysis.

Third, *dramatizing has been identified as an essential dimension in group problem solving.* Fantasy chains, as pointed out earlier, are an essential part of most group processes.

Fourth, *dramatizing has been identified* by Goffman (1974) — his phrase is "frame analysis" — *as a way to organize experience.* Goffman discriminates dramatizing from ordinary activity. Dramatizing is a frame that changes perception of reality; it includes dreams, experiments, ritual, games, tests, rehearsals, deceptions, fiction, and playfulness. In short, communicating in a dramatic way has the magnificent ability to create a mind set that initially has little match up with reality but can eventually become self-fulfilling — a person who "acts" bigger than life frequently "becomes" bigger than life.

Fifth, *the dramatic style serves the effective teacher well.* Overstating, understating, or altering literal meaning in some way for effect is a good device to gain attention and educate at the same time.

SUMMARY

It is easy at this point to see that dramatic style is complicated. It is possible to develop a unidimensional measure assessing dramatic style as long as the defining core of items taps behaviors that cut across the whole domain — that is, that are necessary components.

The dramatic style takes the scholar and researcher to sophisticated theoretical considerations. Much needs to be unraveled here. In addition, the pragmatic applications are not only wide ranging but fascinating. The potential to affect both the physical and psychological quality of a person's life through dramatic communication is a drama in itself.

NOTES

1. This research agrees with Sullivan (1953) that knowledge about the tension of anxiety is a key to understanding interpersonal dynamics. The communication scholar in particular should note the assertion that Sullivan makes; it is not only provocative, but direction setting.

2. If the deviation is too extreme, the phenomenon moves into the realm of "aberrance" or "freakishness." Even here, the extremes are useful because they define implicitly what the outer boundaries of our identities are. Even more intriguing is a notion advanced by Fiedler (1978, p. 137):

All freaks are perceived to one degree or another as erotic. Indeed, abnormality arouses in some "normal" beholders a temptation to go beyond looking to *knowing* in the full carnal sense the ultimate other. That desire itself is felt as freaky, however, since it implies not only a longing for degradation but a dream of breeching the last taboo against miscegenation.

3. Janov (1970, p. 75) explains: "Tears and sobs in conventional group therapy are but the tiny effluvia of that gigantic, still-dormant inner volcano composed of thousands of denied and compacted experiences pressing for release. Primal Therapy unleashes that volcano in steps."

4. Derogatis et al. (1974) report the developmental history of the Hopkins Symptoms Checklist, its reliability and validity coefficients across various contexts, and the current factor structure.

5. In fact, out of the 420 who answered the national survey, about 45 percent thought they could sometimes prevent the onslaught of a seizure through nonmedical means.

6. The data were submitted to principal-components factor analysis and varimax rotation to isolate independent factors. Since this investigation is in its initial stage, no primary or secondary loadings in terms of magnitude of effect were stipulated as decision rules to determine a factor.

7. The derived distances in Table 5.2 are for a two-dimensional solution with semistrong monotonicity. However, the correlations could be input for a three-dimensional solution should one wish to graph the relationship at a higher dimensionality. McQuitty (1957) elementary linkage analysis was used to interpret the smallest space solution.

6 / Attentive Style

the communicative coordinator

Attentive style is
manifested essentially
as *feedback showing respon-*
siveness. Most often, the attentive
style is associated with the auditor role.
However, this need not be the exclusive way
to think about it. It is easy to think of a person
simultaneously speaking and attending.[1] Nevertheless,
throughout this chapter, the attentive style will be discussed
mostly in terms of the auditor. Also, the word "attentiveness" will
be used interchangeably with the phrase "attentive style."[2]

Axiom 10: Attentive style signals an ongoing willingness
to provide feedback that the person's
messages are being processed in an alert
and/or understanding manner.

The word "understanding" is being used in the sense of "grasping the meaning" rather than in the sense of "showing a sympathetic or tolerant or indulgent attitude toward." The immediate consequent of such signals sustains an interactive process. Even if there is disagreement, the attentive style signals that the communicative process is working.

While attentive style is only one of the components of the communicator style domain, its prominence in many important interpersonal processes warrants detailed analysis. Accordingly, the purpose of this chapter is to further establish the construct in its own right.

First, the *attentiveness domain is defined* in terms of the pertinent components found in the literature. Second, the *attentiveness construct is placed in the perspective of other stylistic variables* relating to communication. As indicated in previous chapters, by understanding the structural relationships that constitute an attentiveness construct, we can gain a more dynamic picture of the attentive style of communication. Third, *a model of the attentiveness domain is presented* based upon variables used in a pencil-and-paper measure of the construct. Attentiveness, as a stylistic component, is introduced also through a self-report questionnaire. A 30-item, pencil-and-paper measure is presented that focuses upon three clusters: (1) behavioral signals, (2) sensitivities, and (3) self-evaluations.

ATTENTIVENESS DOMAIN

Three interrelated bodies of literature provide the defining characteristics that are used to stipulate the domain of the attentive style construct. The three topics are (1) feedback, (2) listening, and (3) empathy. The elements of commonality drawn from each area introduce precise parameters of this style subconstruct.

Feedback

The literature is sparse on the subject of attentive style, but it is relatively abundant on the topic of feedback. As a result, research about feedback is used to discover connections to attentiveness. Often the connections are relatively easy to make, but sometimes they emerge only inferentially. In essence, the following relationship holds: Attentiveness always entails feedback of some sort. However, a person can give feedback without manifesting a high amount of attentiveness.

Feedback, for instance, can indicate to the speaker the degree to which the listener is processing and understanding the points being made, and is agreeing with them (Rosenfeld, 1978; also see Yngve, 1970). It can indicate the respondent's involvement, state of confusion, thoughtfulness, and affective reaction to what has been previously said (Leathers, 1979). Such indications would likely lead the speaker to conclude that the receiver was attentive.

The speaker often nonverbally requests such feedback. For example, as a speaker nears the end of a cognitively difficult passage, eye gaze is reestablished, as if the speaker were calling for a reaction (Kendon, 1967). Typically, the nonverbal request is given, which can manifest itself through behaviors ranging from verbal responses to simple acquiesence (Dittman & Llewellyn, 1974; also see Duncan, 1974). Again, if such feedback is forthcoming, the speaker would likely conclude that the receiver was attentive.

The attentive style is active and reactive. The surprising consequent of attentive style is that it has a strong form-giving function.

Postulate 11:   Attentiveness, manifested through various kinds and degrees of feedback, regulates a speaker's speech as it is happening.

That is, it shapes not only the quantity, but the quality of a conversation.

The first clue that attentiveness does something to the speaker's messages becomes apparent when attentiveness is withdrawn, omitted, or denied. Essentially, when a speaker is denied feedback several phenomena can be observed (Krauss & Bricker, 1967; also see Krauss, Garlock, Bricker, & McMahon, 1977; Krauss & Weinheimer, 1966):

- The speaker may become upset and disrupted, especially if such signals are useful, critical, or needed.
- The speech becomes less structured and coherent. This is most likely to happen when the speaker depends upon the auditor for ongoing guidelines.
- The speaker may communicate less accurately because unwarranted assumptions are made about what the auditor knows or understands.
- The conversation may become less efficient.
- The conversation may develop in a monologue fashion, without backtracking to paraphrase or clarify receiver's confusions.
- Topics are not wrapped up as quickly because understanding has not been signaled.

In short, manifesting in attentive style through responsive feedback gives form to the others messages because it acts as a governor[3] that signals the degree of understanding. With attentiveness, conversations tend to be more structured, coherent, accurate, efficient, and dialectic. Accordingly, **the attentive style is not merely a matter of showing the other person that listening is done, but it actively entails an influential, participant process.**

One of the emergent questions is, how can the form-giving function of attentiveness be demonstrated? Kraut, Lewis, and Swezey (1982)[4] point the way in a study of responsive feedback. They summarize their research this way:

> To examine how feedback influences conversation, we had 76 speaker subjects watch a movie and then summarized it to one or two listeners. The listeners provided varying amounts of feedback to the speaker. When two listeners were present, one could influence the speaker through feedback and the other could only eavesdrop on the conversation. When speakers received more feedback, their narratives were more comprehensible; that is, both listeners understood the movie better.

Kraut et al. found that the feedback individuates the messages. The person with the active, attentive style understands the movie better than the eavesdropper who listened to the same conversation. The authors argue that **"feedback produced these effects by coordinating what the speaker said with what the listener needed to know"** (Kraut et al., 1982, p. 719; emphasis added). Not surprisingly, the auditor has the capacity to teach the speaker how to talk efficiently about the movie.

In other words, the attentive style (manifested as feedback), not only shapes the messages by individuating them, but also the **effects spiral back on the receiver such that the receiver who is actively involved in signaling attentiveness learns more!** The above conclusions do not necessarily mean that "nonattentiveness" is bad. But it is likely to be perceived as increasingly dysfunctional to the extent that the speaker wants or seeks adequate feedback but is denied.

In the experiment, listeners who actively manifested an attentive style were (1) better able to summarize the speaker's conversation, (2) more complete in their summaries, and (3) more accurate in their facts. In addition to learning more, they were more likely to perceive the speaker's summaries to be clear. In essence, two people reacted qualitatively differently to the same stimulus as a function of different, form-giving processes.

It is as though the feedback cycle pressured both the speaker and auditor to participate more, but not the eavesdropper. Kraut et al. (1982) found that when the speakers gave better summaries, the active listeners' summaries were also better, but the eavesdroppers' summaries were not. As speakers included more idea units in their summaries, the active listeners' summaries were of higher quality, whereas the eavesdroppers' were not.

This same pattern occurred for all but one of the measures of listeners' comprehension and significantly so for the overall measure of listeners' comprehension, for the accuracy and completeness of their summaries, and for their assessment of speakers' clarity (Kraut et al., 1982).[5]

Empathy

As mentioned above, research on attentiveness is sparse. Conclusions about what should be expected regarding behaviors in the attentiveness domain, however, can be inferred from related concepts. The literature on empathy is particularly useful. Because of the conceptual closeness between empathy and attentiveness, certain directions emerge that shape this analysis.

The assumption is that a person who is perceived to be empathic will also be perceived to be attentive. However, a distinction should be noted. The empathic communicator must be attentive, but the attentive communicator need not be empathic.

Most treatments of attentiveness are found within the realms of counseling and psychotherapy literature addressing empathy and listening. Attentiveness is seldom examined as a concept in its own right.

Research by Truax and Carkhuff (1967) concerning empathy indicates that the concepts of attentiveness and empathy overlap along certain behavioral dimensions — the therapist's verbal and nonverbal facility to communicate empathic understanding in a language attuned to the client's current needs. Empathy thus appears to be a combination of understanding the other's feelings and indicating that understanding to the other. In short, attentive, behavioral cues signal that the receiver is being empathic.

Because the empathy literature comes from the areas of counseling and psychotherapy, the emphasis is on "positive reinforcement." This is not to say, however, that attentive cues must always be of a positive nature. One can imagine an attentive style being invoked during an argument or dispute. For example, the opponents during a debate will likely display many of the same stylistic behaviors as an empathic counselor or therapist without projecting a facilitative or therapeutic climate.

Listening

Listening behavior also is frequently characterized by attentiveness, but need not be. Conversely, attentive behavior need not be marked by listening activity. A person can signal attentiveness without really listening.

Furthermore, the speaker can signal attentiveness while talking. One could adopt an attentive style while debating, criticizing, or fighting that might preclude empathy; the debater, critic, or fighter might choose to neglect the personal feelings of the other and focus on the nonverbal rather than the verbal aspects of the message.

Rogers (1951) was one of the first researchers to explicate systematically some of the stylistic components of attentiveness. His approach emerged primarily as the important function that role listening played in therapeutic communication. He begins with the premise that "without attention there can be no communication" (Rogers, 1951, p. 349).

Rogers's original list of behavioral cues has undergone considerable expansion as a result of more current empirical research. This list now includes eye contact, forward trunk lean, physical proximity, verbal following (restatement and interpretation), listener silence, and gestures (see Bayes, 1972; Cook, 1964; Haase & Tepper, 1972; Hackney, 1974). Attentive cues thus appear to entail a combination of verbal and paraverbal cues that are directed toward the speaker in a manner that is both obvious and to some degree reinforcing.

For Rogers (1951, p. 349), the attentive communicator "conveys to the speaker that his contribution is worth listening to, that as a person he is respected enough to receive the undivided attention of another." The attentive communicator signals this by nodding his or her head, looking directly at the speaker, and restating what the speaker has just communicated.

While a person may be truly attending to another's communication, it is reasonable to suggest that such activity will not have the stylistic impact suggested by Rogers *unless it is accompanied by the corresponding behavioral signals.* As pointed out above, attending per se can be different from manifesting an attentive style.

Attentiveness as a stylistic concept can be clearly distinguished from the related concept of listening by comparing the corresponding activities of each. "Good listening" behavior entails at least the following four components: (1) thinking ahead of the speaker, (2) weighing verbal evidence carefully, (3) reviewing the completed portion of discourse, (4) listening "between the lines" for implicit meanings (Nichols, 1957).

In contrast to attentiveness, listening concerns intrapersonal, cognitive behaviors that have no overt behavioral manifestations and consequently no stylistic impact on the communicative exchange. A person could engage in the four processes of listening without signaling attentiveness; a person could listen without appearing to listen.

THEORETICAL CONSIDERATIONS

Attentiveness as Reinforcement

Attentiveness has been focused upon by proponents of behavior modification. This viewpoint treats attentiveness as a *reinforcement tool* that involves the amount of time spent with a subject and/or the physical proximity to the subject. Research has found that attentiveness is effective in maintaining peer isolation for a nursery school child (Allen, Hart, Buell, Harris, & Wolf, 1964), modifying the behavior of hyperactive children (Kennedy & Zimmer, 1968), and reducing classroom disruptions (Whitley & Sulzer, 1970).

In the Allen et al. (1964) study, attentiveness was used systematically as reinforcement. Teacher attention was used as a positive reinforcer. When it was given contingent upon interaction with another child in the nursery school and withheld when the child attempted solitary play or interaction solely with an adult, interaction with children rose markedly and adult interaction decreased.

In the Whitley and Sulzer (1970) study, it was also argued that the attentive style provides an essential ingredient in the operant conditioning model.[6] To test the notion, the teacher was counseled to use attentive style to change the behavior of a disruptive ten-year-old student. This meant that attention would be paid to the child only when the behavior was appropriate. The attentiveness was manifested by being near the child, looking at him, giving directions to him, and praising him. The intervention worked.[7]

This chapter does not treat the full range of behavioral dynamics relating to attentiveness, but it supports the notion that attentiveness is an influential stylistic device in human communication. In short, the attentive style has the capacity to reinforce, maintain, modify, and control. These functions are the essence of the axiom that is restated below.

Form-Giving Functions

The attentive style signals the willingness to provide feedback, the willingness to be responsive. The willingness itself is a form of feedback. However, the specific information embedded in the feedback can carry complex and dense messages, including instructions, commands, or directives. Because of these *reactive* possibilities inherent in attentive style, it has the capacity to draw distinctions. In essence, the attentive style is form giving. It reflects the functions suggested in Axiom 2 (Chapter 1):

One message system gives form to another when the literal meaning of one system is reinforced or changed.

In this case, the attentive style functions as a message system that reinforces or changes the ongoing gestalt from the speaker. As such, it (1) entails social motive, (2) influences at multiple levels, and (3) supplies information that is necessary for the speaker's reality checks.

SOCIAL MOTIVES

This perspective which treats attentiveness as a way for the receiver to shape messages from the speaker, assumes that when people communicate it is a nonrandom event for both the speaker and the receiver.[8] When people provide feedback it is a nonrandom event. It is an event that makes distinctions. Accordingly, a variation of Assumption 1 (Chapter 1) is suggested:

There can be no feedback without motive.

In other words, if the responsive feedback is ongoing by both parties in the conversation, either mutually or independently, reciprocal cues not only simultaneously distinguish, but *distinguish with social motive.*

What are some of the social motives? The speaker communicates to provide information, give orders, persuade, impress, change feelings, teach, sell, and so on. The listener communicates to gain information, understand, show interest, express sympathy, learn, confirm, deny, negotiate, and so on. Most often, it is relatively easy to identify social motives even though they may be multiple and complex.

Whatever the motive, responsive feedback is needed to assure a conversation rather than a monologue. This is not an idle phenomenon in light of Assumption 2 (Chapter 1):

There can be no motive unless contents are seen to differ in value.

For the style researcher, this assumption directs attention to the two core questions embedded in the definition: (1) What is the motivation? (2) What are the value differences? In short, these assumptions carry an evaluative consequence with them that lays the groundwork for a discussion of the moral impact of communicator style in the Chapter 10.

MULTIPLE LEVELS

Because speech is hierarchically organized, the form-giving impact of attentiveness may manifest itself at many levels. It could affect the *organization* of the message. For example, feedback can indicate that chunks of information should be omitted; thus the order of information could be sequenced differently. If the speaker instructing another on the fine points of building a house sees that the receiver has some knowledge of framing a house, then the explanation need not follow the original sequence of explications.

Feedback can affect the *structure* of the message. For example, it can indicate that a particular topic, such as finances, should not be explored very much. The speaker can then restructure the message. In similar ways, feedback can influence the *choice* of particular words, the contextual presentation, or the persona.

Finally, feedback can influence the *way* the speaker presents the gestalt. Thus the receiver can maneuver stylistic components of the speaker by signaling varying degrees of attentiveness. Researching the form-giving function of attentiveness is difficult because the consequent change in message may occur at any of the hierarchies. This is why Postulate 1 (Chapter 1) — **stylistic components function with a hierarchical impact** — is intrinsic to style theory.

REALITY CHECKS

There are two sources of feedback to monitor in an interaction. The speaker generates reality checks because of the dual sources. The first source is the self listening and attending to the self. It represents the classical notion of feedback of the mechanism self-monitoring. The person listens to the self as a "generalized other" by projecting how he or she may be coming across to the other. This source of feedback establishes the anchor for the comparisons.

The second source of feedback is from the receiver, the person who manifests an attentive style. This source provides information that either matches the expectations or deviates from them. The comparative differences, if great enough, probably trigger indications for the speaker to either change or continue with the message gestalt.

What is important here is that the monitoring is cybernetic. That is, the referent points of self-monitoring are compared to norm information from the other. The other's reactions provide the test to verify what the self's feedback expectations are. When both sources of monitoring are noted, the exchange is ongoing, guiding, somewhat complex, and interactive.

Both sources of feedback can generate information that might cause the speaker to modify the conversation. These modifications, like the hierarchies of speech, may take many forms. For example, the person may redirect the goal of the conversation. Or the speaker might concentrate more to achieve better efficiency. This might be observed by noting the amount of backtracking that occurs, the increased intensity in persuasiveness, or the deviations from the conversational agenda. I used the last modification, for instance, when I was lecturing a class of about 200 students. The size of the class itself compounded the problem of keeping the students interested. Many times I have slipped into a more trendy topic to reestablish interest in the class.

Attention Versus Attentiveness

Attentive style may be appropriately distinguished from the generic concept of "attention." Attention is primarily concerned with the human processes of reception and cognition — the neurophysiological activities through which information is received and given meaning (see Baken, 1966; Deutsch & Deutsch, 1963; Makworth, 1970; Norman, 1976; Ryle, 1949; White, 1964).[9] A person can attend to information without signaling an attentive style. The eavesdropper typifies this — the person who attends without manifesting attentiveness.

Much empirical research in communication has focused on audience attention to the interlocutor and his or her message during the speech act.[10] Even though social science has shown empirical favoritism toward the concept of attention, distinguishing attentive style as a construct is useful to the understanding of human communication. A strong predictive relationship has been found between attentive activity and projection of a positive communicator image, interpersonal attractiveness, and effectiveness in teaching and psychotherapeutic contexts (Lieberman et al., 1973; see also Norton, 1977; Norton & Pettegrew, 1977; Pettegrew, 1977b).

The distinction is that an attentive style not only involves doing something actively, such as processing information, but also reactively, such as indicating that the information is being processed. An attentive style involves more than the passive reception of another's message; the attentive communicator behaves in specific ways that signal to the other that attention is being paid to the message.

Skinner (1953, pp. 123-124) maintains that attention and "paying attention" are not behavior; they are what he calls "a controlling relation":

> When our subject describes an object at the edge of the page even though we are sure he is not looking at it, or when he tells us that the clarinets have fallen a beat behind the violins, we need not demonstrate any spatial arrangement of stimulus and response. It is enough to point to the special controlling relation which makes such a response possible.[11]

In like manner, an attentive style is not a behavior in itself. Rather, the domain of attentiveness is a set of behaviors that have been stipulated to represent the construct. If the behaviors compatible with the stipulation are manifested, then it is said that attentiveness is shown.

Summary of Parameter Distinctions

Attentiveness is conceptually related to but not synonymous with empathy, listening, feedback, or attention. Attentiveness is an intentional and active process; it functions simultaneously with listening activity, but not exclusively. The speaker, for example, can signal alertness or sensitivity *while talking*. Only attentiveness serves a *stylistic* function in this process. In a precise sense, only attentiveness signals the process of reception. Conversely stated, inattentiveness is a combination of behavioral and psychological activities that indicate that an individual has tuned out and has adopted an indifferent attitude toward speaker and message. With these distinctions in mind, the following sections formally stipulate the domain.

DEFINITION

Attentive style is responsive interaction reflecting alertness and/or awareness. Attentiveness is a constellation of verbal, non-verbal, and paraverbal signals that indicate that a person's message is being noticed in an alert and/or understanding manner. The precise definition found at the beginning of this chapter is embedded in the mapping sentence below (Elizur, 1970; Gratch, 1973; Levy, 1975).[12]

MAPPING SENTENCE OF ATTENTIVE STYLE DOMAIN

Attentive style is the **A** (a₁ cognitive assessment)

by **B** $\begin{pmatrix} \mathbf{b_1} & \text{self} \\ \mathbf{b_2} & \text{target} \\ \mathbf{b_3} & \text{participant observer} \\ \mathbf{b_4} & \text{nonparticipant observer} \end{pmatrix}$

which **signals that there is an ongoing willingness to provide feedback that the person's messages are being processed in an alert and/or understading manner**

in **C** $\begin{pmatrix} \mathbf{c_1} & \text{general face-to-face} \\ \mathbf{c_2} & \text{intimate} \\ \mathbf{c_3} & \text{marital} \\ \mathbf{c_4} & \text{instructional} \\ \mathbf{c_5} & \text{therapeutic} \end{pmatrix}$ settings with respect

to the directive focus of **D** $\begin{pmatrix} \mathbf{d_1} & \text{verbal} \\ \mathbf{d_2} & \text{paraverbal} \\ \mathbf{d_3} & \text{nonverbal} \end{pmatrix}$

behaviors including **E** $\begin{pmatrix} \mathbf{e_1} & \text{duration} \\ \mathbf{e_2} & \text{frequency} \end{pmatrix}$

of the respective behaviors.

The commitment and expectation entailed in the mapping sentence is that components reflecting the facets can be used to obtain data to evaluate subjects. For example, in facet D, behavioral signals provide indicators of attentiveness. These signals are primarily drawn from the counseling and psychotherapy literature. The nonverbal behaviors (d_3) include smiling, head nodding, using verbal following (restatement and other nondirective phrases), body and trunk lean, direct eye contact, and relating similar experiences or feelings. These signals serve to demonstrate that a person is deliberatley reacting in such a way that the other communicator knows he or she is being listened to and focused upon.

Second, sensitivities provide indicators of attentiveness. If a person is attentive to another (even in a conflict situation), he or she should be sensitive to — but not necessarily in agreement with — the feelings of that person. The attentive communicator should be more knowledgeable about what the other person means than the inattentive communicator; an attentive person should be more "co-oriented" with the other and very likely, although not necessarily, more empathic.

Third, it is assumed that the attentive person will also evaluate him or herself as such. The fact that the attentive individual is providing both specific behavioral cues to attentiveness and is sensitive to the feelings and emotions of the other communicator assumes that he or she is consciously performing this activity. Consequently, the person should claim to be extremely attentive and should indicate that he or she really focuses on others during communicative interactions. In the next section, the attentiveness construct is placed in perspective by showing its relationship to other communicator style variables.

ATTENTIVE STYLE IN RELATIONSHIP TO THE COMMUNICATOR STYLE STRUCTURAL GESTALT

By placing any style variable in the larger context of the communicator style structural gestalt, one obtains a holistic picture of the role that it plays. As presented in Chapter 3, the communicator style construct includes nine independent variables (dominant, open, relaxed, dramatic, contentious, friendly, attentive, animated, and impression leaving). It also includes one dependent variable — communicator image.

Figure 3.2 (Chapter 3) indicates that attentive and friendly are closely related. This suggests that the attentive communicator usually manifests a friendly style such as acknowledging, encouraging, deliberately reacting to, and accommodating others. Attentiveness anchors one end of a dimension in the configuration.[13] Dominant (talking frequently, coming on strong, taking control in social situations) anchors the opposite end of this dimension.

This does not mean that a given style of communicating could not include these two variables together; a "dominant-attentive" style occurs often. The sensitive but aggressive salesperson communicates in such a way that he or she is seen as coming on strong but willing to interact responsively. The dominant-attentive combination suggests that the person is engaged in a more complex communicative activity — multiple signals are indicated.

Method

In this section, the facets of the mapping sentence are incorporated to structure operationally the pencil-and-paper self-report measure. The self-report method was chosen for several reasons. First, because this research involves construct explication for the heretofore poorly defined concept of attentiveness, it makes good sense to begin at an elementary level. Only after our knowledge and expectations about the attentiveness have matured is it reasonable to adopt more advanced methods, such as coding schemes based on live or videotaped communicative interactions.

Second, the multi-item Likert scaling procedure is well tested, does not make stringent assumptions about the statistical properties of the individual items, and has proven to work well for social-psychological attributes (Nunnally, 1967, chaps. 1, 2).

Finally, because attentiveness embraces a conscious activity on the part of the communicator, it makes sense to understand this activity from the perspective of the respondent.

SUBJECTS

Two sample populations were obtained to test the attentiveness measure. First 170 noncollegiate adults voluntarily filled out the measure.[14] Second, 158 students from introductory communication classes at the University of Michigan voluntarily completed the measure. This procedure provided two different samples for comparison. The validity check indicated that there were no important differences between the two samples.

MEASURE

The attentiveness measure consists of three parts. In part one, behavioral signals, sensitivities, and evaluations composed a 30-item test relating to attentiveness. Tables 6.2-6.4 report the exact wording of these items. In addition, it was thought that any communicator manifesting "other-oriented" attentive behavior might do so because he or she was passive, submissive, or too anxious to talk. Hence items reflecting these possible assessments were also included (Table 6.1). Finally, two filler (introductory) items were included. A six-point Likert scale was used for all items.

In part two, attributes of the attentive style were measured using 18 semantic differential scales. A five-point scale was employed. Table 6.5 reports the attributes for each behavior.

In part three, five context-bound questions were asked about listening behavior (an important component in most attentive activity). A seven-point Likert scale ranging from "I do almost all of the listening" to "I do almost none of the listening" was used regarding the person's (1) most intimate friend, (2) more dominant parent, (3) less dominant parent, (4) boss, and (5) stranger.

In summary, the measuring instrument was constructed so that "good" items could be identified that reflect the attentiveness construct. The measure has a lot of redundancy built into it. However, because the immediate task centers on construct explication and establishing content and construct validity, these items were included.

Results

Three types of analysis are reported. First, a structural analysis of the variable set defining the attentiveness construct is made to understand the interrelationships between individual items and clusters of items. Second, the predictive relationships between individual items and a general measure of attentiveness were explored through regression analyses. Third, an analysis relating the listening component of attentiveness to various contextual relationships was made.

STRUCTURAL ANALYSIS

A principal-axis factor analysis and McQuitty's (1957) elementary linkage analysis were used to interpret the structure of the 30-item domain. Four of the factors in this analysis were easily interpretable.[15]

Factor 1 explains 7.1 percent of the variance for attentiveness. Table 6.1 shows the six variables that determine this factor. The items were included in this analysis for heuristic purposes; it was thought that being a passive/submissive communicator might be a strong correlate of being an attentive communicator. This, however, does not seem to be so. Items 10, 16, and 21 in the inactivity factor are related only to other items within the same factor; they are unrelated or negatively related to 26 of the 30 total items. Item 14 in this factor did only slightly better; it was unrelated or negatively related to 24 of the 30 tiems.

Being passive/submissive/too anxious is marked by inactivity (not doing something during the communicative process). Being attentive/alert/listening/sensitive to, on the other hand, is a characteristically active process.

Being passive, submissive, or too anxious to say anything may be sufficient components, under some circumstances, in under-

TABLE 6.1   Factor 1: Inactivity

Variable	Orthogonal Loading	Oblique Loading	Mean	Standard Deviation
10 I am a very passive communicator.	−.74	.99	4.20	1.20
16 I am a very submissive communicator.	−.67	1.05	4.10	1.03
21 I often listen because I am too anxious to say anything.	−.52	1.02	4.14	1.11
14 Many times I pretend not to be listening (even though I am) to the other person.	−.31	.86	4.22	1.21
20* I [do not] have a lot of energy when I communicate.	.45	−.70	2.74	1.03
3* I [do not] have a habit of asking for clarification from the other person if I am unclear on what was said.	.24	−.57	2.61	.93

*Items 20 and 3 may be bad items. A tentative interpretation, however, is to reverse the wording of the items.

standing attentive behavior, but they are not necessary components.[16] One can be attentive and passive/submissive/too anxious or inattentive and passive/submissive/too anxious. This suggests that factor 1 does not contribute to the development of the attentiveness construct.

Table 6.2 presents the twelve variables that make up factor 2, which explains 10.7 percent of the variance in attentiveness. Most of the variables that define this factor concern signaling the other that one is being attentive. Item 27 is the most representative variable in this factor. The various attentive signals include smiling (15), nodding (19), providing nondirective phrases (22), leaning toward the speaker (25), eye contact (30), relating similar experiences (17), and restating the other's message (11). These items accurately characterize the behavioral cues of attentive activity found in the psychotherapeutic literature.

Factor 2 suggests a communicative style that is ongoing, interrelated, and obviously deliberate. It is clear that behavioral cues entail an important component of most attentive activity.

Factor 3 explains 7.7 percent of the variance in attentiveness. Table 6.3 reports the statistics for each item in this factor. The five variables reflect one's empathic abilities — one's sensitivity to others. Three of the items, 31, 24, and 26, highlight knowing what the other meant or felt by his or her communication. These items

TABLE 6.2   Factor 2: Attentiveness Signals

Variable	Orthogonal Loading	Oblique Loading	Mean	Standard Deviation
15 I have a habit of encouraging the other person to continue talking by frequently smiling during the conversation.	.65	.95	2.82	1.13
19 I have a habit of encouraging the other person to continue talking by frequently nodding my head during the conversation.	.53	1.01	2.70	1.11
27 Usually, I deliberately react in such a way that people know that I am listening to them.	.50	.84	3.00	1.04
22 I have a habit of encouraging the other person to continue talking by saying phrases like "I see," "Uh-huh," "I understand," or "That's very interesting."	.49	.96	2.93	1.22
25 I have a habit of encouraging the other person to continue talking by leaning toward the person.	.48	1.04	3.83	1.11
5 I want people to know that I am listening to them.	.45	.70	2.14	.91
30 I have a habit of encouraging the other person to continue talking by looking at him or her.	.44	.59	2.44	.90
4 Other people often come to me when they need somebody to listen to them.	.39	.82	2.63	1.00
17 I have a habit of encouraging the other person to continue talking by frequently relating similar experiences during the conversation.	.37	.95	2.81	1.03

closely parallel empathic abilities treated in great detail by the therapeutic communication literature.

Factor 4 emerges as the most cohesive factor and also contains the most redundancy. It explains 10.2 percent of the variance in attentiveness. The items in factor 4 entail the respondent's evalua-

TABLE 6.2 Continued

Variable	Orthogonal Loading	Oblique Loading	Mean	Standard Deviation
23 I frequently notice a lot of different ways to interpret what a person says.	.37	.96	2.92	1.11
8 When I communicate in a general one-to-one situation, I always am a careful listener.	.36	.65	2.54	1.13
11 I have a habit of restating what the other person said if I am unclear on what was said.	.34	.98	3.31	1.22

tion of his or her attentive behavior. The assessments are expressed in terms of being a careful listener and being very attentive to others. Table 6.4 presents the statistics for each individual item in this factor. Items 28 and 29 are the most representative variables in factor 4. Item 7 is a bad item; the wording is ambiguous and difficult for respondents to interpret.

Figure 6.1 shows a graphic representation, using McQuitty's elementary linkage technique, and the Pearson product-moment correlations for the variables in factors 2, 3, and 4. The decision rule for this analysis required that a correlation had to be equal to or greater than .30 to be included in a link and an item must load at least .50 on a factor.

No items from factor 1 satisfied the decision rules. Ten variables from the factor analysis have loadings of at least as high as .30 for any given link. This model strongly suggests that the facets delineated in the mapping sentence work well in constituting the attentiveness construct. Equally informative is the fact that an attentive style of communication does not appear to include components of passivity.

REGRESSION ANALYSES

Two sets of regression analyses are presented. The first analysis shows which behavioral attributes on the semantic differential scales best predict attentiveness. These predictor variables were standardized. A "total attentiveness score" was created as the dependent variable by standardizing and averaging all items in factors 2, 3, and 4 (except item 7 — a bad item). A stepwise regression analysis was then performed. Table 6.5 reports the results of this analysis.

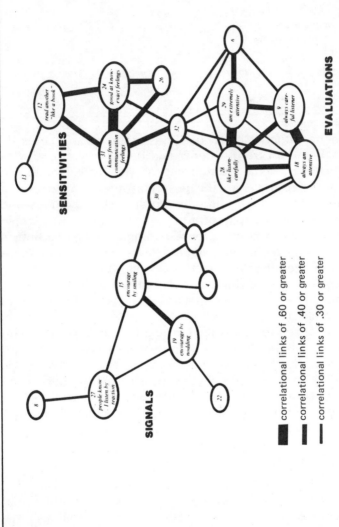

SENSITIVITIES

- 13
- 12 *read another "like a book"*
- 24 *good at knowing evaluations feelings*
- 26
- 31 *know from communication feelings*
- 32

SIGNALS

- 8
- 27 *people know I listen by reaction*
- 19 *encourage by nodding*
- 22
- 15 *encourage by smiling*
- 4
- 5
- 30

EVALUATIONS

- 6
- 29 *am extremely attentive*
- 9 *always careful listener*
- 28 *like listen carefully*
- 18 *always am attentive*

■ correlational links of .60 or greater

▮ correlational links of .40 or greater

— correlational links of .30 or greater

NOTE: Numbers in the ovals refer to the items in Tables 6.2–6.4. Only the variables in the larger ovals met the criteria of high factor loadings and correlational links of .30 or greater.

Figure 6.1 Correlagram of Attentive Style Variables

172

TABLE 6.3   Factor 3: Attentiveness Sensitivities

Variable	Orthogonal Loading	Oblique Loading	Mean	Standard Deviation
31 I am very good at knowing the exact feelings of other people from their communication.	.77	.97	3.22	1.03
24 I am very good at knowing the exact feelings of other people.	.77	1.03	3.44	1.09
12 Usually I can read another person "like a book."	.59	.91	3.60	1.24
26 I can always repeat back to a person exactly what was meant.	.44	.82	3.93	1.03
13 I try to read between the lines when I am listening to another person.	.31	.59	2.90	1.22

Three behavioral attributes emerged as significant predictors of attentiveness. Posture was the best predictor, accounting for 19 percent of the variance. Verbal behavior (restatement and non-directive responses) accounted for 5 percent of the total variance in attentiveness, and eye behavior (direct eye contact) accounted for 4 percent of the total variance.

This finding is commensurate with previous research, which has suggested that nonverbal behaviors are more influential in communicating a feeling of empathy than verbal behaviors (Haase & Tepper, 1972). This is especially true for posture; leaning toward the speaker, maintaining a relaxed posture, and showing interest via body attitude go a long way toward expressing an attentive style of communication. These cues can be reinforced through both eye contact and verbal (other-oriented) behavior. It is reasonable to conclude, therefore, that nonverbal cues might be more intimately linked to an attentive style of communication than are verbal cues, but this conclusion needs substantially more research for support.

In the second regression analysis, the attentive-not attentive semantic differential scale was treated as the dependent variable and the three remaining scales for each of the remaining scales for each of the behavioral attributes were used as predictor variables. Table 6.6 reports the results of the regression analysis for eye behavior, facial behavior, verbal behavior, and posture.

TABLE 6.4   Factor 4: Attentiveness Evaluation

Variable	Orthogonal Loading	Oblique Loading	Mean	Standard Deviation
9 When I communicate in a general one-to-one situation, I always am a very careful listener.	.69	1.02	2.63	1.10
29 I am an extremely attentive communicator.	.65	.78	3.03	1.01
28 I really like to listen very carefully to people.	.64	.78	2.73	1.00
18 When I communicate in a general one-to-one situation, I always am very attentive.	.59	.83	2.72	1.02
32 Other people would say that I am an extremely attentive communicator.	.49	.58	2.91	1.04
6 Even when I am doing most of the talking, I am a very alert communicator.	.46	.71	2.73	1.02
7 Often people think I am listening to them when I am not.	−.39	−.93	3.64	1.33

NOTE: The most representative items are included in factors 2, 3, and 4 (except item 7). A total attentiveness score can be determined by standardizing and averaging these items. Such an attentiveness index can be usefully integrated into developmental studies of communicative competence as well as serve as a dependent measure (in its own right) for studies that seek to investigate how an attentive style of communication is acquired. Because attentiveness is such a desirable quality, the items tend to be positively skewed. The use of modifiers such as "always" and "never" should make the distribution of the items more normal. The internal reliability (Hoyt coefficient) for the items in factors 2, 3, and 4, excluding item 7, is .91.

In every instance, attentiveness was predicted by the "tendency to show interest" scale. This attribute seems to be the pervasive impression accompanying attentiveness across a wide variety of behavioral cues. In other words, **what all attentive behaviors appear to have in common is their ability to signal interest in the speaker's messages.** These results, however, should be interpreted with caution.[17]

ATTENTIVENESS IN CONTEXTS

If attentiveness is to be a useful construct in its own right, it will have to be tested in communicative situations and contexts that are functionally related to real-life encounters. While this issue can

TABLE 6.5   Attributes Regressed on Attentiveness

Variable	R^2	Standard Error	Significance Level
Eye Behavior			
Tends to show interest	.45	.59	.00
Tends to be maintained	.53	.55	.00
Tends to be direct	.54	.54	.01
Facial Behavior			
Tends to show interest	.45	.51	.00
Provides a lot of feedback	.46	.50	.01
Verbal Behavior			
Tends to show interest	.49	.50	.00
Encouraging	.56	.47	.00
Provides a lot of feedback	.57	.47	.00
Posture			
Tends to show interest	.51	.52	.00

NOTE: For each of the four regression analyses above, the dependent variable is represented by the words in italics. For example, facial behavior is the dependent variable in the second regression analysis. For eye behavior, $F_{(3, 307)} = 117.9$; $p < .001$. For facial behavior, $F_{(2, 307)} = 130.6$; $p < .001$; For verbal behavior, $F_{(3, 306)} = 136.8$; $p < .001$. For posture, $F_{(1, 303)} = 310.7$; $p < .001$.

only be adequately addressed by more detailed subsequent research, the present exploratory study points to some directions.

The subjects were asked to indicate how much listening they did across five communication contexts: with their least dominant parent, their most intimate friend, a stranger, their most dominant parent, and their boss. While listening is not synonymous with attentiveness, it is an essential component of most attentive behavior and, therefore, an important index of attentiveness. Furthermore, listening behavior is the easiest of the attentiveness components to differentiate across contexts. Table 6.7 reports the means and standard deviations for each context.

The results of this analysis suggest that listening behavior increases as a function of role status. For example, the least amount of listening was done with subject's least dominant parent, while the most listening was done with his or her boss. Perhaps the role of an individual determines listening behavior more than the importance of any particular message.

It is important to note that the same effect may not be replicated for other covariates of attentiveness. The boss may garner

TABLE 6.6   Summed Attribute Scores Regressed on Attentive-Not Attentive Variable

Variable	R^2	Standard Error	Significance Level
Attentive-Not Attentive			
Posture	.19	.44	.00
Verbal behavior	.24	.43	.00
Eye behavior	.28	.42	.00

NOTE: In each instance, the summed attribute score is made up of the variables outlined in Table 6.5—interest, maintenance, and directness. $F(3, 254) = 32.7$; $p <$ .001. Facial behavior and the overall rating did not make it into the regression equation at the .05 level.

the lion's share of an individual's listening behavior, but may receive almost no empathy. Future research must address how each of the attentiveness components operates across contexts.

Discussion

An attentiveness domain can be organized according to behavioral cues, sensitivities, and evaluations. Furthermore, sets of "good" predictors that make sense and have empirical support from previous research can be generated. Finally, the listening component of attentiveness appears to function as a result of role status within particular contexts.

The present research indicates that the attentive style of communication is a complex process involving both sending and receiving messages during the interpersonal transaction. The attentive communicator focuses his or her regard toward the other while simultaneously signaling interest, concern, sensitivity, and notice verbally, nonverbally, and paraverbally.

The impact of an attentive style can be deeply therapeutic. As Shave (1975, p. 80) has demonstrated, therapeutic communication is more intimately related to listening than to talking, "for somebody must be there to listen, and be perceived as listening, at least in part, to initiate and to continue the transference phenomenon."

Or the impact can be trivially pragmatic, as when a husband attentively sits through his wife's account of her bridge party so that she won't object to his going bowling with his friends.

Across a wide variety of contexts, the attentive style can suggest that a person is being empathic, tolerant, caring, interested, and other oriented in an active rather than a passive way.

The following points highlight the dynamics of the attentive style component: (1) It coordinates conversation, (2) it reflects

TABLE 6.7   Means of Attentiveness Across Contexts

Context	% of Listening	Mean	N per cell	Standard Deviation
Least dominant parent	60%	3.8	273	1.5
Intimate friend	63%	3.6	313	1.1
Stranger	67%	3.2	314	1.5
Most dominant parent	67%	3.2	287	1.3
Boss	73%	2.9	259	1.3

NOTE: The N per cell varies because of missing data—not every person had a boss, for example.

interpersonal affiliations, (3) it is frequently solicited, and (4) it refers to multiple phenomena.

ATTENTIVE STYLE COORDINATES CONVERSATION

Attentive style not only shapes the semantic contents of the speaker's message, but it coordinates the conversation through signals that regulate speed, redundancy, and length of interaction. For example, if a listener continues to show interest in the speaker's speech, it is a tacit demonstration that there is an ongoing commitment to engage in the conversation. As Kraut et al. (1982) remind us:

> Conversationalists coordinate much of what they have to say to each other on the spot. To achieve whatever goals they have in a conversation, whether they are exposition, persuasion, or impression management, people generally want their partners to understand them

The converse is also true. Inattentiveness marked by bored looks and little or no feedback causes most speakers to stop talking or to shift the tenor of conversation.

ATTENTIVE STYLE REFLECTS
INTERPERSONAL AFFILIATIONS

In addition to the information from feedback about the conversation per se, the attentive style is often a good indication of the interpersonal affiliation between two people. A smile or a head nod are not merely nonverbal cues that regulate, but are also implicit demonstrations of (1) understanding in the sympathetic or tolerant sense, (2) interest in the person independent of the immediate content of the message, and (3) a desire to escalate the state of the relationship.

ATTENTIVE STYLE IS FREQUENTLY SOLICITED

Many times messages are framed so that they are unilaterally presented, such as a speech to a live audience. In this situation, the good speaker frequently solicits feedback. The first planned laugh from the audience is a clear signal that the speech is on track. Sometimes, the speaker will deliberately ask the audience for feedback: "Do you know what I mean?" "Is the point clear?" "Okay [said softly so as to indicate that the speech won't go on until it is all right with everybody]?"

The good speaker also might weave in information that he or she knows about the audience, such as common premises ("Guns don't kill, criminals do"), histories ("When I went to high school here in 1962 . . . "), or codes ("This country needs more law and order"). This kind of information might predictably get a reaction that the speaker plans on and expects.

In intimate relationships feedback is sometimes demanded, especially in conflict situations. One partner may not allow the other partner to withdraw into passivity. At its extreme, the partner may push the withdrawn partner to violent reactions, just to get feedback.

ATTENTIVE STYLE REFERS TO
MULTIPLE PHENOMENA

To the extent that a speaker feels a need to be clear, unambiguous, and concise — in keeping with Grice's (1975) maxims — he or she must assess how the speech is affecting the receiver in terms of both knowledge and understanding. The assessment may embrace many components. Both the speaker and the receiver can process feedback that is explicit or implicit and direct or indirect. Model 6.1 helps in visualizing the multiple phenomena available to the communicants.

These components may be intrinsic to the receiver and may function as feedback in the true cybernetic sense, or they may be inferences drawn from the environment, context, situation, or time. The strongest indication of attentive style is when the feedback is direct. The weakest indication of attentive style is when the feedback is indirect and implicit.

Direct, Explicit Feedback. When feedback is direct and explicit, it serves an immediate form-giving function. It provides an immediate indication that understanding has occurred; it permits an immediate way to eliminate ambiguity; all a person has to do is ask, "What did you mean?"

FEEDBACK

		EXPLICIT	IMPLICIT
FEEDBACK	**DIRECT**	the clearest signal of attentiveness— verbal and to the point	nonverbal and paraverbal signals— apparently responsive
	INDIRECT	responsive, but entails some ambiguity— metaphorical, ambivalent, etc.	most inferential information available, but ambiguous

Model 6.1   Types of Feedback

Direct, Implicit Feedback. All the nonverbal and paraverbal indications of understanding fall into this category. The feedback is apparently responsive to the conversation at hand. However, if the receiver is on "automatic pilot," the feedback may seem appropriate and interactive, when in fact it is passive and possibly random.

Indirect, Explicit Feedback. The feedback in this category may be immediate, but it needs to be decoded more than a direct answer. The feedback may take a metaphorical form. For example, Aureliano in Garcia Marquez's *One Hundred Years of Solitude* (1971) only realized the meaning of a piece of information near the moment of his death. Garcia Marquez writes:

> And then he saw the child. It was a dry and bloated bag of skin that all the ants in the world were dragging toward their holes along the stone path in the garden. Aureliano could not move. Not because he was paralyzed by horror but because at that prodigious instant Malquiandes' final keys were revealed to him and he saw the epigraph of the parchments perfectly placed in the order of man's time and space: **The first of the line is tied to a tree and the last is being eaten by the ants.**

Thus feedback can be provided, but the speaker may not be able to interpret it, may be oblivious to it, or may misunderstand it. As a consequence, the speaker may even deny that feedback is available, even though the information is available if it could be processed.

In such situations, the line between manifesting an attentive style and providing feedback needs to be recalled. The attentive style signals that there is an ongoing willingness to provide feed-back that the person's messages are being processed in an alert or understanding manner, but the content-specific feedback that is being sought may not be given. One type of feedback indicates that the message is being processed in an understanding, alert way; the second type of feedback concerns the literal content of the message.

Indirect, Implicit Feedback. In this category, the speaker is least likely to conclude that attentive style is being signaled, although information may be available on which the speaker could capitalize. For example, the speaker may draw implications merely from the other's physical presence (Clark & Marshall, 1981). It is easy to invite intimacy with particular physical posturing; conversely, it is useful to become more defensive through physical maneuvering. In like manner, humans can signal myriad other emotional, spiritual, psychological, psychic, or health states through physical posturing and postures.

Many forms of therapy, in fact, rely upon clues from physical signals. Probably one of the most extreme perspectives is from Reich (1972), who connects character traits to "muscular armor" that is used as a defense against emotional excitation. Reich ar-gues, for instance, that rigidity of the body signals emotional deadness.

External information also predisposes assessments of what a conversation should be. Demographic or geographic information often determines how and what a speaker might say. When Mark Twain went out West, he characterized a certain part of the Rocky Mountains this way:

> It was the very paradise of outlaws and desperadoes. There was absolutely no semblance of law there. Violence was the rule. Force was the only recognized authority. The commonest misun-derstandings were settled on the spot with the revolver or the knife. Murders were done in open day, and with sparkling fre-quency, and nobody thought of inquiring into them. It was considered that the parties who did the killing had their private reasons for it; for other people to meddle would have been looked upon as indelicate [Twain, 1871, pp. 65-66].

Such information structures conversation parameters, shapes ex-pectations, and determines forms of feedback.

Prior information also gives the speaker a perspective that can influence the shape of the conversation before it ever happens. For instance, if I heard that you really like basketball, but hate boxing, then I have access to some information that easily lends itself to a conversational agenda of specific small talk.

The fact that each of these pieces of information, whether from inferences about an environment or context, from gossip or factual information, or from the infinite subtlety of nonverbal signals, can give form to a message reflects the need for Axiom 3 (Chapter 1) in style theory:

> **Form-giving messages can be antecedent to, simultaneous with, or subsequent to another message.**

In these processes, speakers make inferences from characteristics of their partners, the context, the situation, and the time that are neither evolutionarily adapted nor necessarily intended for the immediate exchange of messages. For example, if a person has an irrational but predisposed bias against midgets, this characteristic does not inherently affect communication; nevertheless, it can taint the social interaction.

FUTURE DIRECTIONS

There is a wide variety of hypotheses to test concerning the attentive style construct. In all the studies, the research should carefully discuss manifestations of attentive style and the functions of the many types and nuances of feedback integral to the communicative process.

In addition, the following relationships should be explored. First, *the attentive communicator is more socially effective, cooperative, and successful* (Krauss & Glucksberg, 1977). The assumption is that attentiveness is wanted. It can be a reward in itself; it signals that the communicative process works. The reward function of attentiveness should not be underestimated by communication scholars. What might pass for uninteresting discourse may in fact be vital and critical because of the attentiveness inherent in the process.

Second, *the communicator/counselor showing attentiveness is optimally therapeutic* (Ivey, 1971; see also Nichols, 1957; Truax & Carkhuff, 1967). This perspective favors an interactional model of therapy in which elements of attentive style are incorporated *as part of the means of maneuvering* the client. Also, the communicator/counselor will maximally capitalize on the clues and "state" of attentiveness provided by the client. Milton Erickson epitomized this perspective, raising it to a communicative art (Haley, 1973).

Third, *the attentive communicator is more obsessive-compulsive* (Shapiro, 1975). This is a speculative connection, but an intriguing one. I have a colleague who is so attentive that she drives me to distraction by continually anticipating and finishing my sentences for me or simultaneously with me. I have reached the point of stopping the sentences halfway to see how they will come out with her. Whatever the case, if it is possible to be too attentive, then the questions relating to consequents should be explored and the motivations should be analyzed.

Fourth, *the attentive communicator tends be a leader in groups because active participation is signaled.* The participant signaling an attentive style should be perceived as more influential in a group than the participant who is merely attending but not signaling it.

Fifth, *the attentive communicator tends to talk more in social situations* — as a result, he or she may be perceived by others as more powerful or as possessing more leadership ability. Again, this would be in contrast to the person who is simply attending but not signaling it or the inattentive person.

Finally, *the form-giving functions that are transmitted through attentiveness need to be carefully identified and analyzed.* Kraut et al. (1982) are exemplary in this regard. There are general form-giving functions that result from attentiveness, such as increased efficiency in the conversation. Now, specific form-giving functions need to be explored. To what extent can the receiver craft particulars in the conversation through attentiveness?

Although many studies will be needed to establish the attentiveness construct firmly, including behavioral observation and more critical analyses, the self-report data from the attentiveness measure is a good starting point. It works well and is compatible with previous conceptual work in the literature.

Criteria-related and construct validity must be demonstrated further. Criteria-related validity can be shown partially, but not entirely, by correlating the attentiveness measure with other established measures of listening, empathy, and attentiveness.[18] Establishing construct validity is an unending process. But, if data and analyses are obtained relating to some of the future directions outlined above, this work will advance the cause substantially. In short, attentiveness is an important element in the communication process. It serves an active, confirming function — testifying to the worth of the other's communication — and a coordinating function.

NOTES

1. When a person is speaking, that person can be simultaneously and continually reading the other person's reactions and responding to those reactions even while talking. Further, the person can be responsive in different ways. He or she can begin to acknowledge the other person's reactions through verbal content, or can continue to talk and nonverbally provide yet another set of messages that give form to the verbal information in ironic, sarcastic, serious, or other ways. Thus the ongoing form-giving process in itself represents feedback or a way to signal attentiveness.

2. If a person manifests an attentive style, attentiveness is signaled; conversely, if attentiveness is signaled, the person is showing an attentive style.

3. There is an irony with the attentive style. At first glance, it is assumed that it is the less powerful influence. Yet, because of its capacity to govern, in the sense of feedback, it has a strong ability to control. In the cybernetic sense of a machine system, the governor provides feedback to monitor the system. It is an elegant mechanism attached to a machine to afford automatic control or limitation of speed or power. It is often an attachment actuated by the centrifugal force of whirling weights opposed by gravity or springs.

4. Kraut et al.'s (1982) outstanding article addresses the issues pertinent to the notion of attentive style, although the authors do not use this phrase. Throughout the first part of the chapter, I paraphrase much of Kraut et al.'s analysis and parallel their organization of points. This is one of those studies that I would have liked to have done.

5. Kraut et al. (1982, p. 728) conclude that "the data are evidence that speakers can use listener feedback to tailor what they say to what listeners need to know. Active listeners gave feedback that indicated how well informed they were about the topic at hand. Speakers modified what they had to say on the basis of this feedback." In addition, they maintain that "the person giving the feedback benefits more than another person who can overhear the same conversation but has no opportunity to influence it. Active listeners understand the communication better and are more influenced by variations in its quality" (p. 728). The consequence is that "along with other functions, feedback can regulate the informational density of speakers' communication" (pp. 728-729).

6. Whitly and Sulzer (1970) use the term "paying attention" rather than "attentive style," but the exchange of phrases in this instance is equivalent. The phrase itself, "paying attention," is interesting because of the word "paying." It clearly suggests that attentiveness functions metaphorically like money.

7. The attentiveness worked well as part of the operative conditioning in this study. In fact, when the teacher inadvertently gave attention after a set of disruptive behaviors, disruptive behaviors increased. The suggestion is that disruptive behavior essentially is a demand for a measure of attention, a reward. If attention is given, the child essentially obtains a reward for disruptive behavior.

8. The issues of unconscious, accidental, and habitual communication are discussed in Chapter 10.

9. The complexities of attentiveness have led some researchers to refer to it as a "polymorphous activity." White (1964, pp. 6-11) says that to "simply say that someone is attending, or paying attention, gives no more clue as to what activities he is engaged in than simply to say that he is practicing. What 'attending' tells us is that his activities and energies, whatever they are, are directed to and focused on

something which occupies him." White, in essence, calls for more precision when discussing the phenomenon of attending.

10. For typical treatments of attention in communication, see Ross (1974), Scheidel (1967), and Simons (1976).

11. Skinner (1953) says that "the criterion is whether the stimulus is exerting any effect upon our behavior. When we stare at someone without noticing him, listen to a speech without attending to what is said, or read a page 'absentmindedly,' we are simply failing to engage in some of the behavior which is normally under the control of such stimuli."

12. A mapping sentence functions two ways in theory building. First, it forces the researcher to specify the elements of the construct under investigation. Second, it identifies specific facets of the construct, the components of which can be expanded or modified to extend and enrich the theory and improve the measuring instrument.

The various facets of the mapping sentence, a, b c, d, and e, indicate the orientation of the subconstruct and suggest where parameters within the domain can be made increasingly sophisticated in order to generate a richer theory about attentiveness. For example, facet B could be expanded to include b_2 (other perception: experts, trained raters). Facet C could also include religious, conflicting, negotiating, ritualistic, and logistic settings of communication, to name but a few. Also, the nonverbal facets of D could be expanded to include a stronger emphasis on modification and reinforcement of behavior such as the time spent with the target person. Facet E indicates the type of units the researcher might gather — nominal units or ration units.

13. For a detailed discussion of dimensionality in nonmetric multidimensional scaling, see Lingoes, Guttman, and Roskam (1977).

14. The adults were waiting at a metropolitan airport in Detroit. Thus the sample is not random from the larger adult population and probably represents a relatively affluent set of people.

15. For a good treatment of simple structure in the factor analysis, see Mulaik (1972) and Rummell (1970). The factor solution was both orthogonally rotated and obliquely rotated to achieve a simple structure. Initially, an eight-factor solution emerged. From this foundation a four-factor solution was specified to find out possible associations for the items in the weak factors. Since this stage of the research is exploratory, no cutoff point for excluding items is offered. In addition to the orthogonal and oblique loadings presented for each factor, the mean and standard deviations of each item are reported.

16. For example, the trait of "communication apprehension" may explain "attending" behavior in some interactions. The person attends to stimuli in order to create the defense mechanisms needed to avoid communication. But this passive type of attending is not what is included in the notion of attentiveness found in this chapter (see McCroskey, Daly, Richmond, & Falcione, 1977; for a detailed treatment of necessary and sufficient causation, see von Wright, 1971).

17. While it is wise to consider possible effects due to subjects' response styles, there is good evidence that suggests that such effects are inconsequential in most research procedures (see Roger, 1965). None of the semantic differential scales was reversed on the measuring instrument. Consequently, subjects may simply have answered consistently according to what seemed readily applicable to the majority of questions.

18. Caution must be exercised, however, for two reasons. First, most of these measures are primarily concerned with the therapeutic context. Second, as indicated above, there are definitional nuances across the various topics.

III

APPLICATIONS OF
STYLE WORK

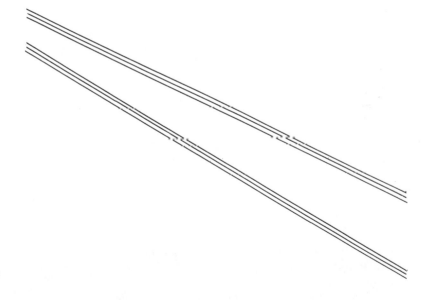

7 / Reality Filter

perception of communicator style

This chapter provides strong evidence that **the way one communicates affects the perception and assessment of social reality.** A series of three studies demonstrates that a person with a "low dominant" style misperceives both the way the self and the other interact in conversations. The most striking finding is that the person with a low dominant style misperceives the amount of dominant signals the self provides and receives. The low dominant person thinks that he or she communicates in the same way as a high dominant person. This misperception has far-reaching implications. For example, if a person does not talk as much as another, but thinks that he or she does, then that person might wonder why he or she does not receive the same kinds of rewards as the other. Social reality does not match the expectations for the low dominant person. The resultant attitudes may entail bitterness, paranoia, or a sense of gross unfairness. Needless to say, establishing convincing evidence for the above conclusions can be illusive, but the studies in this chapter provide cumulative and replicated findings.

Few researchers have examined **perceptions as a function of style.** This is not to say that communication scholars have not asked others to judge their interactant partners regarding communicative behavior. Of course, perception is involved, but the research phrased as a perceptual problem is often an afterthought confounded by social desirability issues. Little attempt is made to establish a research problem or generate data centered on perception, especially perception of communicator style. The following studies point to directions some researchers have taken.

Bushard (1959) observed that enlisted men in small military units (eight- to ten-man squads) after brief exposures and limited interactions could be differentiated by communication patterns. The most dominant persons were quite talkative, outgoing, and aggressive.

Further, these individuals were markedly critical of those they perceived as verbally and socially inept. They were not the most intelligent members of the group, but they did have the greatest social skill. As a result, they maintained prominent positions but were not often among the true group leaders. **Here is an instance of being rewarded or punished by peers because of the way one communicates.**

The second kind of interpersonal style was displayed by the leaders, who were usually intelligent, tended to be verbally reserved until others had spoken, and frequently revealed greater perceptivity in their judgments of others.

The third kind of interpersonal style was reflected by persons of little verbal intelligence. Such persons tended to remain silent, but usually became increasingly ill at ease until they were ultimately moved to make a contribution. In essence, Bushard (1959) found a relationship between type of communicator style and leadership ability. In each instance, a form of dominant style marked an essential difference across the three profiles.

Bales (1970, 1956, 1950) touches upon some aspects of the dominant style effect upon perception with his analysis of types of group roles. In two decades of research, he created a system to place people into a theoretical space as a function of the type of interactions they manifest. The theoretical space consists of three dimensions: (1) positive-negative, (2) up-down, and (3) backward-forward.

In short, the dimensions reflect these characteristics:

- *Positive:*   This person seems friendly, sociable, and informal. Others are approached as equals.

- *Negative:*   This person seems unfriendly and disagreeable. He or she is rather self-centered and isolated, detached, unsocial, and defensively secluded.

- *Up:*   This person seems active, talkative, and powerful, but not clearly either friendly or unfriendly. He or she seems to be trying to move toward material success and power.

- *Down:*   This person seems self-effacing and completely non-self-assertive, passive, and powerless. He or she accepts others in the group and the nature of things as they are without requesting anything for the self, but also without any enthusiasm or desire.

- *Forward:*   This person seems primarily task and value oriented. He or she is direct, to the point, instrumental, analytical, and problem solving.

- *Backward:*   This person seems heretical and disbelieving. He or she refuses to admit the validity of nearly all conservative group beliefs and values (Bales, 1970, p. 221).

Based on these dimensions, Bales derives 27 unique combinations. Some of the combinations are characterized by misperception. For example, the UNF Type (a person in the up, negative, and forward space of Bales's model) is predicted to *misperceive*. According to Bales (1970):

> In actuality he distorts his perception of his own personality so as to put the bad and feared impulses into others and then often infuses his own aggression, fear, and even contempt for others into his actions toward them.

The UNF Type is seen as dominating and unfriendly; he or she takes the initiative in the value- or task-oriented direction. In terms of the way the person communicates, Bales (1970) writes:

> The person in the UNF role has a prominent place in the group. His total interaction initiated is high, though not necessarily the highest in the group. He tends, even so, to "overtalk." His tendency to talk to the group as a whole, rather than particular members, is high, but his total interaction received from others is only average. Either he tends to prevent replies, by overtalking, or others tend to withhold replies, or both.

Bales points out that dominance is associated with talking a lot. But dominance as a personality trait may not necessarily cause talking. Bales (1970, p. 168) explains that "it is just as important to note that both the personality trait (as perceived by the others) and the behavior are alike in that they affect others in the group in such a way as to make them feel that their power is reduced. In other words, dominance may be simultaneously a power determinant and a power effect."

Although Hayes and Meltzer (1972) do not look at style of communication in the same sense that Bales looks at type of group roles, they examine a behavior closely related to and entailed by the dominant style subconstruct — namely, talkativeness. They demonstrate that sheer amount of talk can accurately predict judgments of activity, dominance, prominence, and assertiveness.

Hayes and Meltzer (1972, p. 554) argue that talkativeness is curvilinearly related to evaluative dimensions: "Persons who talk a great deal or very little are rated unfavorably and they are described as having predominantly unpleasant attributes. The most favorable evaluations are given to persons who contribute somewhat more than their share to the conversation."

This suggests that there probably is an optimal level of talkativeness in which the person is perceived by the others in the most favorable light. It seems reasonable to conclude that if the person's own perception of that level coincides with that of the group's perception, then that person is closely aligned with the expectations of that context. The emergent question is: **Does the person who is sensitive to style perceptions in interaction benefit from the awareness?** The consequences of accurate perception of style on one hand and misperception on the other have yet to be researched sufficiently by the communication scholar.

Finally, although the following studies by Goslin (1962) and Lieberman et al. (1973) do not directly phrase their research in terms of style as a covariant of misperception, they suggest relevant hypotheses for this research. Goslin investigated accuracy of self-perception as a function of social acceptance. He required junior and senior high school students to be in each other's company five hours a day for a minimum of eight months: "The children not only knew each other fairly well, but were operating as effective group units" (Goslin, 1962, p. 284).

Goslin found that *the rejected students perceived themselves differently from the way they were perceived by the group. Also, the rejected students were unaware that they were being perceived differently.* An amplification of this research would be to see whether certain enduring communication styles affected the accuracy of perception among the students.

Lieberman et al. (1973), in an elaborate project, studied 18 different encounter groups (251 subjects) to determine whether the way the leaders conducted themselves made a substantive difference in the relative benefit or harm group members experienced. Four dimensions operationally defined a leader style: (1) stimulation — revealing feelings, challenging, and confronting; (2) caring — protecting, offering friendship, and loving; (3) meaning-attribution — providing concepts for how to understand; and (4) executive function — limit setting, suggesting rules, limits, norms.

Leader style can be used to discriminate in three areas of perception. First, *some leaders misperceived their impact:* "Often leaders saw themselves as more charismatic than they were seen to be by participants or observers" (Lieberman et al., 1973, p. 260). Second, *certain leader types could not assess accurately who in the group benefited from the therapy.* Third, *the style of the leader affected the degree of discrepancy between the participants' view of self and ideal self-image:* "Some leader styles significantly decreased the discrepancy between the person's ideal self and his described self, while other leader styles had the opposite effect of making the discrepancy between self and ideal greater" (Lieberman et al., 1973, p. 257). While leader style is an interesting stratification, the analysis of communicator style of every participant could provide information to deal with more encompassing questions. What kind of communicator benefits the most from specific therapies? What kind of communicator is most vulnerable in therapeutic situations? What kind of communicator perceives most accurately the dynamics of therapy?

As indicated above, there is little research examining directly perceptual accuracy as a function of how one communicates. Piecemeal evidence indicates that

(1) enduring leaders are more intelligent, verbally reserved, and perceptive;

(2) dominance as a personality trait can be used as a power strategy;

(3) too much or too little talkativeness is disliked by others;

(4) students accepted by the group more accurately perceive social interactions; and

(5) leader style influences self-perception and other perception.

Since there is not enough information in the literature to provide a basis for directional hypotheses, to gain a clearer set of expectations about this construct, this study assessed the variations of perception of dominant styles by persons with different scores in a mutual interpersonal encounter.

METHOD

Dominant Style Measure

A crucial step in this research was to define types of dominant style. For the purpose of this study, the Dominant Style Measure (DSM) was used to operationalize the construct. The DSM is a 25-item paper-and-pencil test using a 7-point response scale initially developed and refined by Mortensen, Norton, and Arntson.[1]

The test is internally consistent in measuring a single construct. The respective Hoyt coefficients across five revisions of the test (1127 subjects) were .73, .79, .88, .88, and .89 (Mortensen, 1972). The stabilization of the Hoyt coefficient in the last three revisions indicates that a high degree of confidence can be placed in the internal reliability of this test. The measure also has good criteria-related validity. It correlates adequately with self-esteem, self-acceptance, communication confidence, and dominance (Mortensen, 1972).

Because the DSM contains variables that are experimentally dependent caused by overlapping items (Nunnally, 1967), the infrastructure of the construct was identified by using McQuitty's (1957) elementary linkage analysis to form clusters rather than using factor analysis (McQuitty, 1968). The three clusters emerged represent the essence of the DSM.

FORCEFUL

In this cluster, which accounts for about 25% of the test, the items reflect a person's need to be in control:

17. I would describe myself as dominant in social situations.
15. I try to take charge of things when I am with people.
18. When I am with others I am inclined to talk forcefully.
10. In most social situations I tend to come on strong.
4. In most social situations I tend to direct the course of conversation.
2. I have a tendency to dominate informal conversations with other people.

For a person to obtain a high DSM score, he or she must be predisposed to describe the self as dominant and forceful; he or she sees the self as coming on strong, directing the course of conversation, and trying to take charge.

MONOPOLIZING

This cluster accounts for about 23 percent of the test. A person who receives a high DSM score sees the self as talking for long periods of time, offering long comments, and preferring not to listen. The cluster is closely aligned with the forceful cluster except that the items are phrased in terms of the amount of talking. In fact, some researchers define dominance in terms of frequency of speech (Knott & Drost, 1965; Mann et al., 1967).

Representative items include:

3. When I am with other people I generally talk often.

21. In most social situations I tend to speak for long periods of time.

24. I probably [do not] speak for shorter periods of time than the average person.

22. I am [not] inclined to let other people talk for long periods of time.

7. In most social situations I generally speak quite frequently.

In some situations, the forceful cluster and the monopolizing cluster could be independent. That is, a very forceful person by virtue of status, prestige, or power could control the conversation without speaking very often. Conversely, a chatterbox could fill a conversational period without being forceful (in the sense of influencing the ultimate outcome).

In this study, "dominance" is anchored to the items in the test. It is treated as a predisposition that may manifest itself not only through frequency of speech, but also as a function of perceived forcefulness.

INVOLVEMENT

This cluster accounts for 32 percent of the test. The items reflect a person's predisposition to be involved with the ongoing movement of a conversation. Typical items include:

5. When I am with others it generally [does not take] me quite a while to warm up enough to say very much.

8. I [do not] tend to hesitate when I speak.

13. I [do not] tend to feel inhibited when I talk with others.

14. I generally find that I [do not] express myself quite freely.

1. I am [not] inclined to let other people start conversations.

6. I generally [do not] rely on others to keep conversations going.

The brackets indicate which items were reversed in scoring.

By definition, then, a person with a high DSM score is predisposed to see the self as forceful, monopolizing, and an involved conversationalist. These scores provided the basis for designing an experiment to examine one kind of perceptual accuracy in dyads.

The independent variable of dominant style was determined by stratifying the sample of those who took the DSM pretest into three categories — high, middle, and low. Any person scoring greater than one standard deviation from the mean of all items on the DSM was classified as "high." This meant that the person saw the self as very forceful, a frequent talker, and high in involvement. Any person scoring less than one standard deviation from the mean was classified as "low." Any person within a standard deviation of the mean was classified as "middle."

Dependent Variable

The dependent variable in this study was a 15-item version of the DSM administered after the subjects mutually completed a task. The questionnaire consisted of the most representative items from the cluster analysis — that is, those items that had the highest and most intercorrelations with other items in the cluster. A 7-point response scale for each item was used again.

The post hoc DSM provided information concerning (1) how the subjects viewed themselves in the interpersonal encounter, and (2) how the subjects viewed the other person in the same encounter. The DSM pretest and the DSM posttest were used to pinpoint the apparent discrepancies in perceptions by each subject.

SUBJECTS

The questionnaire assessing dominant style was voluntarily completed by 100 undergraduate speech communication students at the University of Michigan. The scores were normally distributed. From this pool of subjects, 24 dyads were constructed.

Design

The design employed 48 subjects in 24 dyads. The first condition, in which a subject with a high DSM score was paired with a subject with a low DSM score, involved 12 dyads. Since the mean for the sample was 4.41 and the standard deviation was .50, any subject with a score of 4.91 or greater was defined as high. Any subject with a score of 3.91 or less was defined as low.

To control for sex effects, combinations of mixed-sex and same-sex dyads were considered. In the second condition, composed of 12 dyads, subjects with middle DSM scores were paired. Again, sex effects were controlled. Any subject scoring between 1.91 and 3.91 was defined as a middle.

Procedure

A three- to six-week period passed between the DSM pretest and the dyadic encounter. The stimulus was a case study concerning American values. In it, the person was asked to determine five objects that best symbolized American values. In pretests, this case study always produced lively discussions.

First, the subjects were given five minutes to complete the task individually. This procedure gave each subject time to understand the task and to commit himself or herself to some solution. Second, the subjects were given ten minutes to interact and complete the same task mutually. The subjects were left alone during this phase. After the ten-minute period, the subjects were asked to respond to two 15-item dominant style measures.

Both measures employed the same questions. The first questionnaire measured the self-perceptions of the subject's dominant style in the interaction; the second questionnaire measured the subject's perception of the other's dominant style in the interaction. In short, four postmeasures were obtained for each dyad. The difference between the self-rating-self measure and the self-rating-other measure provided an indication of how discrepant the dominant styles were from each other.

RESULTS

Table 7.1 reports the means for each condition. The multivariate analysis of variance showed one significant main effect and one significant interaction. On the average, a person tends to see self as having a significantly higher DSM score than the other. The mean for self-rating-self was 67.7 and the mean for the self-rating-other was 59.7; $F(1,84) = 13.0$, $p < .01$. Table 7.2 shows the means for the interaction. Figure 7.1 shows the graph of the interaction; $F(2,84) = 11.1$, $p < .01$]. No other effect was significant.

A stepwise regression (Cooley & Lohnes, 1971; Draper & Smith, 1966) was done for the self-rating-self and the self-rating-other postmeasures to obtain clues about perceptual differences. With

TABLE 7.1   Means for Postmeasures

	Male		Female	
	Self	Other	Self	Other
High DSM pretest score	70.3	58.0	82.8	50.3
Middle DSM pretest score	62.1	60.1	66.9	59.5
Low DSM pretest score	64.2	65.7	60.0	64.8

TABLE 7.2   Means for Interaction

	Self Rating Self	Self Rating Other
High DSM pretest score	76.5	54.2
Middle DSM pretest score	64.5	59.8
Low DSM pretest score	62.1	65.2

.05 for the F-ratio criterion out of the 15 possible variables, 11 steps of regression were completed for the self-rating-self postmeasure with an R^2 of .54, and 12 steps of regression were completed for the self-rating-other postmeasure with an R^2 of .49. Table 7.3 reports the magnitude of the squared betas, which indicates the relative contribution of each variable to the prediction of the criterion. Only the strongest coefficients were reported.

It appears that the subject had little difficulty assessing the question "Did you seem able to express yourself quite freely?" for both the self and the other person. For the remaining questions, however, it appears that the subject had an easier time rating the other person than the self. While the questions "Did you tend to hesitate when speaking?" explained 36 percent of the variance by itself when the subject rated the other, it explained nothing when the subject rated the self.

The question concerning the amount of speaking time explained 17 percent of the variance by itself when the subject rated the other; it explained only 2 percent of the variance by itself when the subject rated the self.

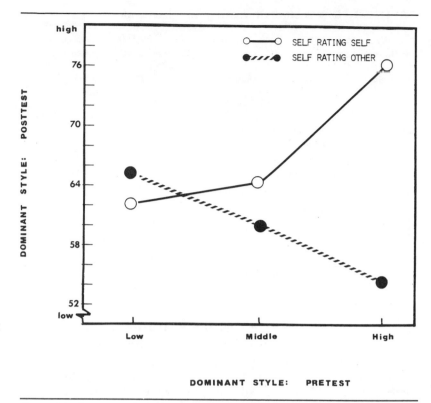

Figure 7.1   Perceptions of Dominant Style Compared Across Pretest and Posttest Conditions by Self and Other

Finally, concerning the variable of warm-up time by itself, it explained 13 percent of the variance when the other was rated, but only 1 percent when the self was rated.

DISCUSSION

As expected, the persons in the second condition saw themselves and the others as falling into the middle range of DSM scores. It was thought that the persons in the first condition (high versus low) would perceive themselves and each other accordingly. However, the person with the low DSM pretest score saw no difference between the self and the other. In fact, he or she rated the self and the other as falling into the middle range of dominant styles. The person with a high DSM pretest score perceived a clear difference between the self and the other. In short, persons report-

TABLE 7.3   Beta Coefficients for Stepwise Regression

Postmeasure Variable for Dominant Style	β^2 for Self Rating Self	β^2 for Self Rating Other
Did you tend to hesitate when speaking?[a]	.00	.36
Did you seem able to express yourself quite freely?	.14	.29
Did you speak more than half of the total time devoted to speaking?	.02	.17
Did it take you quite a while to warm up enough to say very much?	.01	.13
Did you pause often when speaking?	.06	.05
Did you talk forcefully?	.08	—[b]
Did you react quickly to what the other person said?	.06	.00

a. For the self rating other postmeasures, the questions were phrased in terms of the other person.
b. For the self rating other regression analysis, this variable did not meet criterion of .05 for the F ratio.

ing high and low DSM pretest scores perceived one another's dominant style differently in a mutual, interpersonal encounter.

There are two viable explanations for the findings: (1) a social desirability factor confounded the postmeasure, or (2) the person with the low DSM score did not perceive accurately. If, after the dyadic encounter, the person with the low score reasoned that it was undesirable to be labeled as such, then the person might systematically inflate the self score and deflate the other score. **Thus a new riddle emerged from the research: Why does the person with low dominant scores seem to be misperceiving?**

The following considerations should shed light on the first explanation. First, what is the actual adjustment of the individual to the situation? Second, what knowledge does the individual have about his or her own predispositions? Third, how frank is the individual in stating what he or she knows?

It is possible that persons with a low DSM pretest scores may make ongoing, complex, and interrelated adjustments so that by the end of the encounter they may, in fact, be behaving in all respects like persons with high or moderate DSM scores. Indeed, persons with high DSM scores might motivate the change. However, the likelihood of this occurrence is considerably small. Hayes and Meltzer (1972) suggest that such an effect is unlikely because the encounter was rather brief. Also, in the first condition, the person with the high DSM score *testifies* that the other person does have a low DSM score.

Other types of adjustments include selective forgetting, denial, and, possibly, repression. If the individual does not have adequate knowledge about the self concerning verbal dynamics, he or she might not be able to articulate or report the relationships. The researcher might have to teach the subject to be more sensitive to the processes. For example, if the dyadic encounter were videotaped, the subject could dispassionately analyze his or her verbal interactions.

Finally, more precise evidence could be marshaled if the researcher could be assured of the frankness of the individual. Hayes and Meltzer (1972) point out that socially inept people, that is, people who experience difficulty in speaking, learn to be quiet. In turn, their lack of activity then becomes a cue indicating social and personal ineptitudes. The validity of this viewpoint has not been empirically demonstrated, but it does suggest that social desirability rather than perceptual differences may account for the failure of the subjects with low DSM scores to respond as expected.

The second explanation has more radical and far-reaching implications. A major implication is that the person with the low DSM score is deficient in the interpretation of the communicative interaction. The person may not be completely tuned in; he or she may be ignoring substantive feedback. If this analysis is correct, then the style variables touch many behaviors and attitudes — such as problem solving and therapeutic problems — that affect many other behaviors and attitudes.

One might be tempted to suggest, contrary to the second explanation, that high DSM scorers did not act as their pretests suggest and their self-reports attest. Consequently, the low DSM scorers reported accurately. If this is correct, then not only are high-scoring persons perceptually deficient, but those with low DSM scores are functioning as moderately scoring persons in the experimental situation. While this explanation cannot be wholly discounted, it is not the most parsimonious interpretation of the data.

To obtain more evidence concerning what is perceived, a more precise methodology is required. The regression analysis points to some directions. For example, it cannot be assumed that the subject is fully aware of what constitutes "hesitancy" in the verbal interactions. The regression analysis indicated that hesitancy was the single greatest factor in explaining variance when the subject rated the other person, but it was not a factor when the subject rated the self. It could be that whenever there is a period of silence, the subject attributes that silence to the other person rather than to him- or herself. Obviously, a tight operational definition is needed.

In a like manner, the question "Did you seem able to express yourself freely?" requires more precision. The answer to this item is tainted by ambiguity either way the subject responds. One implication is that the other person was relatively fluent. A second implication, however, is that the subject may have hindered the other person during the interaction. It is socially desirable to allow another person to express him- or herself freely. In short, each of the DSM posttest items requires further analysis and amplification.

Moreover, a more precise methodology will not rely solely upon self-report data. If the present study had been supplemented by unobtrusive observation, raters, testimony from friends, and the like, more precise conclusions could be drawn. For example, trained raters observing the subjects through one-way mirrors would provide evidence to support or reject the above alternative explanations. A videotape of the encounter would provide a means for the subjects themselves to review the interpersonal process objectively. Finally, interviewing friends of the subjects would provide additional helpful data.

This study detected an effect in which the person with a low DSM score either (1) feels compelled to compensate by manipulating his or her DSM posttest score and/or that of the other person or (2) fails to perceive enough cues to allow accurate assessment of the dominant style in a dyadic encounter.

Given the above possibilities, Miller (1977) replicated the study. The replication served multiple purposes. First, it demonstrated that the initial phenomenon probably did not happen by chance alone. Second, by introducing additional procedures, the most viable explanation of the phenomenon emerges.

MILLER'S STUDY

Miller used the following five items — these are the items found in the CSM reported in Chapter 3 — to determine dominant style scores:

1. In most social situations I generally speak very frequently.

2. In most social situations I tend to come on strong.

3. I have a tendency to dominate informal conversations with other people.

4. I try to take charge of things when I am with people.

5. I am dominant in social situations.

Miller replicated the original study, but introduced improvements by doing the following. *First, he stratified the low, middle, and high scorers more efficiently.* A dominant style score was generated by summing the five items. A person with a middle dominant style score had to fall within a half standard deviation of the mean. Then, to prevent misclassifying subjects, a "buffer zone" was stipulated as scores falling between a half standard deviation from the mean and one standard deviation from the mean. No scores within these parameters were used. A person with a high dominant style score had to fall between one standard deviation and three standard deviations. Similarly, a person with a low dominant style score was defined as a score past the "buffer zone" and within one standard deviation and three standard deviations in the negative direction.

Second, the dyads were videotaped so that objective data could be obtained from raters other than the participants. Subjects were videotaped through a one-way mirror with full knowledge of the interactants.

Third, raters were chosen based on dominant style scores. The reason this was done is surprisingly critical to the research question at hand. If a person with a low dominant style score does indeed misperceive the style of others, it is important not to have a "dispassionate" rater coding style scores who has a low dominant style score. Consequently, three raters, two female and one male, each possessing middle-range scores on the dominant style items, were selected.

Fourth, a longer period passed between the pretest and the dyadic encounters – ten to twelve weeks, instead of three to six weeks. The longer period provides some protection against a reactive interaction between the test scores and the stimulus.

Fifth, the tapes were coded blindly and in random order to prevent primary or recencey effects.

Findings

Essentially, the same phenomenon was observed. Table 7.4 reports the results. Figures 7.1 and 7.2 provide the comparison between the original and Miller's study.

By having the three raters score the dyads also, it is possible to see whether the raters agree with the participants. Miller (1977) reports the following:

After viewing videotapes of pretest high and low scorers interacting, the observers rated those who scored high on the pretest as

TABLE 7.4   Means for Interaction from Miller's Study

	Self Rating Self	Self Rating Other
High DSM pretest score	14.0	11.2
Middle DSM pretest score	12.1	10.8
Low DSM pretest score	11.7	11.4

being high scorers during the encounter. Those who scored low on the pretest were perceived as low scorers during the encounter. Subjects who scored in the middle range on the pretest . . . were seen as scoring in the middle range. In short, three raters . . . perceived pretest high scorers as high, pretest middle scorers as middle, and pretest low scorers as low.

This means that it is probable that the person with the low dominant pretest score distorts his or her own score in the posttest. Furthermore, an analysis of the amount of time that each person talked during the videotaped interaction reflects the phenomenon observed by the raters. That is, the high scorers talked the most, the middle scorers the second most, and the low scorers the least.

However, part of the riddle remains. Is it social desirability that motivates the low scorer to distort, or is it misperception? Miller's (1980) next study sheds more light on the question. He essentially replicated the above study, but this time he amplified it in the following way:

Participants were asked to return seven to ten days after the interaction to view the tapes [their own and others] and rate the interactants. Each subject served as a rater and observed three different videotapes: one tape in which the subject interacted with the high or low dominance other, and two with other subjects who participated in the values discussion [Miller, 1980].

Then the subjects were asked to rate two additional videotapes of high and low scorers interacting.

In other words, the lower scorer had the opportunity to see the self one step removed from the interaction and four other low scorers in four other tapes. The order of viewing for the first three tapes was random. **Would the low scorer perceive the other low scorers as such or would the low scorer also inflate the scores?**

Figure 7.3 shows what happened. In the "Immediate Postinteraction" condition, the low scorer saw little difference

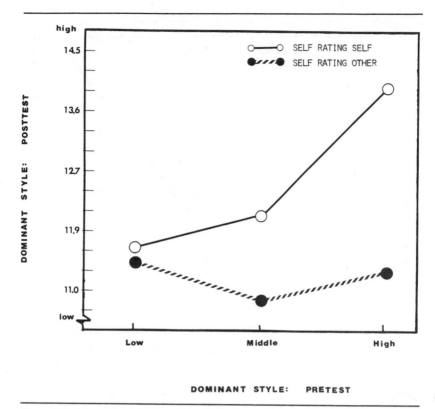

Figure 7.2   Perceptions of Dominant Style Compared Across Pretest and Posttest Conditions by Self and Other: Replication

between the self and the other, indicated by about .5 on the graph. The high scorer saw approximately a two-point difference between the self and the other with the other being perceived as "low dominant."

After viewing and rating the "delayed replay interaction" videotape, the low scorer brings the response patterns into correspondence with those of the high scorer. That is, the "high scorer" is seen as a "high scorer" and the "low scorer," namely, the self, is seen as a "low scorer." There is now approximately a two-point difference in the appropriate direction; the "high scorer" sees the same two-point difference.

After viewing the "framed delayed preplay interaction," the "low scorer" reports an even larger difference between the self and the "high scorer" — a seven-point difference. The "high scorer" sees the same two-point difference.

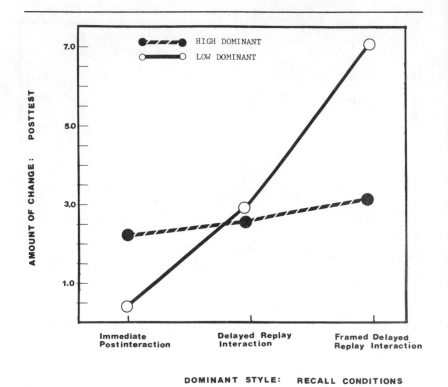

Figure 7.3   Amount of Change in Perception Across Three Recall Conditions by High and Low Dominant People

The high scorer does not change across the three time conditions in rating either the self or the other. That is, the high scorer throughout sees the self as a high scorer, which is compatible with the pretest score. Further, the high scorer sees the other as a lower scorer, which is compatible with the pretest score.

However, **the low scorer changes radically.** The low scorer starts rating low scorers as such. And, even more dramatically, the low scorer starts rating the high scorer as such, which is compatible with the pretest score and the "dispassionate" rater's score. **It is as though the lower scorer is learning how to perceive the stylistic reality of the interaction.** However, it is as though the low scorer only learns the directionality of the difference and misperceives the degree.

Miller (1980) says:

Two explanations are possible for initial noncorrespondence in the perception of the other by the pretest low scorers. First, they may have experienced an experimental demand characteristic that precluded full attention to the awareness of the others' dominance cues. Why this should be true for pretest low scorers but not pretest high scorers is not clear.

He adds:

A more plausible explanation . . . is that the pretest low scorers may be less attuned to the social dynamics that characterize the communication behavior of their pretest high scoring colleagues. In other words, pretest low scorers may be inclined to overlook or simply not recognize social skills they do not themselves possess.

At this point, the riddle is still not solved. It is evident that the low scorer is doing something different and that he or she can be influenced to change what he or she is doing. But two hypotheses are still competing. Is the low scorer misperceiving or is he or she engaged in some complex rationalizing (a variant of social desirability)?

Miller's designs are approaching resolution of this question. The next step is to track what the low scorer does as a function of viewing order of videotapes. For example, if the low scorer saw the self on the tape and then saw two other low scorers, would that differ from the low scorer seeing two other low scorers before seeing the self on tape? The consequent of varying the order of viewing would shed some light on the development process.

SUMMARY

The evidence is good that certain people as seen by themselves or evaluated by others to communicate in a certain way — in this case, in terms of a dominant style — report seeing different stylistic behavior. Such phenomena have serious pragmatic consequents. If the stylistic discrepancy is caused by misperception, then the groundwork for serious communication difficulties is laid. If the stylistic discrepancy is caused by a need to resolve social pressures, then a different, albeit still communicative, impact is a mediating factor in the process. In some ways, the latter hypothesis is more interesting because it may involve a series of "masking" moves that a person who feels stylistically deficient generates.

If this phenomenon holds up, its impact upon therapeutic situations, teacher-pupil relationships, conflict-resolution contexts, and other human transactions will be important. The results invite some directional hypotheses.

- **A person with a low dominant style score tends to misperceive the communication styles of others.** This theme, along the lines of research by Lieberman et al. (1973), could be expanded to test power differences, self-esteem problems, and ability to empathize.

- **A person with a low dominant score is not attractive to group members.** This type of research would be similar to Goslin's (1962) study.

- **A person with a low dominant score is not effective.** Effectiveness could be covaried in terms of leadership (Bushard, 1959), getting things done, or making maximum contributions.

In summary, the dominant style construct differentiated among respondents such that an interesting phenomenon was uncovered. The DSM was used in a variety of important ways. First, it provided the initial pool of respondents. In effect, people testified about their dominant style behavior. Based on the scores, subjects were stratified and randomly selected within the stratification to participate in a dyadic interaction. Second, the DSM was used not only for self-report after the interaction, but also as a means to obtain data as observed by another person. Third, the DSM was used to provide a validity check for the three trained raters. It became important not to have raters who themselves had low dominant style scores.

The replications and extension of the phenomenon illustrated a way to converge on a research question. Each step refined and more clearly focused the evidence. While single studies may be provocative in their own right, social science is served better when series of studies are incorporated to support generalizations and arguments. The three studies discussed here increase confidence that perceptual questions relating to style work are good directions for communication scholars to explore.

NOTE

1. David Mortensen and I worked on the development of this test (1971) — originally labeled an "intensity test" — which covered the first three revisions. Mortensen and Paul Arntson continued the refinement of the test with revisions four and five. Since then, Miller and I have independently analyzed the test and have made further modest revisions.

8 / Social Magnetism

style determinants
of attraction

Every person has a
particular style of
communication that remains
within certain parameters such
that consistently recurring associations
can be attributed (Chapter 2). Since one's
style of communication is a persuasive part of
one's behavior, it is reasonable to expect that it affects
how attractive a person appears to be. It can also be posited
that some communicator styles are stronger covariates of attraction than other styles.[1]

It is relatively easy to guess how attraction relates to styles of
communication. An ornery, contentious style tends to be offen-
sive; a friendly, soft-spoken style tends to be appealing. When
style-related components do not entail obviously positive or negative valences, it becomes increasingly difficult to anticipate which
combination of communicator style variables best predicts
attraction.

A small amount of research in the literature directly investigates
attraction as a function of communicator style. This chapter discusses three successive studies that provide strong evidence that
one's communicator style is an important effect determinant of
attraction. The implications are of consequence. If the way one
communicates influences the degree of attractiveness, then a mul-

titude of interactive social situations are affected, including therapeutic dynamics, teaching, intimate activity, persuasive processes, and problem-solving situations.

Attraction is investigated typically as a function of attitude similarity (Byrne, 1969a, 1969b; Byrne & Griffitt, 1973), economic similarity (Byrne, Clore, & Worchel, 1966), need similarity (Izard, 1961), and personality similarity (Griffitt, 1966, 1969). Researchers who attempt to make a statement about the relationship between communication and attraction often discover the obvious, highlight only physical manifestations, or tangentially relate communication variables.

Some researchers suggest that opportunity to communicate as manifested by physical closeness correlates positively with interpersonal attraction (Gullahorn, 1952; Newcomb, 1961). Other researchers have found that attractive persons are perceived as more sincere, more stable, and warmer (Dion & Berscheid, 1974; Dion & Walster, 1972). One group of researchers tried to determine whether a given behavior of an individual or his physical appearance was a better determinant of attraction (Mims, Harnett, & Nay, 1975). However, the communication context (a debate) and the broad classification (nice versus obnoxious) limited the generalizability of their findings that the physical variable was the better predictor of attraction.

Still others have researched the effects of individual expressive styles on attraction. Typical findings indicate that *expressive cues can induce liking for a communicator* (see Lowe & Goldstein, 1970; Holstein, Goldstein, & Bem, 1971; Mehrabian, 1968, 1969). Most of these studies, however, isolate certain discrete variables while neglecting a more holistic consideration of social interaction.

Another area of research involving communication and attraction has focused on the vehicle of expression as the most important component in interaction. For example, it has been found that how one communicates is more influential than what is actually communicated with regard to social effectiveness and the success of the transaction (Leginski & Izzett, 1973).

Also, media affect style considerations (Williams, 1975). The more immediate the medium (face-to-face interaction), the more positively people are evaluated. Less immediate media (telephone communication and videotaped communication) produced significantly less positive evaluations (Williams, 1975, pp. 126-127). The findings suggest that more immediate media permit a wider range of the person's style of communication to influence his or her evaluation by others.

In the therapeutic context, the communicator style of professional compared to paraprofessional therapists was discovered to be a determinant of the client's attraction to them. Simonson and Bahr (1974, pp. 362-363) conclude that the attractiveness of a therapist is not merely a function of content, but rather "involves the subject's **knowledge of the therapist's style of interaction,** which he might or might not like" (see also Pettegrew, 1977b). In this study, style was defined in terms of self-disclosure and openness.

Finally, the personality literature provides implications regarding the relationship of communicator style to attraction. Attraction is positively related to such personality dimensions as self-concept, self-esteem, and dominance-submissiveness (Byrne & Griffitt, 1973). *Communicative behavior* is also associated with the attractive personality (see Bales, 1970; Bushard, 1959; Reusch, 1957; Shapiro, 1965; Watzlawick et al., 1967; Weblin, 1962).

What research there is suggests that there is a strong empirical link between the way one communicates and how others regard one's attractiveness. This association, however, needs to be investigated in light of a holistic construct such as communicator style.

SHORT VERSION OF
THE COMMUNICATOR STYLE MEASURE

The longer version of the CSM reported in Chapter 3 is the 51-item pencil-and-paper measure. In that version, 5 items are summed for each of the 9 independent variables; 6 items are summed to obtain an index score for the dependent variable.

In the shorter version of the CSM, *the five representative items for each independent variable are summarized in paragraph form, as are the six dependent variable items.* After the subject reads the capsule description for all style variables, he or she responds on a Likert-type scale by indicating the degree to which the target person represents the particular style component. Another short version of the CSM can be found in Chapter 9.

In this study, the short form of the CSM was slightly modified — that is, the respective paragraphs for some of the style components do not exactly match the items in the longer version of the CSM.

Research Objectives

The following three independent studies were designed to investigate the relationship between communicator style and attraction.

- The first study measures the strength of the relationship between the various communicator style variables and attraction.

- The second study assesses the relative attractiveness of four distinct style types and the predictive relationship between the individual style variables and attraction.

- To test the validity of the communicator style self-report in regard to attraction, teachers were asked to evaluate students representing the four style types (self-report) from their own perspectives.

The studies build upon one another and are increasingly complex.

STUDY 1

Method

This study investigated whether an effect could be found between communicator style components and attraction. A measure of attraction (Byrne, 1971) was given simultaneously with the short version of the communicator style measure. Two conditions were studied.

CONDITIONS

In the first condition, people were asked to respond to the questionnaire with their best friends in mind. "Best friend" was defined as the person the subject liked the best among his or her acquaintances.

In the second condition, people were asked to respond to the questionnaire with the persons they liked least among their acquaintances in mind. In oral instruction, the subjects were told: "Recall a set of your acquaintances. In your mind rank order these acquaintances in terms of liking. The person at the bottom of the ranking can be thought of as a 'least liked friend.' " A validity check showed that the manipulation in phrasing worked. The respective means for all attraction variables were significantly different beyond the p < .01 level.

SUBJECTS

Questionnaires were filled out by 97 volunteers from beginning communication classes at the University of Michigan. For the first condition, 19 males and 26 females completed the measures. For the second condition, 24 males and 28 females completed the measures.

MEASURES

Two measures were used: (1) an attraction measure and (2) a communicator style measure. Byrne's Interpersonal Judgment Scale was used to measure interpersonal liking. The instrument includes four filler items and two items measuring attraction — likability and desirability as a work partner. A seven-point Likert scale was used.

For the communicator style measure, seven independent variables (dominant, dramatic/animated, relaxed, open, attentive, impression leaving) and one dependent variable (communicator image) were used. For this study, the dramatic and animated style variables were combined because of the conceptual closeness. Again, a seven-point Likert scale was used.

Finally, for each of the style variables, a question was asked concerning where the person should be put "ideally." For example, the subject was asked on the dominant variable to indicate where the target person would fall, and then the subject was asked to indicate where the target person should be "ideally." Using the modifier "ideally" provided an indication of how much change a subject would like to see for any particular style variable.

Results

Hotelling's T^2 statistic (Overall & Klett, 1972) showed that the communicator style variables in the mean vector differed significantly across the two conditions; $T^2 = 42.1$; $F(6, 90) = 6.7$; $p < .01$. This is an overall indicator that the style components are related to attraction components as operationalized in terms of "best liked" and "least liked" friend. The mean vectors for the style variables with the modifier "ideally" also differ across the two conditions; $T^2 = 67.2$; $F(6, 90) = 10.6$; $p < .01$.

Limitations of Study 1

There are two problems with this study. First, asking the subject to think of a "least liked friend," was awkward and semantically difficult to analyze. Second, treating the communicator style variables *additively* only provides a crude indicator of the relationship between the style variables and the attraction variables. By adding the style components, many phenomena can be obscured.

Discussion

The results from Study 1 suggested a strong enough relationship that further exploratory studies were undertaken. Positive communicator style attributes were strongly associated with people who are liked. They are seen as more dramatic, animated, relaxed, open, and attentive, and as having a better communicator image.

Two processes probably affected the evaluations. First, the person who is liked really does have a good style of communicating. Second, the person who is liked may adventitiously receive the benefit of an inflated rating.

The subjects did not want to change the style components of the "best liked friend." In fact, the ratings for the best friend did not change when the modifier "ideally" was included for each style component.

However, the ratings for the "least liked friend" did change for some of the style components. Subjects preferred the target person to be less dominant and impression leaving and to be more attentive. In short, the person should signal a greater degree of other orientation.

This relationship was indicated further by the strong correlations between the attentiveness style variable and desire to work with (.57). In other words, people are attracted to those who deliberately communicate in such a way that others know that they are being listened to.

STUDY 2

Method

The previous study showed a relationship between communicator style variables and attraction variables, but the conclusions are general and must be interpreted cautiously. In Study 2, four **types of communicator style** were generated by combining specific subconstructs. Subjects were then asked to indicate which style types they were most attracted to. This procedure eliminated the semantic problem of dealing with the phrase "least liked friend." By introducing **types of communicator style,** a more sophisticated methodology is brought to bear on the problem.

SUBJECTS

The questionnaire was filled out by 63 volunteers from beginning communication classes at the University of Michigan.

GENERATING TYPES OF COMMUNICATOR STYLE

The dependent variable in this study was the **type of communicator style.** Four types of communicator style were generated from an earlier analysis of the long version of the communicator style measure, which sampled 1086 subjects. This is the same data set used in Chapter 3.

A THAID analysis (Morgan & Messenger, 1973) was done on the data. THAID is a form of regression analysis that employs a sequential binary split algorithm.

> The primary idea behind the binary split algorithm is that the data be sequentially partitioned into two parts, determined by an independent variable's code, so as to optimize locally a criterion function for the dependent variable [Morgan & Messenger, 1973, p. 9].

The THAID solution is shown in Figure 8.1. Communicator image is the dependent variable used in the analysis. The single best predictor among the nine independent variables is dominant. In the THAID model, 569 subjects saw themselves as dominant, and 517 subjects saw themselves as nondominant.

The THAID analysis next treats the dominant group as the dependent variable and the remaining eight style variables are predictors. Open emerged as the best predictor of the dominant group, with 380 of the 569 subjects seeing themselves as dominant and open. Similarly, 189 of the dominant group saw themselves as dominant and not open.

In like manner, the not dominant group is treated as the dependent variable and the eight remaining style variables as predictors. Relaxed entered the model as the best predictor of the not dominant variable — 252 of the 517 subjects saw themselves as not dominant and relaxed. The remaining 265 subjects viewed themselves as not dominant and not relaxed.

These four unique combinations of style variables were used to operationally define the **types of communicator style** in Study 2 — namely, a dominant/open style (Type 1), a dominant/not open style (Type 2), a not dominant/relaxed style (Type 3), and a not dominant/not relaxed style (Type 4). The temptation at this point is to attach names to the different types. However, given the relatively young stage of research, naming the types would only serve to reify unnecessarily.

The commitment to this model means that particular style types are ignored, even though their inclusion would exhaust all

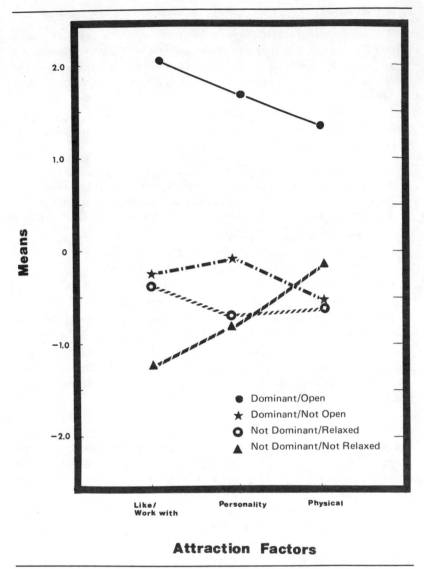

Attraction Factors

Figure 8.1 THAID Model for Communicator Style Variables

combinations of the defining variables. In other words, the model indicates that the dominant/relaxed, dominant/not relaxed, not dominant/open, and the not dominant/not open types are not sufficiently heterogeneous to warrant examination.

MEASURES

The questionnaire used in Study 1 was also used in this study. Two changes were made for Byrne's attraction measure and the short version of the communicator style measure. First, no items included the modifier "ideally." Second, a five-point scale, ranging from "much above average" to "much below average," was used for all items.

PROCEDURE

Each type of communicator style was printed in bold letters at the top of the measure. Four measures, representing each of the four styles, made up the questionnaire. The instructions asked the subjects to "think of a person whom you know best, representing the designated style of communication."

The subjects were then asked to write the name of that person next to the target style. The filler, attraction, and communicator style variables were defined on the cover sheet of the questionnaire. The subjects were instructed to read the definitions carefully before naming and rating the target persons. All subjects completed the same scales for the four target persons.

VALIDITY CHECKS

Three validity checks were built into the questionnaire. First, it was expected that for the dominant/open (Type 1) and dominant/not open (Type 2) styles the means for the dominant item should be greater than the means for the dominant items for the not dominant/relaxed (Type 3) and not dominant/not relaxed (Type 4) styles. The expectation was confirmed. The respective means were 4.5 and 2.4; $t(252) = 21.2$, $p < .01$.

Second, Type 1 and Type 2 should differ for the open item. The expectation was confirmed. The mean for Type 1 on the open item was 4.3; the mean for Type 2 on the open item was 2.1; $t(126) = 15.4$, $p < .01$.

Third, Type 3 and Type 4 should differ for the relaxed item. This expectation was also confirmed. The respective means were 4.0 and 2.1; $t(126) = 15.2$, $p < .01$.

Results

Two kinds of statistical analyses were used. First, central tendency differences were assessed among the four communicator style types. Second, a regression analysis was used to explore the predictive relationships between dependent and independent variables for all style types combined to obtain a general sense of the total data set.

MEAN DIFFERENCES ACROSS STYLE TYPES

An attraction score was constructed by averaging the liking and working with scores from Byrne's measure. A one-way ANOVA on the attraction score shows significant differences among style types; $F(3, 248) = 16.2$, $p < .01$. Scheffe's method for post hoc comparisons ($p < .01$) showed that Type 1 was most attractive, and that Type 2 was more attractive than Type 3 and Type 4.

A similar pattern occured in a one-way ANOVA for communicator image; $F(3, 248) = 26.2$, $p < .01$. Type 1 had the best communicator image ($p < .01$), Type 2 had a better communicator image than Type 4 ($p < .05$), and Type 3 had a better communicator image than Type 4 ($p < .01$).

Figure 8.2 shows the graphed means for both attraction and communicator image variables across style types. Table 8.1 reports the means across types.

REGRESSION ANALYSIS

Multiple classification analysis (MCA; Andrews, Morgan, Sonquist, & Klem, 1973), a form of regression analysis, was employed to predict attraction from the ten style variables. This technique was chosen because it overcomes some of the traditional problems of multiple regression, such as correlated predictors, that cause difficulty in estimating the total variance explained.

> A key feature of the MCA technique is its ability to show the effect of each predictor on the dependent variable both before and after taking into account the effects of all other variables [Andrews et al., 1973].

Table 8.2 reports the results of the MCA.

Friendly emerged as the best overall style predictor of attraction. By itself, it explained 36 percent of the total variance. Attentive and relaxed were the next best predictors of attraction, respectively explaining 22 percent and 16 percent of the total variance. These percentages are variance explained by the particular predictor variables with the effects of all other variables removed; they are not weights in an additive regression model.

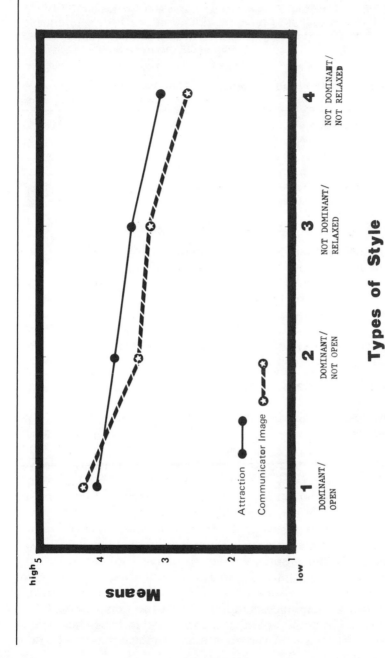

Figure 8.2 Mean Ratings for Attraction and Communicator Image Across Style Types

217

TABLE 8.1   Means for Communicator Image and Attraction
             Across Style Types

	Types of Communicator Style			
	Type 1	Type 2	Type 3	Type 4
Dependent Variables	Dominant/ Open	Dominant/ Not Open	Not Dominant/ Relaxed	Not Dominant/ Not Relaxed
Communicator image	4.2	3.5	3.2	2.7
Attraction	4.1	3.9	3.4	3.2

NOTE: The attraction variable is the average of two variables: (1) liking and (2) desire to work with.

Limitations of Study 2

As usual, it is fairly easy for researchers using self-report data to be lulled into a false sense of security. The major problem with Study 2 is that all the variables, both the attraction and style variables, are presented to the respondent as one set. It is not difficult for the respondent to give the researcher the relationships that are expected — respondents tend to be generous this way. There is good information in Study 2, but it needs to be interpreted cautiously.

Discussion

The results of Study 2 show that types of communicator style influence how attractive a person is perceived to be by a friend. The dominant/open style (Type 1) was the most attractive style, while the not dominant/not relaxed style (Type 4) was the least attractive.

When viewed from a societal perspective, the findings are not surprising. The person who interacts in such a way that he or she takes charge of a conversation, comes on strong, and talks frequently demonstrates communicative competence. Furthermore, if the person interacts in such a way that he or she makes the self vulnerable by being open, the person signals confidence and control. Such a style is rewarded in a competitive society that values hierarchies, sustains Horatio Alger myths, and rewards leadership.

The regression analysis indicates that the person who is perceived to be friendly, attentive, and relaxed in his or her style of communication is seen as more attractive than a person who does

TABLE 8.2   Multiple Classification Analysis of Communicator Style Variables on Attraction

Predictor Variables	B^2	N^2	Predictor Variables	B^2	N^2	Predictor Variables	B^2	N^2
Friendly	.16	.36	Contentious	.02	.01	Open	.01	.03
Attentive	.04	.22	Dramatic	.01	.03	Impression leaving	.01	.13
Relaxed	.02	.16	Animated	.01	.03	Dominant	.01	.02

NOTE: B^2 indicates the approximate additive weights that each predictor variable contributes. N^2 indicates the percentage of variance explained by the particular predictor variables by itself. R^2 (unadjusted) equals .48; R^2 equals .43.

not interact this way. The dominant/open (Type 1) communicator scored highest in each of these categories, although not significantly.

STUDY 3

Method

Study 3 represents an extension of Study 2. In Study 2 the subjects specified target persons representing style types and evaluated the target persons. *In Study 3, a step was taken to avoid the bias of having the respondents rate the same target person on both sets of measures.* Instead, the sample of people rating the style scores was different from the sample of people rating the attraction scores.

The communicator style scores of the target persons were determined by self-report. The attraction scores of the target persons were generated from other respondents who knew the target persons. Also, the attraction scores were obtained without the respondents knowing about the target person's style scores.

TARGET PERSON

The long version of the CSM (51 items) was filled out voluntarily by 508 students enrolled in beginning communication classes at the University of Michigan. Based on these scores, a pool representing the four style types from the THAID model was created.

To obtain relatively pure style types, a student had to score greater than one-half standard deviation from the mean in the appropriate direction for the defining variables. The criteria resulted in the following pool of target persons: (1) 67 subjects in the dominant/open style (2) 14 subjects in the dominant/not open style, (3) 11 subjects in the not dominant/relaxed style, and (4) 54 subjects in the not dominant/not relaxed style. Eight subjects were drawn randomly for the perspective pools for each style type.

RESPONDENTS

The respondents were 20 faculty and teaching assistants who had the above students in their classes. They participated voluntarily.

MEASURE

A nine-item attraction measure was constructed for Study 3. The items were chosen in light of three attraction dimensions found in the literature:

- liking and working together (Byrne, 1971)
- personality (Griffitt, 1966, 1969; Byrne & Griffitt, 1973)
- physical features (Byrne, London, & Reeves, 1968; Byrne, Ervin, & Lambert, 1970; Stoebe, Inski, Thompson, & Layton, 1971)

Three items were selected for each factor (refer to Table 8.3 for the exact wording of each item).

Four variables relating to communicator style also were included in the measure: (1) dominant, (2) open, (3) relaxed, and (4) communicator image. The variables served two purposes. First, they operated as a validity check for each of the styles. A dominant/open (Type 1) style, for example, should be perceived as both dominant and open. Second, they camouflaged somewhat the true nature of the measure.

PROCEDURE

Ten weeks after the initial pool of target persons had been generated, the respondents were asked to participate in a research project. They were not told the nature of the study. They were given no indication that the target person had been selected in any special way. None of the teachers associated this study with the communicator style measure given out in their classes on the first day of the semester. None of the teachers guessed the research hypothesis when asked about it after the evaluations. In short, the teachers "blindly" evaluated the target persons.

At the top of each measure, the name of the respective target person who was in the teacher's class was printed. Under the name, an instruction requested that the teacher evaluate the target person along a 15-point scale for 13 items. Most of the teachers evaluated only one or two students.

VALIDITY CHECKS

Table 8.3 shows the correlation coefficients for the attraction items. In a cluster analysis (Sneath & Sokal, 1973), the items grouped into three posited factors. Thus the attraction measure was structured as expected.

Also, the mean differences of dominant, open, and relaxed verified the validity of the THAID model. For the dominant variable, the means differed significantly; $F(3, 28) = 11.9$, $p < .01$). For the relaxed variable, the means differed significantly; $F(3, 28) = 4.0$, $p < .05$). Finally, for the open variable, the means differed significantly; $F(3, 28) = 3.9$, $p < .05$). In other words, the a priori structuring of the types matched the post hoc perception of the types.

Results

Two nonparametric Friedman tests were done on the data. This test was selected because of the small sample size in each condition. In the first test, the style types were compared across all nine attraction variables. The groups differed significantly ($\chi^2 = 17.9$, $p < .01$). Table 8.4 reports the standardized means.

In the second test, the four styles were compared for the summed items for each attraction factor. The groups differed significantly ($\chi^2 = 6.6$ $p < .05$). Figure 8.3 shows the graphed scores.

Discussion

The dominant/open style (Type 1) was the most attractive in all categories. It was anticipated that this style would be evaluated highly for two of the attraction factors. **The surprising finding was that the style type was evaluated highly also in the physical attractiveness factor.** Why should a disproportionate number of handsome or pretty people show up in the dominant/open category?

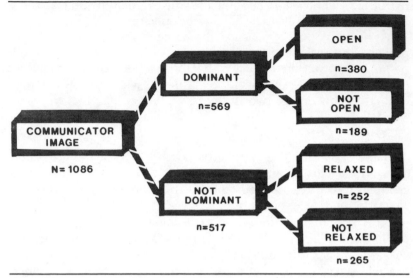

Figure 8.3   Ratings for Each Attraction Factor Across Types

Two explanations are suggested. First, the dominant/open style is sufficiently engaging that the perceiver inflates all the target person's attraction scores, including those related to physical features — in effect, *a carryover phenomenon because of the way one communicates.*

A second possibility is that people who are physically attractive receive strokes, feedback, and ego gratification from others such that they develop a style of communication that reflects confidence about themselves to the point where they manifest a dominant and open manner of communicating.

Type 1 is the only style that entails two positive variables. Being dominant seems to be a socially desirable behavior. As mentioned in the previous chapter, it covaries strongly and positively with high self-esteem, self-acceptance, and communication calmness (Mortensen, 1972). To the extent that dominant related to these traits, it should be valued by others. An optimally dominant person should be liked because confidence, self-worth, and teleological behaviors are manifested.

In like manner, being open is a socially desirable behavior, connected with honesty, sincerity, and authenticity. However, there may be a point where a person could be too dominant or too open, reflecting a curvilinear relationship. For this study, the level of being dominant and open was appropriate, and not counterproductive.

TABLE 8.3   Correlation Coefficients of the Attraction Variables

	(1)	(2)	(3)	(4)	(5)	(6)	(7)	(8)	(9)
(1) I like this person.	—								
(2) I would be willing to work with this person outside of class.	.9								
(3) I would find it easy to become a good friend of this person outside of class.	.8	.7	—						
(4) This person is a pleasing conversationalist.	.8	.7	.7	—					
(5) This person is popular with other members of the class.	.6	.7	.6	.7	—				
(6) This person has an attractive personality.	.8	.8	.7	.9	.8	—			
(7) This person is sexually attractive to members of the opposite sex.	.6	.6	.6	.6	.7	.7	—		
(8) This person is handsome/ pretty.	.8	.7	.6	.6	.6	.7	.7	—	
(9) This person is attractive physically.	.7	.7	.6	.6	.7	.7	.8.	.9	—
	(1)	(2)	(3)	(4)	(5)	(6)	(7)	(8)	(9)
	Liking/ Work With			Personality Attraction			Physical Attraction		
	Three Groups of Attraction Variables								

NOTE: In the cluster analysis, items 1, 2, and 3 grouped in the liking and working together factor; items 4, 5, and 6 grouped in the personality attraction factor; items 7, 8, and 9 grouped in the physical attraction factor.

A person who is dominant but not open (Type 2) could be seen as interpersonally unreliable, undependable, untrustworthy, or insecure. This style of communicating may be debilitating in that ambiguity is not resolved for the other. If a person does not reveal things about him- or herself, then he or she projects uncertainty. Being closed, tight-lipped, or silent could create an image of mistrust, possibly inferiority. Any one of these characteristics could affect the level of perceived attraction.

A person who is not dominant but is relaxed (Type 3) may manifest a rather bland manner of communicating. This person may prefer to follow rather than lead, listen rather than talk, or execute tasks rather than initiate them. The positive valence of relaxed could be misconstrued as passivity or social ineptitude.

TABLE 8.4   Means for Attraction Variables Across Style Types

| | Types of Communicator Style | | | |
Attraction Variables	Type 1 Dominant/ Open	Type 2 Dominant/ Not Open	Type 3 Not Dominant/ Relaxed	Type 4 Not Dominant/ Not Relaxed
Liking/working with				
(1) Like	.7	−.1	−.1	−.5
(2) Work with	.7	−.2	−.2	−.3
(3) Friend	.7	−.1	.0	−.6
Personality attraction				
(4) Conversationalist	.4	.1	−.1	−.4
(5) Popular	.7	−.1	−.4	−.2
(6) Personality	.7	−.2	−.3	−.2
Physical attraction				
(7) Sexually	.5	.1	−.5	−.1
(8) Handsome/pretty	.4	−.3	.0	−.2
(9) Physically	.5	−.3	−.1	−.1

NOTE: For exact wording of items, refer to Table 8.3. $N = 8$ for each style type.

A person who is not dominant and not relaxed has two negative factors. Being uptight, jittery, fidgety, agitated, excitable, tense, or anxious often causes others to react in the same way or to begin to dislike the person due to psychological and social discomfort.

Again, the conclusion is that one's style of communicating is an important effect determinant of how one will be perceived in terms of attraction. *The way one communicates not only directly influences whether one will be liked, chosen as a work partner, seen as popular, and seen as having a pleasing personality, but also affects adventitiously whether one will be seen as handsome or pretty.* Furthermore, particular style types may be more suited for certain interactive situations, such as those that demand competent and competitive social skills.

ADDITIONAL EVIDENCE

Since the above three studies were conducted, a handful of researchers have reached similar, pertinent conclusions. In the study discussed here, Reis, Wheeler, Spiegel, Kernis, Nezlek, and Perri (1982) found a sex difference relating to physical attractiveness and social interaction. In the second study discussed, Stohl

(1981) provides evidence that style differences can be detected across levels of attraction for children 3, 4, and 5 years of age.

Sex Differences

The findings of Reis et al. (1982) have pragmatic consequences in terms of both quantity and quality of interactions. The following points paraphrase their findings:

- For males, as physical attraction increases, **quantity of interaction** increases with females and decreases with males.

- For both sexes, as physical attraction increases, **quality of social experience** increases. Attractive males have more intimate and disclosing interactions across all partners. Attractive females have more satisfying, pleasant, intimate, and disclosing interactions.

- Physically attractive males are **more assertive.**

- Physically attractive males are **less fearful of rejection** by the opposite sex.

- Physically attractive females are **less assertive** and **less trusting** of the opposite sex.

- **Social competence** mediates part of the influence of beauty on males' interaction patterns.

The surprising direction that this study takes is that the attractive male seems to accrue more advantages in certain communicative situations than does the attractive female. Reis et al. (1982) offer this explanation:

Attractive males were generally more assertive and less fearful of women. It therefore seems likely that they would approach women more readily. Given a women's likely responses to being sought by a socially desirable person, the attractive male would probably gain approval.

The rewards and punishments take a different turn for the physically attractive female. Reis et al. explain:

Attractive women were less assertive than unattractive women and reported more other-initiated opposite-sex encounters . . . they were more likely to wait to be approached by others, perhaps because of cultural stereotypes about their social demand.

This explanation is in keeping with Deaux's (1977) notion that males are **status assertive** — that is, seeking to enhance their social standing through their relationships. Females, on the other hand, are what Deaux calls **status neutralizing** — that is, striving to eliminate differences in social rank.

The consequences of status neutralizing activities have negative associations in terms of a power perspective, but there are positive implications:

- Attractive females report more satisfying and pleasant interactions.

- Attractive females have more choice among potential partners. This means that they have a greater freedom to socialize with rewarding friends and rebuff others.

- Attractive females have a greater feeling of personal control over social time.

The sex differences suggested by this work raise a critical issue. They confound the question of how style and physical attractiveness affect each other. Style interacting with physical attraction may do different "communicative work" for males than for females.

Developmental Differences
Across Young Children

Style differences can be detected across levels of attraction for 3-, 4-, and 5-year-olds (Stohl, 1981). This means that the way a child communicates may affect how both peers and adults perceive him or her. Very early in a person's life the way one communicates can affect perceptions of attraction, which, in turn, have lifelong consequences. At this point, directionality of impact needs further research: Does style influence perceived attraction more than perceived attraction affects perceived style? It probably is not an either/or phenomenon, but mutually influential.

These findings are "teasers." Why should a child who is perceived to be relatively unattractive also be perceived to be relatively unfriendly, less relaxed, less attentive, and not as good a communicator? Is this set of covariates "real" or inadvertently imposed by the perceiver?

In short, this line of work indicates clear directions for the researcher attempting to understand the relationship between style profiles and perceived attraction. In particular, three research hypotheses point the direction to further research (Stohl, 1981):

- The more communicatively noticeable a child's style, the more attractive the child is to peers.

- The more communicatively sociocentric a child's style, the more attractive the child is to teachers.

• As a child gets older, attractiveness becomes less dependent upon noticeable styles of communication and more dependent upon sociocentric behavior.

SUMMARY AND CONCLUSIONS

From the results of the studies presented in this chapter, several conclusions emerge. *First, certain communicator style variables appear to be strong covariates of attraction variables.* This is intuitively appealing, since the way one communicates is such a pervasive part of one's interpersonal image. In Study 1, subjects expressed satisfaction with the communicator style of their "best liked" friends, while indicating how their "least liked" friends might become better communicators. Specifically, they should become less dominant and impression leaving and more attentive.

Second, certain communicator style types are both distinctive and stable enough to elicit evaluative differences in regard to their relative attractiveness and communicator images. In the second study, it was found that the dominant/open style (Type 1) was the most attractive and had the best communicator image; the not dominant/not relaxed style (Type 4) was the least attractive and had the worst communicator image. These findings were replicated in Study 3 in regard to three different indices of attraction — physical, personality, and liking to work with. It is important to recognize that this effect was obtained from both students rating their acquaintances and teachers blindly rating their students.

Third, a particular domain of communicator style variables recurrently emerge as best predictors of attraction: attentive, friendly, and relaxed. These predictors point to specific areas of one's communicator style that can be manipulated to alleviate problems relating to a poor sense of self-worth, dysfunctional communication processes, and not being liked by others.

It is important to remember that these findings may be mediated by context, situation, and time. For example, style characteristics influencing attraction should vary depending upon a therapeutic, academic, business, political, or religious context. In a like manner, they should also vary depending on whether the situation is loving, hating, playing, selling, lying, persuading, instructing, asserting, and so on.

Finally, a time component is likely to influence style considerations. It is reasonable to hypothesize that as a person gets older his or her style of communication probably changes. A more adventuresome speculation is that communicator style varies with one's life cyclical episodes — there may be cyclical periods in one's life in which one exhibits a more or less expressive style of communicating, for instance.

In conclusion, strong evidence indicates that communicator style is an effect determinant of attraction. It might have been somewhat surprising if the data had not supported this conclusion, since our workaday world so graphically reveals that it is often not what you say but how you say it that makes the difference. The task now becomes one of identifying optimal combinations of style variables that can predict consequents such as effectiveness, empathy, conflict resolvability, emotional comfortableness, and healthy personality in addition to attraction.

NOTE

1. For example, a contentious style would not be as attractive as a friendly style.

9 / Commanding Attention to Educate

style impact on teaching

> As the teacher in
> such a situation [anar-
> chy] is frightened of the
> pupils and fawns on them, so the
> students make light of their
> teachers, as well as of their attendants.
> And, generally, the young copy their elders and
> compete with them in speeches and deeds while the
> old come down to the level of the young; imitating the
> young, they are overflowing with facility and charm, and that's so
> that they won't seem to be unpleasant or despotic [*The Republic of Plato*, 563a; A. Bloom, trans.].

Borrowing the pessimistic tone from Plato, the question is: To what extent does the teacher have to fawn and charm in order to teach content? Or, in a more objective tone: Does style contribute to effective teaching? The overwhelming evidence indicates that it does.

The primary reason to do style work is not to verify that effective teachers do things right stylistically, although this is a necessary connection to make theoretically. Pragmatically, the effective teacher does not need to know what characterizes good teaching. This information, however, **provides an ideal with which to contrast the ineffective teacher;** as such, it provides a critical frame. Axioms 4 and 5 (Chapter 2) are important to the researcher because they remind him or her that a sense of style is never operative in a vacuum.

Three studies that support this conclusion are synthesized in this chapter. In the first study, a style profile of ineffective teachers is presented. In the second study, a particular style subconstruct is related to teacher effectiveness — namely, the dramatic style. Finally, in the third study the relationship between the dramatic style and teacher effectiveness is further established.

LITERATURE REVIEW

Excellent reviews of the literature regarding the general problem of evaluating teacher effectiveness are available, including Roberson (1971), Null and Walter (1972), Rodin and Rodin (1972), Gage (1972), Gessner (1973), Kauffman, Hallahan, Payne, and Ball (1973), Coppernoll and Davies (1974), Centra (1973), Hind, Dornbusch, and Scott (1974), Scriven (1974), and Rippey (1971).

None of these researchers studies style per se as it relates to teacher effectiveness, although the researchers cited in Table 9.1 allude sometimes to dimensions, components, or characteristics that entail stylistic elements. Table 9.1 references 6 large-scale studies representing 13,245 respondents, with respective sample sizes of 500, 1260, 354, 7948, 2301, and 882.

In each of these studies, the researchers examined components that either directly or indirectly relate to communicative processes in general and to style processes tangentially. It would be a fallacy of intent to maintain that these researchers should have studied the communicative processes with more focus. What the set shows is that communicative elements interpenetrate the research concerns in various forms.

Flanders (1973), for example, presents a comprehensive model for analyzing listening. This component falls into the attentiveness domain (Chapter 6) in the communicator style construct. Breed, Christiansen, and Larson (1972) examine the effect of a lecturer's gaze direction upon teaching effectiveness; this falls into the animated domain (Chapter 3). Costin, Greenough, and Menges (1971) investigated whether "a professor who tells good jokes will get a good rating." This component falls into the dramatic domain (Chapter 5).

TABLE 9.1   Six Large Sample Studies of Teacher Effectiveness

Style-Related Study	Key Variables	Variables
Rico (1971)	1. cognitive	1. impression leaving
	2. affective	2. attentive, friendly
	3. motivational	3. –
	4. disciplinary	4. dominant
	5. innovative	5. –
Isaacson, McKeachie, Milholland, Lin, Hofeller, Baerwaldt, and Zinn (1964)	1. skill	1. –
	2. rapport	2. attentive, friendly
	3. structure	3. precise
	4. overload	4. –
	5. feedback	5. friendly
	6. interaction	6. dramatic
Frey (1973)	1. work load	1. –
	2. student accomplishment	2. –
	3. organization planning	3. –
	4. teacher presentation	4. precise
	5. teacher accessibility	5. attentive
Finkbeinder, Lathrop, and Schuerger (1973)	1. general course	1. –
	2. attitude toward	2. –
	3. attitude toward method	3. precise
	4. rapport	4. friendly, attentive
	5. attitude toward workload	5. –
Meredith (1975)	1. instructor impact	1. animated, open friendly
	2. humanistic outcomes	2. attentive
	3. instructional expectations	3. communicator image
	4. intimacy	4. friendly
	5. openness	5. open

(continued)

TABLE 9.1 Continued

Style-Related Study	Key Variables	Variables
	6. interest value	6. impression leaving, dramatic
	7. vocational technical outcomes	7. —
	8. student morale	8. —
Greenwood, Bridges, Ware, and McLean (1973)	1. facilitation of learning	1. precise, attentive, friendly
	2. obsolescence of presentation	2. —
	3. commitment to teaching	3. —
	4. evaluation	4. precise, dominant
	5. voice communication	5. voice
	6. openness	6. open
	7. currency of knowledge	7. impression leaving
	8. rapport	8. friendly, attentive

STUDY 1

The primary reason for Study 1 is to see which style variables strongly profile the ineffective teacher. The hope is that if the teacher wants to improve, then behavioral directions can be pointed to concerning the way he or she communicates in the classroom. An idiosyncratic profile can be used to compare to an ideal profile rather than abstractly guessing what a teacher needs to do or vaguely exhorting the teacher to do something different.

Method

Students in introductory communication classes evaluated the instructor in terms of effectiveness variables and communicator style variables. The assumption is that a profile of style variables would systematically distinguish the effective teacher from the ineffective teacher.

UNITS OF ANALYSIS

The unit of analysis is the teacher in the respective class. The student is not the unit of analysis because his or her perception is not independent. That is, other students in that class influence an individual's perception of the teacher. The teacher per se is not the unit of analysis because a teacher's performance varies from class to class as a function of time of day, mood, class structure, and other idiosyncratic variables.

The units of analysis are 111 classes averaging 25 students per class. This represents 2775 students who voluntarily filled out the measures. The responses were anonymous.

MEASURES

The students responded to 59 items standardized by an evaluation process done each semester for all teachers by Purdue University. There were 22 items related to course evaluations, addressing reading assignments, grading procedures, amount of material, sequencing of lessons, and specific units. There were 37 items related to teacher evaluation. Embedded in the 37 items were 13 single-item communicator style variables and 1 overall teacher effectiveness variable.

Table 9.2 reports the style variables used. A five-point scale was used, ranging from "strong agreement" with the item to "strong disagreement" with the item.

PROCEDURE

Each measure was standardized and computer scored. The instructor asked the students during the last week of the semester to fill out the measures evaluating both the class and the teacher. The instructor designated a student to collect the measures and return them to the departmental secretary. The students were told that the instructor would not see the evaluations until after all the grades were in. They were also informed that they did not have to evaluate if they did not want to do so. The instructor then left the room.

ANALYSES

Construction of Units of Analysis. Each unit of analysis was constructed by averaging the responses for the respective items.

TABLE 9.2   Style Variables Used in Study 2

YES! = *strong agreement* with the item
yes = *agreement* with the item
? = *neither agreement nor disagreement* with the item
no = *disagreement* with the item
NO! = *strong disagreement* with the item

My instructor communicates in a very **lively/animated** way.	YES!	yes	?	no	NO!
My instructor has an **effective style** of presentation.	YES!	yes	?	no	NO!
My instructor communicates in a very **friendly** way.	YES!	yes	?	no	NO!
My instructor is **careful and precise** when answering questions.	YES!	yes	?	no	NO!
My instructor communicates in a very **evasive** way.	YES!	yes	?	no	NO!
My instructor communicates in a very **dominant** way.	YES!	yes	?	no	NO!
My instructor communicates in a very **serious** way.	YES!	yes	?	no	NO!
My instructor leaves a very **strong impression** in communicating.	YES!	yes	?	no	NO!
My instructor communicates in a very **humble** way.	YES!	yes	?	no	NO!
My instructor communicates in a very **dramatic** way.	YES!	yes	?	no	NO!
My instructor is a very **good communicator**.	YES!	yes	?	no	NO!
My instructor communicates in a very **attentive** way.	YES!	yes	?	no	NO!
My instructor communicates in a very **argumentative** way.	YES!	yes	?	no	NO!

NOTE: Three additional style items have been included—evasive, serious, and humble. These attributions were generated by asking a sample (n = 112) to give a one-word description of the way someone they liked communicates and a one-word description of the way someone they disliked communicates. These three were mentioned most often. As a result, they are included in this study for exploratory reasons. Also, note that the word "argumentative" is being used instead of "contentious" and the phrase "lively/animated" is being used instead of "animated." In both instances, the new words replace the original descriptors used in Chapter 3.

So, for each unit, the means are being analyzed. As such, the mean represents a substantially more stable score than an individual score.

Stratification of Teachers in the Respective Classes. The teachers in the respective classes were stratified by quartiles. Teachers were designated as "effective" if they scored in the top twenty-fifth percentile on the following item: **Overall, this instructor is among the best teachers I have known.** They were designated as "above average" if they scored above the fiftieth percentile but below the seventy-fifth percentile. They were designated as "below average" if they scored above the twenty-fifth percentile but below the fiftieth percentile. And they were designated as "ineffective" if they scored below the twenty-fifth percentile.

Decision Rules. A series of one-way analyses of variance were conducted on the data for each style variable across the four stratification levels. To protect against chance findings, alpha at .01 was partitioned among the 14 style variables. Consequently, a finding was considered significant if the F statistic exceeded a critical value determined by an alpha level of .001.

In addition, a finding was considered useful only if it reflected a strong linear phenomenon. That is, the respective means across the four stratifications must show either increasing or decreasing monotonicity. This criterion was easily established by inspection of the mean scores.

Results

Using the more rigorous criteria, six communicator style variables systematically covaried across the teacher effectiveness stratifications. Table 9.3 reports the means, expressed as z scores, for the variables that were significantly different across the four percentiles (p < .001).

The strongest difference to emerge is with the lively/animated style variable. The ineffective teacher is not animated or lively. On the other hand, the effective teacher is very animated and lively. The extreme residuals show that the ineffective teacher is also significantly less friendly, dramatic, precise, and attentive. Figure 9.1 shows the graphed results.

The second analyses in this study shows the correlations among the style variables and the evaluation variables. Based on these coefficients, a correlagram was constructed (McQuitty, 1957). No link was allowed into the structure unless it was greater than .75. Table 9.4 reports the coefficients.

TABLE 9.3   Z Score Means for Style Variables

Style Variable	Ineffective Teachers (Bottom 25%)	Below-Average Teachers (Above 25% and Below 50%)	Above-Average Teachers (Above 50% and Below 75%)	Effective Teachers (Above 75%)
Friendly	−1.1	−.3	.5	1.1**
Lively/ animated	−1.2**	−.3	.5	.9**
Precise	−1.2**	.0	.4	.8
Attentive	−1.2**	−.2	.4	.8
Relaxed	−1.1	−.3	.3	.8
Dramatic	−.7	−.4	.4	.9**

**Indicates the biggest residuals for the positive and negative effects. A total of 75 percent of the residuals fall between −1.1 and .8. The remaining residuals in the upper and lower 12 percent are the extreme residuals. The median residual is .1, with 50 percent of the residuals between −.6 and .6.

The evaluation variables are so tightly clustered that they can be considered tapping almost equivalent phenomena. That is, if a person is perceived as having an effective style and as being a good communicator, then the person will be perceived as a good teacher.

As Figure 9.2 indicates, attentive, precise, animated, and friendly are particularly interrelated with a median correlation among the variables at .77. The strongest "bridge" variables between the style domain and the evaluation domain are animated (r = .90) and attentive (r = .90). Dramatic and relaxed define the ends of a continuum. This finding coincides with the simplex outlined in Chapter 3. Dramatic style represents a greater manifestation of energy expenditure than the relaxed style.

Discussion

Only the strongest effects are presented in this study. The phenomenon had to meet a critical value at an alpha value of .001 or less. In addition, the data had to show strong linearity. That is, across each of the four stratifications of teacher effectiveness, the mean value for the style variable had to increment in a strong, increasingly monotonic way.

As a result, robust conclusions emerge: **An ineffective teacher is not very lively or animated, does not signal enough attentiveness or friendliness, and does not have a very precise style. In addition, the ineffective teacher is not very relaxed and does not**

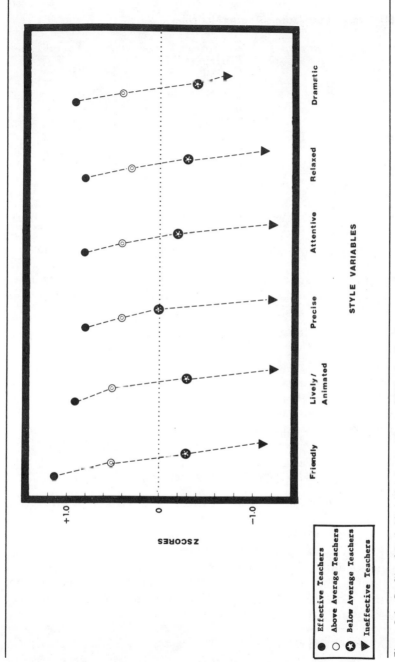

Figure 9.1 Profile of Style Variables Across Range of Effective Teachers

TABLE 9.4   Correlations Among Variables[a]

		1	2	3	4	5	6	7	8	9
(1) Friendly		—	.77	.76	.77	.79	.50	.83	.80	.78
(2) Lively/animated			—	.75	.86	.64	.76	.89	.90	.87
(3) Precise				—	.89	.66	.50	.87	.85	.88
(4) Attentive	r_m = .76				—	.66	.64	.90	.90	.90
(5) Relaxed						—	.43	.74	.72	.73
(6) Dramatic							—	.68	.69	.62
(7) Best teacher								—	.94	.92
(8) Effective style									—	.94
(9) Good communicator	r_m = .84							r_m = .92		—

NOTE: The median correlation is reported (r_m) for the style variables, the evaluation variables, and the intercorrelations between these sets. Because the between-correlation coefficient is greater than the within-correlation coefficient for the style variables, the indication is that this is a linked set rather than a disjoint set.

a. N = 111 classes. All correlations in the table are significant (p < .001).

use a dramatic style. Furthermore, as the teacher improves his or her teaching, these style scores change accordingly. Briefly consider each style variable in the profile.

FRIENDLY STYLE

A friendly style essentially confirms the self of the other. It signals that the person is worthy of recognition, affirmation, and identity. Using a transactional term, it provides "strokes" for the person. Its impact is to imply that the teaching endeavor is a partnership in learning. The teacher, in the one-up position, moves to interact with the student rather than teach at the student.

PRECISE STYLE

By definition, the teacher has something to teach. To the degree that the teacher can unambiguously move the student to that knowledge, the style of communication will be seen as precise. Better teachers are better at explaining content. This is not merely a matter of mouthing an explication. It involves anticipating where a student might have trouble and making a move to surmount that barrier. A precise style also signals that the teacher is in control of the content.

ATTENTIVE STYLE

Attentive style signals that the person is being understood and listened to. Again, it signals that an interactive process is occurring

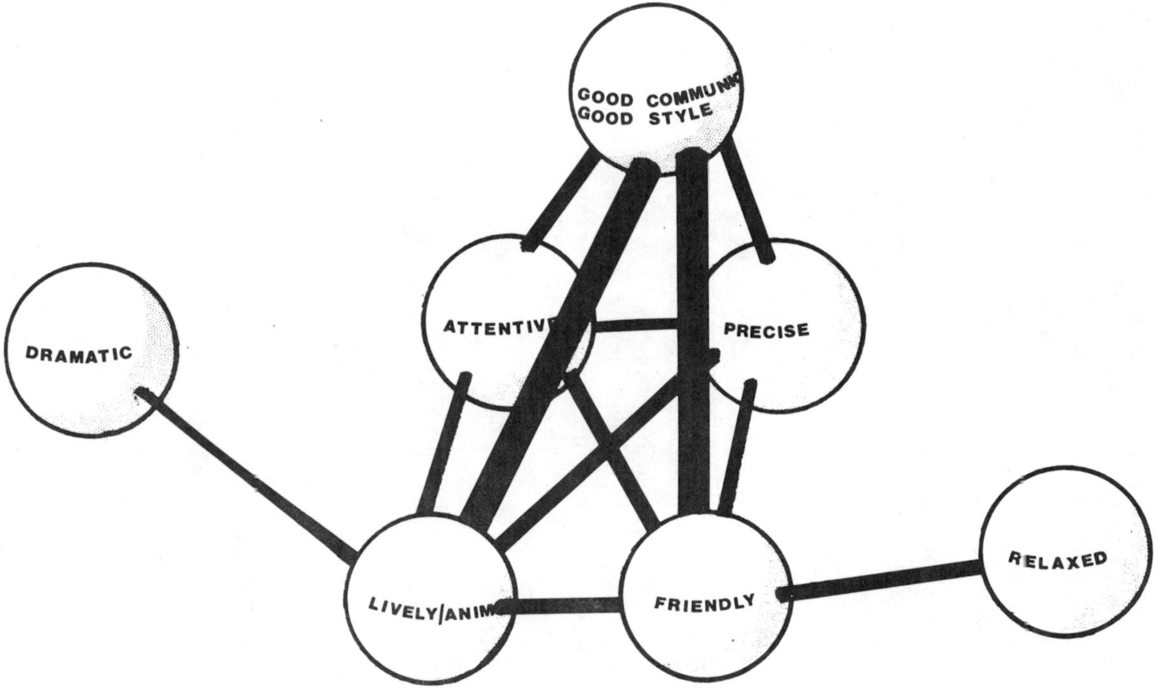

Figure 9.2 Structural Relationship Among Style Variables and Good Communicator and Good Style Variables

rather than a one-to-many process. The attentive teacher tends not only to be more alert, but to actively indicate behavioral alertness. By being actively attentive the person's self is confirmed in a way similar to manifesting a friendly style.

LIVELY/ANIMATED STYLE

This style shows that the teacher is highly expressive both verbally and nonverbally, especially with gestures, facial expressions, and eye behavior. The most frequent association with an animated style is enthusiasm, which is probably the single best predictor of an effective teacher across the greatest variety of studies.

The lively/animated style, by inference, says, "I care enough about this process that I will expend energy for it." The animated style uses gestures and facial and eye expressions to emphasize the literal message or to add redundancy to it. A good teacher who goes beyond repeating an explanation uses this style to indicate critical points in the teaching process. Its form-giving function in the metamessage says, "Now attend to this!"

RELAXED STYLE

A person with a relaxed style tends to be calm and collected in his or her communicative behavior. The person usually is not bothered by nervous mannerisms. As a result, the person is often perceived as confident and in control. As such, the style reflects a person who is at ease with the teaching process.

DRAMATIC STYLE

A dramatic style entails overstating, understating, or altering the literal meaning for a heightened effect. Consequently, it goes hand in hand with an animated style in emphasizing crucial points in an explanation. Also, a person with a dramatic style often tells stories, uses anecdotes, manipulates metaphors, uses sarcasm, irony, puns, and jokes. All this behavior not only emphasizes, but also secures attention.

Summary

It is important to note that the style variables are never perceived in isolation. They are inextricable from one another. A person always manifests some degree of being attentive-not attentive, dramatic-not dramatic, and so on, even if the degree represents the average manifestation of that behavior.

The gestalt of these variables is powerfully associated with effective teaching. The process is not static and it is not simple. It is ongoing, complex, and interrelated. The style behaviors flow sometimes in a rhythm, sometimes mosaically; throughout the teaching process they do a lot of communicative work. Ineffective teachers either are oblivious to the impact of style or do not know how to make the style variables work for them.

STUDY 2

The previous study profiled the ineffective teacher in style terms, but did so with a fairly high level of abstraction. Little information is available regarding specific interventions. It would be useful to explore further each variable in Study 1.

There were many directions to go to at this point. However, the Dr. Fox studies adventitiously focused attention on the dramatic style variable. The original Dr. Fox study sets the stage for the problem. In that research, a professional actor lectured three groups of educators and graduate students with material that was devoid of content of any educational value. The lecture was given in an enthusiastic and expressive manner, which led to the following controversial claim:

The enthusiasm or expressiveness of an instructor can significantly influence rating regardless of the amount of substantive content presented [Naftulin, Ware, & Donnelly, 1973].[1]

The natural tendency is to resist the conclusion. Most scholars do not want to think that enthusiasm or expressiveness is all that is needed for one to be perceived as an effective teacher. The conclusion entails multifaceted issues, however. It would be a mistake to reject enthusiasm or expressiveness as merely fluff in the teaching process. Because both enthusiasm and expressiveness give form, they should be an effective part of the good teacher's communicative repertoire.

The Dr. Fox study controversy is not resolved in this study, but it relates enthusiasm and expressiveness, treated as part of the dramatic style domain, to effective teaching. The problem is that dramatic behaviors are difficult to analyze. The behaviors are as varied as types of entertainment. They range from the teacher who has exceptionally dry wit to the teacher who uses slapstick to illustrate the main points of the daily lecture.

Past Research

The research relating dramatic style to teacher effectiveness is at best tangential. There is only one large sample study in which the dramatic component is treated under an interaction dimension (Isaacson, McKeachie, Milholland, Lin, Hofeller, Baerwaldt, & Zinn, 1964). However, across the 1260 students, the variable did not discriminate well. There have been a handful of minor studies addressing aspects of the dramatic style domain, but the treatment of dramatic behavior is fragmented (Ausubel, 1964; Stephens, 1967; Rosenshine, 1970).

By studying the dramatic variable in the perspective of the larger domain, two general predictions can be made given its relative position in the communicator style structure (see Figures 3.2 and 3.3, Chapter 3):

- The effective teacher tends to be **more active** stylistically.
- The effective teacher tends to be more **sender oriented** in the communicative process.

THE RESEARCH PROBLEM IN STUDY 2

This study examines whether certain dramatic behaviors are systematically associated with effective teachers. The evidence strongly affirms the suggested relationships. Nine out of the ten dramatic behaviors employed in this study covaried with teacher effectiveness.

Method

SUBJECTS

Targets of the evaluation were 25 graduate assistant instructors, ranging in age from 21 to 47 years. A total of 498 students evaluated the target teachers, representing 97 separate classes. All teachers and students voluntarily participated in the study.

PRIMARY MEASURES

Two primary measures were used and administered at different points in time.[2] Ten dramatic behaviors were measured derived from research on dramatic style (see Chapter 5; also see Norton, Baker, Bednar, Salyer, & McGough, 1978). The items were presented on a questionnaire that included the following distractors: (1) 20 items from a solidarity measure, (2) the short form of the Communicator Style Measure, and (3) four items measuring general reactions to the course. The reliability coefficient for the ten dramatic items is .91 (Hoyt coefficient). The exact wording of the dramatic style items can be found in Table 9.8.

The second measure evaluated teacher effectiveness. Five items were used to create an overall teacher effectiveness score: (1) My instructor motivates me to do my best work; (2) My instructor explains difficult material clearly; (3) Course assignments are interesting and stimulating; (4) Overall, this course is among the best I have ever taken; and (5) Overall, this instructor is among the best teachers I have known. The reliability coefficient for the five evaluation items is .90 (Hoyt coefficient).

Procedures

DRAMATIC STYLE BEHAVIORS

The measure for the dramatic style behaviors was administered four weeks before the end of the semester. Each teaching assistant was given twelve questionnaires and was asked to distribute the measures randomly to his or her students in class.

The teacher was also asked to designate one student to collect the measures and return them to the researcher. Finally, the teacher was asked to remind the students that the information was being gathered with his or her permission and the data would not be seen by the teacher.

A teacher was included in the research only if at least six students evaluated him or her. An average of nine students rated each teacher in a given classroom.

TEACHER EFFECTIVENESS

On the last day of class, all teaching assistants took part in a standardized evaluation. Again, the students were reminded that the teacher would not know which students were evaluating him or her. Also, one student collected the evaluations and returned them to the course director. For this questionnaire, an average of 23 students rated each teacher in a given classroom.

Unit of Analysis. As in Study 1, the individual teacher is the unit of analysis (Peckham, Glass, & Hopkins, 1969).[3] A three-step process was used to construct the final unit of analysis. First, the five items for teacher evaluation were standardized and then averaged. The skewness problem was partially alleviated by adding the items together. Also, the transformation to standardized scores forced the mean to zero and the variance to one. The median correlation among the five items is .93.

Second, the means for each teacher in a given classroom were calculated. The assumption is that if a phenomenon is strong enough, then the *average* perception of it will be sufficient for analysis. In short, this decision makes the whole analysis more conservative — only the substantial effects will not be washed out.

Third, means were calculated for each teacher across class-rooms. Some teaching assistants taught three sections, some taught two, and a few taught only one section. The assumption here is that effective teaching endures across classrooms regard-less of many extraneous variables such as time of day, location of classroom, and so on.

In this study, the assumption is probably warranted because effective teachers endured across semesters. That is, people who were perceived as effective teachers in the first semester were also perceived as effective teachers in the second semester. The con-verse was also true. Ultimately, 23 units of analysis were studied.

STUDENT CHARACTERISTICS

As in previous study, the students were in a basic communica-tion course at Purdue University. The syllabus, book, and philoso-phy of the course were relatively constant. Each class must pass three mass standardized exams. Consequently, the topic, size of class (set at about 26), and the level of education were similar for all sections.

Results

MEAN DIFFERENCES BETWEEN EFFECTIVE
AND INEFFECTIVE TEACHERS

The sample was stratified into effective and ineffective teachers. Any teacher scoring above the z-score mean (.10) was *stipulated* as "effective." Any teacher scoring below the mean was *stipulated* as "ineffective." The labels were only meant to be used for convenience and are relative. A teacher falling into the "ineffec-tive" stratum may, in fact, be a good teacher; the label only signals that the teacher is below the mean in this sample.

TABLE 9.5   Central Tendency Statistics for Each Stratum

Dramatic Style Variable	Mean for Ineffective Teacher	Mean for Effective Teacher	Variance	F
This teacher can catch people up in his or her stories.	4.6	5.0	.3	3.2*
This teacher knows how to get people laughing.	5.1	5.5	.2	3.9*
This teacher is very entertaining.	5.0	5.6	.3	6.5**
This teacher does a lot of double takes to create a dramatic effect.	3.4	4.0	.3	6.9**

*$p < .10$
**$p < .05$

One-way analysis of variance was used for each dramatic variable. Table 9.5 reports the central tendency statistics for the significant variables for each stratum.

If all dramatic behaviors are summed to create a total dramatic behavior score, the effective teacher overall is significantly more dramatic ($F = 4.6$; $p < .05$) than the ineffective teacher, with respective means of 3.8 and 3.3.

TRENDS IN THE DATA

The data were smoothed and then each dramatic variable was plotted against the teacher effectiveness variable.[4] Figure 9.3 shows the visual plots. **Getting others to fantasize, catching people up in stories, and being entertaining are strongly positively associated with teacher effectiveness in an overall linear fashion.** Only the linear effect for the fantasy variable should be qualified. There is a strong plateau in the middle of the data for the fantasy variable. This indicates that the effects tend to happen at either end more intensely.

Two plots show weak linearity overall: (1) being sarcastic, and (2) getting others to laugh. The respective correlations are .3 and .5. The shapes of both plots are almost identical. No change is happening for the moderately ineffective teachers. Also, the highly effective teachers tend to use sarcasm more and know how

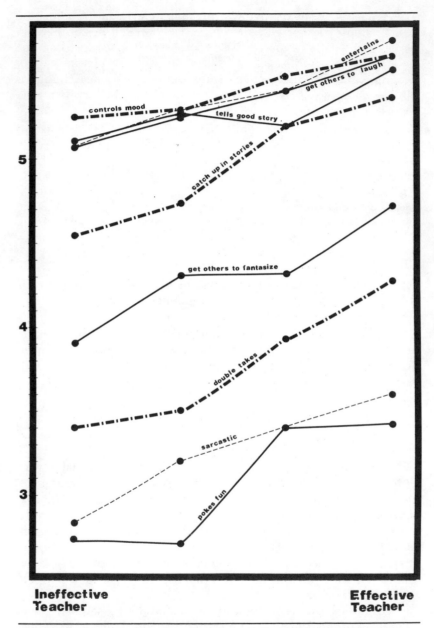

Figure 9.3   Dramatic Behavior Variables Across Range of Effective Teachers

to get others to laugh, but there are no increasing linear effects within group. Change happens the fastest within the group of most ineffective teachers.

Two plots show relatively strong positive linearity using the overall slope and correlation criteria. For the "tells a good story" variable, the correlation is .3. This represents the average dramatic effect. For the double take variable, relatively little change is happening within the ineffective group and relatively fast change is happening within the effective group. This is especially true for the double take variable.

In two variables, controls mood and pokes fun, not much change happens within either stratum; the change happens between strata. It is almost an either/or phenomenon.

The plotted values point to where researchers might expect future effects and suggest the types of phenomena they should anticipate. Only the voices variable failed to show any promise in the plotted values. Each criteria indicated that nothing was happening. The overall correlation was −.1.

Discussion and Conclusions

Two dramatic style behaviors relate strongly to teacher effectiveness both by conventional statistical analyses and exploratory data analysis. The effective teacher is entertaining and probably does a lot more double takes. The first finding is expected because of past research (Rosenshine, 1970; see also Solomon, 1966; Wallen, 1966; Mastin, 1963). The second finding was somewhat surprising. There is no empirical work on double takes. A tentative explanation is offered below.

ENTERTAINING

A cautionary note is in order here. This report does not imply that being entertaining is either a necessary or a sufficient condition to being an effective teacher. One effective teacher who is not entertaining would reduce the argument maintaining that it is a necessary condition to an absurdity. The more interesting argument is that being entertaining is a sufficient condition to being perceived as an effective teacher — in effect, a teacher with certain style but no content. *This question has yet to be answered.*

Bales's (1970) extensive factor-analytic work, reported in *Personality and Interpersonal Behavior,* is useful here. One of the questions in his work is: To what extent do you find the person entertaining? Regardless of whether the person rated self or others rated him or her, if the person was seen as entertaining, that person was classified as a "UB (Up and Backward) type." The entertaining variable in particular and the dramatic style behaviors in general characterize a person in the "UB" space:

The member located in the upward-backward part of the group space by his fellow members seems ascendant and expressive, nontask oriented, perhaps unconventional or even deviant. He seems neither clearly friendly nor unfriendly, but entertaining, joking, dramatic, relativistic, free in his associations, taking pleasure in play, activity, novelty, and creativity. In the realization of his own values he seems to be trying to move toward value-relativism and expression of underlying emotions and feelings. "Life is more a festival than a workshop for moral discipline" [Bales, 1970].

In addition, the following speculations from Bales's work can be adapted to generate questions about future research relating dramatic behaviors to teacher effectiveness:

(1) *Is the effective teacher particularly good at recognizing such tensions and converting them to dramatic behaviors to enhance the learning experience?* In the above attraction, the "UB" person identifies the self with the power that comes from the ability to recognize and express unconscious tendencies in the self and in others, and, thus, escapes from conflict.

(2) *If the effective teacher feels this freedom, does the attitude transfer into dramatic behaviors that enhance the learning experience?* The "UB" person appears to feel a freedom from the constraint of authority.

(3) *Are there instances in which dramatic behavior is counterproductive for the effective teacher?* The "UB" person often takes a risk by joking, which may cause feelings of ambivalence and negative reactions toward him.

The empirical evidence from this report and conclusions from the literature indicate that overall dramatic behaviors relate to teaching effectiveness, but it may not be a simple relationship to establish when specific behaviors are focused upon. The findings for eight of the dramatic behaviors in this way are encouraging and offer specific directions for research.

DOUBLE TAKES

To do a double take, a person needs to react to something. If the person creates a situation in which he or she can "react," then that person is deliberately manipulating the interactions. Johnny Carson is a master of this kind of manipulation. He structures a situation in his monologue that guarantees success regardless of the direction his jokes go. If the joke hits, the audience laughs at this level. If the joke does not hit and the audience boos, then Carson does a double take to their adverse reaction. Carson's "reacting" to their reaction makes the audience laugh at a metalevel. He does about a dozen double takes per monologue, ranging from a subtle coyness to a blatant, feigned fear of the audience. It takes a controlled and confident person/entertainer/ teacher to set up this kind of dramatic behavior.

STORYTELLING

Three variables strongly relate storytelling to effective teaching: (1) tells good stories, (2) catches others up in stories, and (3) gets others to fantasize. All literature teaches through stories, fantasies, metaphors, and poetry. It is not surprising that the effective teacher uses similar vehicles.

The very act of telling a story is somewhat mesmerizing. When a teacher presents a relatively unfamiliar sequence of events to the class, their attention is attracted to the extent that they anticipate the succession and resolution of events. If storytelling relates course content, then the teacher is likely to be perceived as leading a class to knowledge. Bormann's (1975) work on the fantasy chain provides insight here. Also, work by Bandler and Grinder (1975b; Grinder & Bandler, 1976), Watzlawick (1978), and Haley (1978) provokes other ideas regarding this form of dramatic behavior.

GETS TO LAUGH

This study asked the question: Does this person know how to get others to laugh? In a way, the question translates to: Does this person know how to entertain? It does not ask whether the teacher laughs or what the function of laughter in the classroom is. There are conflicting theories of laughter and probably many forms and consequences of different kinds of laughter (Bales, 1970; see also Chapman & Foote, 1976).

Bales, for example, says that laughter is a sudden escape into motor discharge of conflicted emotional states that can no longer be contained. The emotions may be anxiety, aggression, affection, or any other. If this is true, the teacher can manipulate emotions such as those mentioned through laughter. It could be a major communicative behavior that controls disruptive actions in a class; it could be a primary way to indicate empathy. Whatever the case, the research is wide open for the communication scholar.

SARCASTIC AND POKES FUN

In terms of strata differences, sarcastic and pokes fun did not do well in discriminating and the power analysis indicates that it would be very expensive to try to pick up significant differences given the estimators. The researcher can either drop the variable or try to do something about reducing the variance or increasing the minimum magnitude of effect. Also, the plotted values for both variables, although not strong, indicate that something is happening in the right direction.

Consider the sarcastic variable. It would be a mistake to conclude that it might be the key to effective teaching. It may be that when the effective teacher uses sarcasm, he or she does something to mitigate its potentially negative impact. The teacher may be sarcastic, but may signal that the sarcasm is friendly and nonhostile in its intent. In effect, the teacher transforms the negative element to a positive message that gives the person or class a certain amount of playful attention. It would take a confident person to make such a move. In fact, the sarcastic variable correlates strongly with dramatic, dominant, and influential in this study, with respective coefficients of .7, .5, and .4.

CONTROLS MOOD

This variable measures an overall consequence. It does little to provide *specific* information about dramatic style behaviors. In fact, most dramatic behaviors may help control the mood of a class. For instance, the "gets to laugh" and the "gets to fantasize" variables correlate strongly with this variable, with respective coefficients of .7 and .6. The median correlation with all the other dramatic variables is .56.

This variable is interesting because it is at a different level of abstraction from the more specifically defined behaviors. It seems to be a part of each dramatic behavior. If a mood change is effective, it does not lead necessarily to sarcasm. The converse is true. If sarcasm is effective, it leads necessarily to a mood change.

STUDY 3

One of the frustrations of Study 2 is the illusive nature of dramatic style. In light of Study 2 and extensive work with the dramatic style construct as presented in Chapter 5, a sharper focus emerged in Study 3. **The dramatic style of communicating can be treated as either a unidimensional or a multidimensional concept.**

If it is treated as a multidimensional concept, then the elements of the domain may be independent of one another. For example, a teacher perceived as a good storyteller need not simultaneously be perceived as a good actor.

In brief, the research can treat the construct either way as long as the levels of abstraction are carefully attended to and the necessary and sufficent conditions of what constitutes a dramatic style are carefully distinguished. Study 3 contributes to this end.

The second device that is used to provide a better perspective in researching dramatic behaviors is simply an "old reminder" that needs to be carefully attended to — namely, the representative amount of variance about the central tendency of the dramatic behavior. The researcher needs to address the question: **What is the norm range of dramatic behaviors for most teachers?** It is simplistic, for instance, to say that effective teachers are entertaining teachers. It is crucial to identify "being entertaining" relative and relevant to clearly specified central tendency phenomenon. This study provides such a focus.

Method

This study follows the same methods outlined in Study 2. The data were gathered in two steps. First, a measure of teacher effectiveness was obtained during the first semester. Second, a measure of perceived dramatic behaviors was obtained during the second semester.

SUBJECTS

A total of 32 teachers volunteered to participate in the study. Respondents were 1120 students in introductory communication courses at Purdue University. During the first semester, 800 students in the 32 classes voluntarily evaluated the 32 target teachers in terms of effectiveness. The scores for each class were standardized and averaged. During the second semester, 10 students randomly selected from respective class assessed the target teacher's dramatic behavior. These scores also were standardized and averaged. The students for the second semester were not the same as those for the first semester.

UNITS OF ANALYSIS

The units of analysis for this study were the standardized scores for the target teacher, not the individual responses of the respective students. This means that even though a large number of students participated, the N for the analyses is 32. However, because the units are mean scores, the data are stable.

INDEPENDENCE OF RESPONSES

The chances of a response set between the dependent and independent variables were eliminated by obtaining the data for the respective variables in different semesters. The respondent could not "help" the researcher find effects by saying the person is dramatic and is a good teacher.

Embedded in this decision is the assumption that, **overall, the evaluations of teachers tend to endure across semesters.** This is not to say that some teachers may not significantly change across semesters. But in this research, radical jumps in evaluations did not occur. In fact, the correlation between the two scores is high, $r = .92$.

PROCEDURES

During the first semester, the teacher evaluations were administered during the midterm and final tests, which were given en masse in a large auditorium. The teacher evaluations were anonymously given and the respective teachers did not see the summary statistics until after the grades were turned in at the end of the semester. This procedure had the advantage of uniform administration in the same time and same place.

During the second semester, a graduate student distributed the dramatic behavior questionnaires to the different classes while the teacher left the room. Five males and five females from each class were asked to complete the questionnaires. When an equitable sex distribution was unavailable, a disproportionate distribution was accepted.

Students were reminded that the information was being gathered with the teacher's approval and that the teacher would see the summary statistics of the data only after the semester had ended. All respondents completed the questionnaires anonymously and voluntarily. The data were collected between the seventh and eighth weeks of the semester so that the students had time to become familiar with the teacher's style.

MEASURES

Teacher Effectiveness. A hybrid evaluation score was constructed to ensure greater stability in the assessment. Two identical measures of teacher effectiveness were taken the first semester A core item (Overall, my instructor is among the best teachers I have known) was used to define the teacher effectiveness variable. This was done by converting both the midsemester and final evaluations into respective standardized scores and averaging.

Perceived Dramatic Behavior. A total of 12 items assessing perceived dramatic behaviors were taken from a factor analysis of 61 items relating to dramatic style (see Chapter 5). High loading items were taken from each factor to obtain a wide range of perceived behaviors. The items include the following:

- When this teacher talks to the class, he or she knows how to catch their attention. (CATCH ATTENTION)
- This teacher says things in such a way that the class sees multiple meanings in the communication (CREATES MULTIPLE MEANINGS)
- This teacher never swears. (This item is reversed in the subsequent analyses.) (SWEARS)
- It is easy for this teacher to make the class laugh. (MAKES LAUGH)
- This teacher uses a lot of energy communicating to the class. (USES ENERGY)
- Sometimes this teacher acts out a communication physically as well as vocally. (ACTS OUT)
- This teacher often deliberately uses laughter to create a dramatic effect. (USES LAUGHTER)
- This teacher is entertaining. (ENTERTAINS)
- This teacher is very good at manipulating the mood of the class. (MANIPULATES MOOD)
- This teacher likes to get the class laughing. (GET LAUGHING)
- This teacher is often sarcastic. (USES SARCASM)
- This teacher tells a lot of stories. (TELLS MANY STORIES)

The words in capital letters are used to represent the abbreviated items in the figures and tables. There were 15 communicator style items and 9 teacher assessment variables used as background items in the questionnaire that were not analyzed. The 12 dramatic behavior variables have a reliability of .91 (Cronbach's alpha).

DISTRIBUTION OF SCORES

Stratifications. It would have been unrealistic to stratify the 32 teachers into "ineffective" and "effective" teachers based on a mean split of the hybrid evaluation score. The reason for this is that the data are skewed strongly. That is, the students tend to assess the teachers in a strong positive way.

The teachers from the twenty-fifth to the one-hundredth percentile, in general, were seen as effective teachers. It was only below the twenty-fifth percentile that teachers were perceived as relatively ineffective. Consequently, in keeping with the recommendations by Tukey (1977), the sample was stratified into "ineffective" teachers if they fell below the twenty-fifth percentile and "effective" teachers if they fell above that point.

Incidently, other variants of the stratifications were tried, such as creating four equal strata. In this case, the data behaved as expected. The top three strata tended to differ significantly from the bottom stratum. Table 9.7 shows the exact distribution of evaluations. Part of the follow-up analyses included stratifying the sample according to "natural" clustering of evaluation scores and seeing whether the dramatic behaviors systematically increased as expected.

Results

Two primary analyses were done. The first shows the structure of the dramatic style behaviors using smallest space analysis (Guttman, 1982; Lingoes, 1973). The second reports the differences between ineffective and effective teachers in terms of dramatic style behaviors.

A secondary analysis looks at the same data stratified in a larger number of clusters so that idiosyncratic variations of dramatic behaviors can be seen across the continuum ranging from ineffective to effective teachers. The analysis relies upon smoothing techniques as used in Study 3. The general conclusion from these analyses is that certain dramatic behaviors differentiate between ineffective and effective teachers.

The smallest space analysis is shown in Figure 9.4. It can be seen that the variables with the highest correlation are "closest neighbors" in the structural solution. Five dramatic behaviors are strongly associated with the effective teacher variables: (1) CATCH ATTENTION ($r = .35$), (2) MAKES LAUGH ($r = .30$), (3) USES ENERGY ($r = .44$), (4) MANIPULATES MOOD ($r = .39$), and (5) ENTERTAINS ($r = .35$). These are the dramatic behaviors most strongly correlated

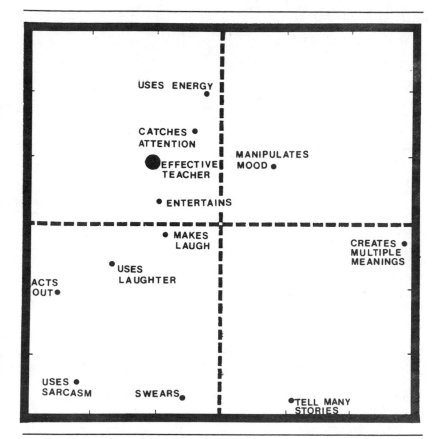

Figure 9.4   Smallest Space Analysis of Style and Effective Teacher Variables

with the effective teacher variable. The remaining correlations with the effective teacher variable are .31, .13, .07, and .02.

This suggests that the "close neighbors" are likely to differentiate between the ineffective and effective teachers and are likely to show a tendency to be increasingly monotonic across the ineffectiveness-effective continuum. This, in fact, proves to be the case, as shown below.

Table 9.6 reports the summary statistics comparing the ineffective and effective teachers. Five of the perceived dramatic behaviors strongly differentiate between ineffective and effective teachers. *For four of the behaviors, there is at least a standard deviation difference between the groups.* For the fifth behavior, there is a .8 standard deviation between the groups.

TABLE 9.6   Central Tendency Statistics for Each Stratum

Dramatic Style Variable	Mean for Ineffective Teacher	Mean for Effective Teacher	Variance	F
This teacher uses a lot of energy communicating to the class.	−1.0	.3	.7	17.0
This teacher is very good at manipulating the mood of the class.	−.8	.3	.8	9.3
When this teacher talks to the class, he or she knows how to catch their attention.	−.8	.3	.8	9.3
This teacher is entertaining.	−.8	.3	.8	8.4
It is easy for this teacher to make the class laugh.	−.6	.2	.9	5.0

NOTE: Each cell reports z scores; as such, they represent standard deviations from the mean. For the ineffective condition, n = 8; for the effective condition, n = 24. Because of the unequal cell size, the average variance is not equal to unity. Only the variables with significant differences are reported.

However, because of the reductionist aspect of the stratifications, it is useful to examine the distribution of the effectiveness scores and then to look at the dramatic behaviors for a larger number of strata. Table 9.7 reports how the effectiveness scores group for the sample.

What constitutes natural strata is arbitrary and can only be stipulated by some reasonable criterion. In this case, the demarcation is relatively easy to suggest. *In the distribution, the closest that any one stratum is to another is .22 standard deviations.* In short, the nine strata are clearly distinct from one another. The question becomes how the dramatic behaviors change across the nine strata. Table 9.8 reports respective medians for each stratum, the smoothed value, and the residual value.

Figure 9.5 shows the graphed results of the respective smoothed values. *The shaded areas on the graph indicate where 50 percent of the medians should fall relative to the particular variables.* In other words, the shaded areas demarcate the values between the twenty-fifth and seventy-fifth percentiles relative to the variable under consideration. *They mark the norm range of behaviors relative to this sample. The indication of norm ranges is*

TABLE 9.7   Profile of Distribution of Effectiveness Scores

Rank-Ordered Standardized Scores for Each Teacher Arranged in Natural Strata	Standardized Scores	Distance to Next Stratum	Rank
(−1.45, −1.37, −1.36)	−1.37	.30	1
(−1.03, −1.03, −.96)	−1.03	.60	2
(−.74, −.66, −.65, −.62)	−.66	.47	3
(−.26, −.19, −.11)	−.19	.25	4
(.06, .07)	.06	.22	5
(.28, .28, .38)	.28	.34	6
(.57, .62, .62)	.62	.37	7
(.92, .92, .99, .99, .99, .99)	.99	.57	8
(1.22, 1.43, 1.70, 1.87)	1.56	—	9

TABLE 9.8   Median Statistics and Smooths Across Strata

Dramatic Behavior Variable		Strata Ranging from Ineffective to Effective Teachers								
		1	2	3	4	5	6	7	8	9
Uses energy	median	−9	−10	−1	1	−2	2	−3	10	2
	smooth	−10	−9	−1	−1	−1	1	2	2	2
	residual	1	−1	0	2	−1	1	−5	8	0
Manipulates mood	median	−7	−2	0	−7	0	9	−3	0	4
	smooth	−7	−2	−2	0	0	0	0	0	4
	residual	0	0	2	−7	0	9	−3	0	0
Catch attention	median	−3	−9	−2	−5	0	11	−4	2	3
	smooth	−3	−3	−3	−2	0	0	2	3	3
	residual	0	−6	1	−3	0	11	−6	−1	0
Entertains	median	−14	−2	2	5	−2	10	2	1	2
	smooth	−14	−2	2	2	2	2	2	2	1
	residual	0	0	0	3	−4	8	0	−1	1
Makes laugh	median	−13	−3	0	13	3	−1	−3	−1	1
	smooth	−13	−3	0	3	3	−1	−1	−1	1
	residual	0	0	0	10	0	0	−2	0	0

important in light of Axioms 4 and 5 (see Chapter 2). The residual values show how good the fit is compared to the given medians.

The USES ENERGY panel in Figure 9.5 indicates that 81 percent of the teachers were perceived to use an average amount of energy (median = −1) in communicating to the class. The better teachers

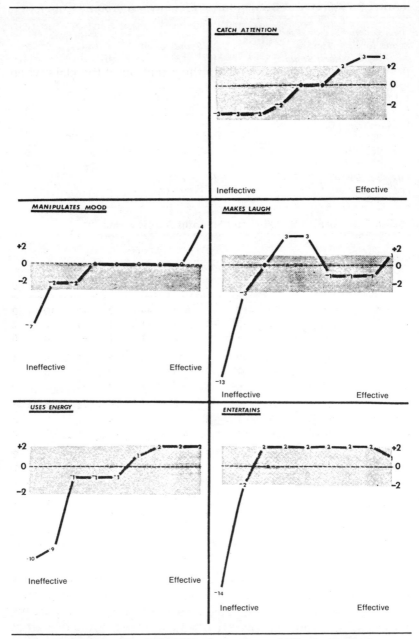

Figure 9.5   Dramatic Behavior Variables Across Range of Effective Teachers

were perceived to use slightly more energy. Only the worst teachers (19 percent) were not perceived to use a lot of energy in communicating to the class.

The CATCH ATTENTION panel shows that most teachers (66 percent) were perceived to catch the attention of the class when they were talking to them (median = −2). However, the better teacher (34 percent) were perceived to be better at catching attention.

The MANIPULATES MOOD panel shows that most teachers (78 percent) were perceived to be about average (median = −0) at manipulating the mood of the class. However, the very worst teachers (9 percent) were not perceived as being good at manipulating the mood of the class. The very best teachers (13 percent) were perceived as being very good at manipulating the mood of the class.

The MAKES LAUGH panel shows that only the worst teachers (9 percent) were not perceived as being able to make the class laugh easily. The remaining teachers were perceived as having average ability or were in the fourth stratum above average ability in ease of making the class laugh. The fourth stratum may be an anomaly in the data.

The ENTERTAINS panel indicates that only the worst teachers (9 percent) were not perceived to be about average in entertaining. *It is not a matter of being highly entertaining, only a matter of being perceived of as about average in entertaining.* That is, most teachers fall within the norm range. They are not "extranormally" entertaining, they are merely within a normal range of being entertaining. Thinking about what constitutes "entertaining" in terms of a norm range deemphasizes the either/or perspective and recognizes the variable for its central tendency.

Discussion

This study indicates that effective teaching relates to specific dramatic behaviors. The structural solution shows that the effective teacher is closely related to the core dramatic style variables. The structure coincides with the expectation that the core variables can be used in a unidimensional way. That is, the person with a high dramatic style score always scores high on three variables: (1) USES ENERGY, (2) CATCHES ATTENTION, and (3) MANIPULATES MOOD.

On the other hand, the dramatic style variables that are not "close neighbors" of the core can function in a multidimensional way. That is, the person with a high dramatic score need not score high on specific dramatic behaviors such as using sarcasm or telling many stories.

Specific dramatic behaviors will prove more useful when intervention is attempted to change the ineffective teacher. The identification of the five communication variables provides a foundation on which to base prescriptive advice for less effective teachers who want help.

Given these findings, the following recommendations should help the ineffective teaching do a better job of teaching:

- **Use more energy when teaching.** The primary problem at this point is operationalizing what constitutes energy. It probably entails being more dynamic, active, open, mentally alert, enthusiastic, and forceful. The dynamic speaker employs vocal variety (emphasis, intonation, rate) and nonverbal variety (gestures) to increase expressiveness.

- **Anticipate how to catch attention.** The genre of communicative behaviors to do this includes use of humor, curiosity, suspense, emotion, analogy, metaphors, surprise, and narratives.

- **Learn how to make a class laugh.** This is not to say that the teacher needs to become a comic or clown. The more important dynamic entails audience analysis. Learning how to make someone laugh requires understanding shared premises. Even if laughter is never evoked, thinking about the problem is useful.

- **Learn what entertains a class.** Again, the advice is not to become an entertainer, but to learn what it would take to entertain the class. It can be easily adapted to any subject matter. A good chemistry teacher can vividly describe the chemical composition of an object, which can be entertaining in its own right.

- **Learn how to manipulate the mood of a class.** The effective teachers know how to do this. It entails many complexities, including a strong sense of timing, a quickness at seeing connections to all sorts of things and processes, and a confidence to try such maneuvering.

CONCLUSION

The studies move toward a sharpened focus both in terms of methodological sophistication and exact conclusions. The findings represent a point where the research provides strong grounds for making practical recommendations. This confidence is reflected by the transition from the tentative suggestions in Study 2 to the exact conclusions in Study 3. The map is better now and new destinations are in sight. The communication scholar is in the ideal position to shed light on improving the quality of teaching.

NOTES

1. This article by Naftulin et al. (1973) has generated an ongoing debate. Some representative articles in this debate include Williams and Ware (1977), Meier and Feldhusen (1979), and Marsh and Ware (1982).

2. Unless the researcher has carefully masked the nature of the study, students easily associate the evaluation variables with the researcher's favorite concepts. It is well documented that the students will help the researcher to find the desired effect. Of course, this "help" aggravates the above problem. Separating the dependent and independent variables improves the study (McCall, 1923; Stanley & Campbell, 1963).

3. Peckham et al. (1969) argue that "the researcher who samples intact classrooms but counts and uses individuals as the units of analysis carries a double burden of assumptions and justifications. Not only must he have sufficient reason to believe that the experimental procedure is free of dependence-producing effects, but he must also produce a rational basis for assuming that the intact classrooms can be considered to be random samples from the same population."

4. Two kinds of smoothing were used with these data. First, interval smoothing was used. The data were ordered on the teacher effectiveness variable, ranging from the most ineffective teacher to the most effective. If the predictor variables are linearly related, then as the teacher effectiveness variable increases, the related variables will increase. Also, as indicated above, the overall slope will be relatively near 1.0.

After the data were ordered, they were divided into "chunks" (intervals) of three. Since there were 23 cases, the last chunk/interval had only two cases. For each interval, the median was recorded. Sometimes the medians would vary slightly, depending upon at which end the intervals of three began. In the cases in which such a discrepancy occurred, two sets of medians were generated by beginning the intervals at the respective ends. Then the average value between the two sets was recorded.

The second kind of smoothing was done on the sets of eight medians from the interval smoothing. The second kind of smoothing (described extensively in Tukey, 1977) is called "running medians of 3." What is important to know here is that minor variances in the data are disregarded and replaced by the most moderate value around an identified variation. In effect, the loss is that the researcher throws away some data, but the gain is that any strong, underlying pattern or trend embedded in the data becomes less obscure (Tukey, 1977; also see Mosteller & Tukey, 1977).

IV

OVERVIEW

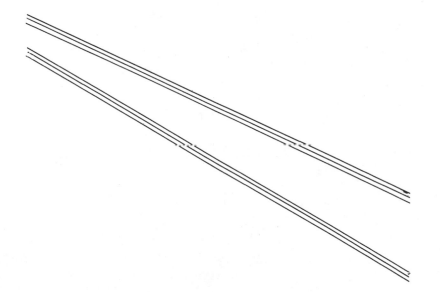

10 / Dialectic Invitations

implications for future study

In review, Chapter 1-3 provided the theoretical statement for communicator style construct. It centers on two senses of style — a micro focus and a macro focus. The micro sense defines style in terms of its form-giving function. The macro sense presents style as the cumulative pattern of form-giving associations that are recurring and consistent. The second three chapters traced the development of three subconstructs in the communicator style domain — (1) open style, (2) dramatic style, and (3) attentive style. The final three chapters pointed to three specific applications of style relating to perception, attraction, and teaching.

This overview does two things. First, it points to natural extensions of the work presented in this book. As such, these are directions in which the style work must go in order to be viable. Second, it briefly discusses ten recurrent issues that should be addressed when doing style research.

NATURAL EXTENSIONS

Form-Giving Function

The fundamental commitment of this book is that the communicative act is a multiplex — that is, two or more signals or messages are transmitted such that content always functions at least at a primary message level and style as a message system informs how to understand, interpret, take, or filter the primary message.

However, more work must be done on the form-giving function of style. This means examining style in the micro sense outlined in Chapter 1, where **the initial claims are that style gives form to content and the form it gives is motivated.** Because the center of style theory is the form-giving function, these notions need further dialogue:

- **In what sense does style make motivated distinctions?**

- **Can motivation always be established?**

The form-giving function serves the style researcher well because it forces the identification of essential elements that define and, as such, carry a persuasive impact.

For example, the dramatic style subconstruct can be overwhelming because there are an extraordinary number of specific ways to exhibit it. Where does one stop in enumerating the complex and many ways of communicating dramatically? How is this subconstruct anchored? What is its essence? The answer is grounded in the form-giving functions of dramatic style.

Even though there are many ways to manifest a dramatic style, ranging from the quiet to the loud, the subtle to the blatant, or the simple to the complex, the elements of commonality across all ways of communicating dramatically provide the anchor for the subconstruct. **The elements of commonality are the form-giving functions of dramatic style** discussed in Chapter 5.

Essentially, the dramatic style always entails the following motivated distinctions: (1) mood is manipulated, (2) attention is demanded, and (3) energy is changed. This applies to telling bad puns, dirty jokes, clever witticisms, acting out a message, insulting, telling a story, and so on. The elements of commonality apply across all forms of dramatic style.

This does not mean that mood will always be manipulated, attention established, or energy changed. For example, a person who is going through an extensive period of bereavement may not be susceptible to such attempts. Also, the person who dramatizes may be inept at it. Mood may not be changed because of inappropriateness or ineptness. Nevertheless, the mood manipulation was attempted.

In like manner, **each subconstruct should be represented so that the form-giving function is identified, because it provides the pragmatic connection in communication.** The form-giving **function relates how to take the content in the message gestalt, which, in turn, has the capacity to affect relationships between people.** This style element is "relational" by indicating how literal meaning should be taken, interpreted, filtered, or understood. **Identification of the elements of commonality for the style behavior is the necessary and sufficient condition for understanding the respective subconstruct.** In this book, several ways were used to do this. Stipulative definitions were used primarily. Also, a mapping sentence was useful. Finally, definitions emerged from the literature or were stimulated by analyzing the data sets.

For the three subconstructs discussed in this book, the following form-giving functions were established:

- *Open style* signals that the message is personal, private, unambiguous, and explanatory. The way the person "openly" communicates indicates that the message should be taken, filtered, or understood to be representational of the self and isomorphic with what the self knows the self to be.

- *Dramatic style* vividly, emotionally, or strikingly signals that literal meaning is being highlighted, emphasized, or altered to manipulate mood, demand attention, and change energy.

- *Attentive style* signals an ongoing willingness to provide feedback that the person's messages are being processed in an alert and/or understanding manner to show that listening is done and to coordinate interaction.

The reader can see why the definitions not only identify core elements, but also entail persuasive elements. The defining elements commit the style researcher to both theoretic perspectives and pragmatic consequences.

NONVERBAL COMMUNICATION

Accordingly, the form-giving function of style may be an organizing paridigm for much of the nonverbal research. Much of the nonverbal work is presented atheoretically. Nonverbal studies are voluminous, but often fragmented. For instance, studies about the face are broken down into eye, mouth, and whole face behavior. The units of analysis often are too small to be pragmatically useful.

Three questions might guide the organization of nonverbal studies:

- How are particular patterns of nonverbal messages form giving?
- What form-giving functions do the patterns provide?
- Are there multiple patterns of nonverbal communication that result in the same form-giving function?

Every subconstruct has accompanying patterns of nonverbal messages. A relaxed style can be signaled partially through eye behavior. A dominant, dramatic, open, and friendly style can also be signaled partially through eye behavior. Future studies will focus on the sets of nonverbal behavior that influence or even determine the respective style multiplex.

For example, many sets of nonverbal behavior contribute to a perceived dominant style. There is no single set of invariant, nonverbal behaviors to trigger this perception. Some sets of nonverbal behaviors may be more parsimonious in establishing perceived dominance than others. This is a researchable question.

OTHER MEDIATING VARIABLES

Only careful work will establish the form-giving impact of style because there are so many ways to frame a message, including time, contextual, and situational considerations. Also, the mutual history between interactants impinges powerfully on any processing. This is the macro sense of style established in Chapter 2. So, what may seem to be a behavior that is not very dramatic for a white-collar group may, in fact, represent extraordinary drama for a lumberjack crew. That is, all the peers in the latter context may testify that a particular person is unusually dramatic, but people outside the context may perceive the opposite.

All these elements interpenetrate the communicative act, sometimes idiosyncratically so that a dispassionate observer or a trained experimenter cannot see it. Sometimes the influence is pervasive. For example, certain comedians cannot stop being "on"; they cannot resist going for the laugh.

The form-giving function is not invariant across interactants. But it may be invariant enough between interactants such that the interactants know when deviation has occurred. A person's being loud and boisterous may seem extraordinary to the researcher, but may seem normal to a close friend of that person. It is for this reason that large samples of behaviors need to be studied so that researchers may feel relatively confident about a particular pattern of style that gives form to messages.

The unit of analysis does not have to be so microscopic that tons of useless information are generated. In natural minute-to-minute interactions, every behavior is not noticed with a high amount of attention. Rather, selective "chucks" of stylistic information are processed.

In like manner, the researcher will gain by processing and coding selective chucks of data. For example, in coding a 30-minute audiovisual tape, a reasonable procedure might be to code the overall stylistic impact over 3-minute periods, rather than to track every twitch, nonverbal adjustment, and so on.

Extensions of the Macro Sense of Style

There is also much work to do with the macro sense of style. The general direction that the macro sense of style will be taken will be to identify optimal style patterns versus dysfunctional style patterns across varieties of contexts, situations, and times. The following list highlights viable areas for extensions:

- *Law:* The way a lawyer communicates probably affects the verdict. I was recently struck with this thought after serving jury duty. Either lawyer had a chance not only to enhance his ethos, but also to shape the way we processed the messages from the opposing lawyer.

- *Education:* The way a teacher communicates affects both learning processes and critical attitudes about the subject matter and the instructor (see Chapter 9).

- *Organizations:* The way people are managed within a hierarchical organization directly determines specific attitudes and may relate to productivity. The confidence in the chain of command in the Russian army is as important a military factor as nuclear capacity. The way messages are communicated are pertinent at every level of any organization.

- *Therapy:* The therapist has the capacity to change a person qualitatively with words and the way they are communicated. Milton Erickson is my favorite exemplar here.

- *Medicine:* Healing entails more than chemical or surgical intervention. "Bedside manner," which centers around style elements, is a potent factor in the process.

- *Marriage:* The way a spouse communicates often is more important than the specific content. Style maintains, controls, and reflects the quality of a marriage.

- *Politics:* The look-alike politicians frequently are distinguished on stylistic impressions rather than on political issues.

- *Mass communication:* The interaction of a medium such as television with a particular style of communication affects success. Johnny Carson, for example, has a style compatible with television that has eluded other talk-show hosts.

Among other consequences, recurring style associations may predict attraction, health, status, power, wealth, and development.

RECURRING ISSUES

The following sections mark areas of advice or debatable points that recur in style work. The arguments below are not meant to be definitive answers, but points of departure for those interested in the dialectic. A dozen areas are briefly discussed.

The Meta Function

The issue of linear combinations versus interactional combinations (in the sense of having a message about a message) is somewhat a moot point. The claim that style serves a meta function — that it frames content — is a stipulative move. **There is no objective reality demonstrating that style frames content.** Everything said about style in this book could be treated as a linear message rather than as a meta message.

For example, if I said, "Shut the door," and said it with anger, the communication researcher can treat the unit of analysis in the following way:

Unit of Analysis = ("Shut the door" + emotion of anger)

In other words, the researcher can construct linear units devoid of any need to discuss "meta" messages. There is nothing inherently wrong with this approach.

In fact, Bales's (1970) extraordinary work opts for units of analysis that do not entail metamessages. He classifies interactions using a 12-category system, as illustrated in Figure 10.1.

Bales (1970, p. 92) says that "the interaction categories do not classify *what* is said, that is the content of the message, but rather *how* the persons communicate, that is, *who does what to whom in*

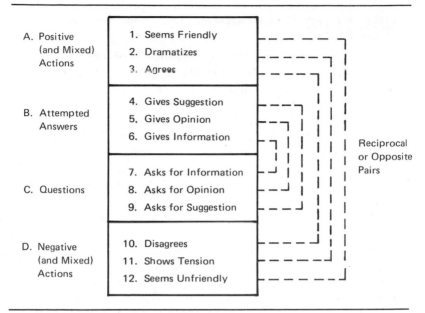

Figure 10.1   Bales's Interaction Process Analysis

the process (time order) of their interaction." So the function of communication is coded — the function of content or the function of how it is said.

Bales maintains that the norm use of each category can be established. For example, he claims that Category 8, asks for opinion, is used about 2 percent of the time by group interactants. This is the summary statistic across 21 different studies using the original IPA system.

The system works well if the researcher conscientiously attends to the coding procedures for each category. I used it in my dissertation examining verbal manifestations of ambiguity tolerance in small groups. One reason that it works is that Bales provides four priority rules so that each interaction can be scored in one and only one category. The rules include the following:

(1) Give priority to a scoring in the dramatizes or shows tension category over a scoring in any other category.

(2) Give priority to a scoring in the seems friendly or seems unfriendly category if an element of interpersonal feeling is present.

(3) Give priority to a scoring in the gives suggestion or asks for suggestion category over a scoring in the gives opinion category.

(4) After an initial act of disagreement or agreement, the scoring reverts to the neutral categories based upon the interaction form of the act.

Bales (1970, p. 135) says "The general effect of these rules is to divert the classification of acts that tend to be most frequent, in the form of giving opinion and information, into less frequently used categories which depend upon more subtle cues and are of greater diagnostic interest." What I sense with the priority rules and his disclaimer is dissatisfaction with the system. The priority rules are designed to recover more emotionally oriented elements. Thus the statement "Shut the door," said with anger, would not be scored in the "gives suggestion" category, but in the "shows tension" category or even the "seems unfriendly" category. Bales wants to recover the way the content was said more than the function of the content.

With his IPA system we have an example of a researcher forcing the units of analysis into a system devoid of metaorientations but, nevertheless, reflecting a yearning to recover metaorientations. A simple restructuring of Bales's system into a model that allows a meta perspective makes the system less cumbersome. For example, consider essentially the same system oriented via content and style functions still using his categories. It might look like the illustration in Figure 10.2.

The advantage of stipulating a meta component is one of parsimony. The phrase "Shut the door," said with anger, can be uniquely categorized without resorting to priority rules. The "gives suggestion" character of the message is not lost. It should make a difference if a pattern of tension was created through constant suggestions versus constant opinion — "Shut the door!" versus "I think it would be a good idea to shut the door." Furthermore, the metaorientation allows less reductionist analyses. The researcher can track both style and content contributions by examining the respective marginals.

Sampling Error

Sampling error discourages many novice social science researchers. Typically, the researcher uses a self-report measure asking the individual to assess general, central tendencies about the self. The researcher assumes that the respondent will be frank, honest, and disclosing. In addition, it is assumed that the respon-

| | STYLE-ORIENTED CATEGORIES | | |
	Seems Friendly/ Seems Unfriendly	Dramatizes/ Shows Tension	Agrees/ Disagrees
Gives Suggestion		"Shut the door"	
Gives Opinion			
Gives Information			
Asks for Information			
Asks for Opinion			
Asks for Suggestion			

CONTENT-ORIENTED CATEGORIES

NOTE: Use positive and negative signs to indicate which reciprocal category is used. Also, note that the Agrees/Disagrees category is not a direct fit for a style component.

Figure 10.2   Revised IPA System Reflecting Both Style and Content Components

dent knows the behavior and is capable of self-monitoring it. From the self-report measure, the respondent is then classified according to the relative score. Often the researcher is excited at this point because a sample of people have been neatly classified.

The next step frequently reduces the excitement because the researcher takes the classified respondents and either puts them in a situation to track behaviors or asks others to assess them. The initial hope is that the self-report score will match the manifested behavior or the other assessment. More often than not the scores do not match, causing the researcher to indict the self-report measure.

However, it is not surprising that the self-report measure that asks the person to generalize a wide range of behaviors or attitudes does not match either a single set of observed behaviors or a single set of other assessments. The researcher is making a sampling error. A "sliver" of all behaviors or possible other assessments is being used to represent a vast and complicated population of behaviors or attitudes.

If the researcher wants to use the Dramatic Style Measure to predict whether an individual will be dramatic in a structured laboratory experiment on self-disclosure or will be dramatic during a one-time, taped visit to the person's work space or will be dramatic during an artificial conversation about capital punishment with a stranger, then the researcher very likely will be disappointed.

If the researcher is serious about using the Dramatic Style Measure to see whether it matches behavior, then **a representative sample of behaviors from all the possible behaviors in the person's life should be taken.** Is the person dramatic over time across situations? Of course, this kind of research is expensive in terms of time, energy, and money.

Range of Norm Behavior

Chapter 2 reminds the researcher to focus on a **range of norm behavior.** The macrojudgment comes from consistently recurring associations. So, simply reporting a mean score on a style component can mislead; it not only reifies a mean score, but obscures the notion that the parameters surrounding the mean score can be critical.

It is not enough, for example, to say that teachers who fall into the most effective stratum obtain better dramatic style scores than the teachers who fall into the next most effective stratum. What is important is whether the first set of teachers obtains a dramatic score significantly beyond some range of the norm dramatic style behavior. Figure 9.5 (Chapter 9) illustrates the point. Dramatic style behaviors across strata ranging from ineffective to effective teachers use a range of norm behavior to anchor the referent point.

Multiplex

Each style element contributes to a multiplex. A person manifests all style components simultaneously, assuming that the respective variables are measured on some continuum. So, a style profile entails multiple indications of a person's score for each variable. Most often the person manifests style behaviors within the range of norm behavior for the respective context, situation, and time. The person, for instance, may exhibit the average range of being attentive, friendly, open, dramatic, relaxed, and so on.

Thinking of style patterns in terms of a multiplex is important because the form of a message gestalt may have been determined by an interaction between two or more style variables. An ineffective teacher may use as much sarcasm in teaching as an effective teacher, but the latter teacher may mediate the sarcasm by defusing it almost immediately with a style signal that reframes the "bite" of the sarcasm.

Future style research will increasingly attend to the style multiplex because it does critical, complex, communicative work. It is for this reason that Postulates 1, 2, 3, and 4 (Chapter 1) are important to style theory.

Factor Analysis

Do not factor analyze the communicator style construct unless a compelling rationale can be provided. Factor analysis by the nature of the algorithm places as many variables on one dimension as it can. As such, it tends to "brutalize" the data structure.[1]

If the researcher needs to convince an editor or a dissertation committee of the structural soundness of the communicator style domain, then use some form of structural analysis compatible with the original report (Chapter 3). For example, smallest space analysis provides a comparison in which the original structure can be used as the target structure and the new structure can be compared to it. Programs that confirm configurations are useful here.

Additivity

The subconstructs are not additive. It does not make sense to add the respective scores from the style components to obtain an overall communicator style score. If the researcher needs to add something, he or she should add only the scores that are strongly correlated with one another, such as the animated and dramatic scores. The scores should be standardized before adding them together. Even with close associations between subconstructs, the researcher should be careful because important nuances may disappear in a combined set of scores.

This is not to say that a discriminant equation could not be generated in which discriminant weights from different style components are added to classify subjects. In fact, this procedure was used to predict sex differences using the style components (Tukey, 1977).

Linearity

Work has not been done to demonstrate this, but it is reasonable to assume that the style components do not function in an entirely linear way. For example, if dominant is being studied to see how it covaries with being a good communicator, it is easy to imagine a person being too dominant. The relationship may look like the illustration in Figure 10.3.

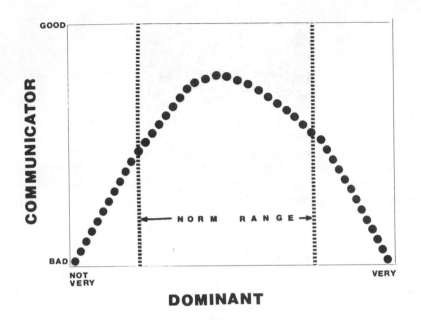

Figure 10.3   Potential Relationship Between the Amount of Dominant Style and the
Quality of the Communicator

If some type of curvilinearity can be associated with the respective style components, this information can be useful in identifying the boundaries where the style behaviors become dysfunctional or extranormal.

Distribution

The issue of distribution is inextricable from the issue of linearity. The distribution of style scores needs to be monitored constantly. In fact, this should automatically be one of the first steps of the style researchers. The style components may not be normally distributed.

For example, the distribution of the attentive style scores tend to logarithmic — that is, most people will indicate that they manifest attentiveness, a socially desirable behavior. In this book, the scores were converted to z scores, thus forcing a normal distribution. In future work, however, two approaches should be considered. First, an optimally useful transformation for nonnormal distributions (Montgomery & Norton, 1981) should be identified. Tukey is a good guide here. Second, increasingly sophisticated psychometric strategies should be developed to obtain a reasonably normal distribution. Both approaches get at the same problem.

Context, Time, and Situation

Clearly, style parameters are mediated by context, situation, and time, as mentioned above. In fact, this is such a strong given that it can be treated and stated as the following axiom:

Axiom 11:   Context, situation, and time always mediate
                    style parameters.

This makes style work interesting. Researchable questions can always be asked along these lines:

- How does a particular context impinge upon style patterns?
- What kind of situation significantly changes the expected style patterns?
- How does time affect style patterns?

The last question is especially important to social scientists focusing on developmental issues.

A long-term model may eventually include context, time, and situation variables as part of a predictor equation along with the appropriate interaction effects. As for now, even though the larger picture is alluring, style research is in the state of taking relatively small steps. Any one study may not be impressive in itself, but the cumulative knowledge will be.

Triangulating Information

Naive researchers often administer a self-report test, obtain one sample of behavioral or attitudinal data, and then indict one or the other sets of data (usually the self-report data) as inadequate. The fallacy is that they have no standard to compare the data sets. Why should the behavioral or attitudinal set be held up as the criterion to invalidate the self-report set or vice versa? **Just because one is different from the other does not mean that one is incorrect.**

It is for this reason that the two data sets need to be compared against some reasonably determined criterion set. Even the criterion set is not inviolately objective — it never can be wholly objective. Nevertheless, a criterion set can be established by a reasonably good rhetorical argument.

For example, people may testify that they have a "good" marriage via self-report instruments such as the Partner Communication Scale, or a set of behaviors may be observed to obtain data about a "good" marriage such as how the couple fight in front of television cameras. These two data sets may not show the same thing. This does not mean that one of the data sets is superior. If this is the researcher's concern — that is, finding out which data set is superior — he or she must compare both data sets to a criterion set, such as the number of eventual divorces among the sample. It is probable that either the self-report or the behavioral observations will be the best predictors. At this point, the researcher has some evidence that one data set is inferior in terms of the stipulated dependent variable.

Monitoring Ability

People often respond to questions without understanding what the question is asking. It is easy to get responses on a seven-point scale to a question such as "Are you a Machiavellian?" If the person cannot or does not monitor the self's behavior, then the researcher obtains poor data that may even have high internal reliability.

The Communicator Style Measure is also vulnerable. It is for this reason that the CSM does not simply ask the respondent whether he or she is contentious. A lot of respondents would not have a good idea what was meant. Rather, the contentious subconstruct is a hybrid notion that is generated by adding scores from five highly interrelated, less obtuse items. Each item is at a lower level of abstraction than suggested by the nominal label attached to the hybrid construct. The lower level of abstraction was chosen because it is relatively easy to monitor the behavior in which one is interested.

So, for the contentious construct, the person is asked about how argumentative the self is, how easy it is to disengage in an argument once it is started, and how quick a person jumps into a discussion to disagree. Then, based on the average standardized score from each of these items, the person is assigned a contentiousness score.

For this reason, the long form (Appendix B) of the CSM provides the most information to the style researcher using these instruments. Work is still being done to discover the degree of self-monitoring a person does in communicating. Several possibilities are open. First, the person may be aware of the self's communicator style such that the self-reports will be accurate. Third, the person may be oblivious to the way he or she communicates. In addition, only parts of each possibility may be true. The person, for instance, may be aware of the self's friendly style, but oblivious to the self's dramatic style.

Nuances

Finally, I take the liberty of closing with the following dialogue inspired by feedback from a friend. The names are hypothetical:

Knapp:	Rightly or wrongly, I got the impression that dominant style reflects the notion of seeking dominance — i.e., striving, overpowering, etc.
Norton:	Rightly.
Knapp:	Once one has the attribution of dominance or power, then the manifestation of that dominance (maintaining it) takes on dual characteristics: (1) behaviors that reflect those used to obtain dominance when dominance is threatened or (2) perhaps used every now and then just to remind people what it could be like.
Norton:	Postulate 6.
Knapp:	I guess that it is kinda like training a dog. First you yell at it, spank it, hold it in place, burn it with cigarettes, etc., but when the dog treats you as if you are the "master," then you become very different — issuing commands with the flick of an ash, forgiving minor mistakes, even showing affection on occasions.
Norton:	Postulate 6

SUMMARY

This book marks a beginning. As such it represents a first map with the accompanying weaknesses. But it also has the important strength that it provides the basis for better maps in the future. The use of the axiomatic structure to present this initial theoretical statement offers only a convenient point of departure; it forces the articulation of hierarchical relationships. Other theoretical structures may be just as viable.

Future work should include the development of various subconstructs in the style domain and refinement of the theoretical foundation, as well as an increased focus on applications. Unless style work is grounded in pragmatic endeavors, it strikes me as merely a distracting academic exercise. **Style work should "touch the flesh," or at least hold forth the promise that it can lead to positive change in the quality of people's lives.**

NOTE

1. I agree with Guttman's (1982) critique when he says that (1) factor analysis is a specialized case of smallest space analysis; (2) factor analysis often requires greater dimensionality than smallest space analysis; (3) factor analysis depends upon "tampering" with commonalities to achieve small dimensionality; (4) factor analysis requires the input of product-moment coefficients; (5) factor analysis does not highlight regionality in a space, even when it exists; and (6) the factor-analytic scoring problem "is plagued by interminacy of the relation of the desired score space to the calculated space for variables."

APPENDIX A:

THEORETICAL SUMMARY

The following assumptions, definitions, axioms, and postulates[1] have been introduced in this book. They are ordered here as they appeared.

Communicator style is broadly conceived to mean "the way one verbally, nonverbally, and paraverbally interacts to signal how literal meaning should be taken, interpreted, filtered, or understood."

Definition 1:	A message system provides information. (Chapter 1)
Definition 2:	A communication "gestalt" is the interaction of information from the respective message systems. (Chapter 1)
Assumption 1:	There can be no distinction without motive. (Chapter 1)
Assumption 2:	There can be no motive unless contents are seen to differ in value. (Chapter 1)
Axiom 1:	Any message system can draw a distinction either by literal meaning or by stylistic means. (Chapter 1)
Axiom 2:	One message system gives form to another when the literal meaning of one system is reinforced or changed. (Chapter 1)
Axiom 3:	Form-giving messages can be antecedent to, simultaneous with, or subsequent to another message. (Chapter 1)
Postulate 1:	Stylistic components function with a hierarchical impact. (Chapter 1)
Postulate 2:	Whenever a gestalt is ambiguous, one style component in the hierarchy moves more to the center of attention and is valued more. (Chapter 1)

Postulate 3:   Whenever the gestalt deviates from normal expectations (it is surprising), one style component in the hierarchy probably commands more attention and operates with greater leverage. (Chapter 1)

Postulate 4:   An ambiguous gestalt motivates the receiver to interactively and inferentially supply premises that alleviate ambiguity. (Chapter 1)

Definition 3:   A consistently recurring pattern occurs when any set of behaviors is likely to occur again within a predictable time period. (Chapter 2)

Axiom 4:   A consistently recurring pattern gives form to an interaction by creating anticipations or expectations about the way one communicates. (Chapter 2)

Axiom 5:   A consistently recurring pattern of style behaviors depends upon enough behaviors to establish at least one norm. (Chapter 2)

Axiom 6:   Style in the sense of consistently recurring associations manifests itself only as the function of a central tendency or a deviation from the central tendency. (Chapter 2)

Postulate 5:   Expectations about consistently recurring patterns in style become increasingly stable as a function of associating with the communicator. (Chapter 2)

Postulate 6:   Style expectations can influence the literal message more powerfully than the immediate style exhibited. (Chapter 2)

Postulate 7:   If the style expectations are different for various receivers, then the immediate style that is exhibited can be differentially interpreted by the various interactants. (Chapter 2)

Axiom 7:   The content component establishes the parameters of the referents in the self-disclosing process. (Chapter 4)

Definition 4:   Qualitative information about the self is information that is representational of the self. That is, it is information about the self that is isomorphic with what the self knows the self to be. It is information that indicates that the self is what the self appears to be. (Chapter 4)

Definition 5:   A message is risky if the self becomes vulnerable to another person because of it. (Chapter 4)

Postulate 8:	Personal, private, unambiguous, and explanatory information has the greatest potential to be risky. (Chapter 4)
Axiom 8:	Open style signals that the message is personal, private, unambiguous, and explanatory. The way the person "openly" communicates indicates that the message should be taken, filtered, or understood to be representational of the self and isomorphic with what the self knows the self to be. (Chapter 4)
Definition 6:	Open style signals that qualitative information about the self is available. (Chapter 4)
Postulate 9:	As open style is increasingly signaled, interpersonal options increase. (Chapter 4)
Definition 7:	Dramatic style vividly, emotionally, or strikingly signals that literal meaning is being highlighted, emphasized, or altered. (Chapter 5)
Axiom 9:	Dramatic style signals a deviation from some norm. (Chapter 5)
Postulate 10:	Dramatic style either manipulates tension or is manifested as a result of tension. (Chapter 5)
Axiom 10:	Attentive style signals an ongoing willingness to provide feedback that the person's messages are being processed in an alert and/or understanding manner. (Chapter 6)
Postulate 11:	Attentiveness manifested through various kinds and degrees of feedback, regulates a speaker's speech as it is happening. (Chapter 6)
Axiom 11:	Content, situation, and time always mediate style parameters. (Chapter 10)

In summary, style is used in two senses — a micro sense and a macro sense. **The accumulation of "microbehaviors" gives form to literal content, adding up to a "macrojudgment" about a person's communicator style.**

NOTE

1. In general, assumptions and definitions are given or stipulated. As such, empirical evidence cannot be provided. Reasonableness is the criterion. Axioms also do not depend upon empirical evidence; they connect notions and operate almost at the level of truisms. However, empirical evidence can be used to establish or refute postulates that are testable.

APPENDIX B:

STYLE MEASURES

COMMUNICATOR STYLE MEASURE

You have impressions of yourself as a communicator. The impressions include your sense of the way you communicate. This measure focuses upon your sensitivity to the way you communicate or what is called your communicator style.

The question are not designed to look at *what* is communicated; rather, they explore the way you communicate.

Because there is no such thing as a "correct" style of communication, none of the following items have right or wrong answers.

Please do not spend too much time on the items. Let your first inclination be your guide. Try to answer to answer as honestly as possible. All responses will be strictly confidential.

Some questions will be difficult to answer because you honestly do not know. For these questions, however, please try to determine *which way you are leaning* and answer in the appropriate direction.

The following scale is used for each item:

YES! = strong agreement with the statement
  yes = agreement with the statement
    ? = neither agreement nor disagreement with the statement
   no = disagreement with the statement
 NO! = strong disagreement with the statement

For example, if you agree with the following statement, "I dislike the coldness of winter," then you would circle the "Yes" as indicated:

NO!   no   ?   (yes)   YES!

Some of the items will be similarly stated. But each item has a slightly different orientation. Try to answer each question as though it were the *only* question being asked.

Finally, answer each item as it relates to a *general face-to-face* communication situation—namely, the type of communicator you are most often.

If you want feedback about this measure and your particular profile, print your name below. Think you for helping out.

NAME _____

I am comfortable with all varieties of people.	NO!	no	?	yes	YES!	1
I laugh easily.	NO!	no	?	yes	YES!	2
I readily express admiration for others.	NO!	no	?	yes	YES!	3
What I say *usually* leaves an impression on people.	NO!	no	?	yes	YES!	4
I leave people with an impression of me which they definitely tend to remember.	NO!	no	?	yes	YES!	5
To be friendly, I habitually acknowledge verbally other's contributions.	NO!	no	?	yes	YES!	6
I am a *very* good communicator.	NO!	no	?	yes	YES!	7
I have some nervous mannerisms in my speech.	NO!	no	?	yes	YES!	8
I am a very relaxed communicator.	NO!	no	?	yes	YES!	9
When I disagree with somebody I am very quick to challenge them.	NO!	no	?	yes	YES!	10
I can always repeat back to a person *exactly* what was meant.	NO!	no	?	yes	YES!	11
The sound of my voice is *very easy* to recognize.	NO!	no	?	yes	YES!	12
I am a very precise communicator.	NO!	no	?	yes	YES!	13
I leave a *definite* impression on people.	NO!	no	?	yes	YES!	14
The rhythm or flow of my speech is sometimes affected by my nervousness.	NO!	no	?	yes	YES!	15
Under pressure I come across as a relaxed speaker.	NO!	no	?	yes	YES!	16
My eyes reflect *exactly* what I am feeling when I communicate	NO!	no	?	yes	YES!	17
I dramatize a lot.	NO!	no	?	yes	YES!	18
I always find it *very easy* to communicate on a one-to-one basis with strangers.	NO!	no	?	yes	YES!	19
Usually, I *deliberately react* in such a way that people *know* that I am listening to them.	NO!	no	?	yes	YES!	20

Usually I do not tell people much about myself until I get to know them well.	NO!	no	?	yes	YES!	21
Regularly I tell jokes, anecdotes and stories when I communicate.	NO!	no	?	yes	YES!	22
I tend to *constantly* gesture when I communicate.	NO!	no	?	yes	YES!	23
I am an *extremely* open communicator.	NO!	no	?	yes	YES!	24
I am vocally a loud communicator.	NO!	no	?	yes	YES!	25
In a small group of strangers I am a *very good* communicator.	NO!	no	?	yes	YES!	26
In arguments I insist upon very precise definitions.	NO!	no	?	yes	YES!	27
In most social situations I generally speak very frequently.	NO!	no	?	yes	YES!	28
I find it extremely easy to maintain a conversation with a member of the opposite sex *whom I have just met.*	NO!	no	?	yes	YES!	29
I like to be strictly accurate when I communicate.	NO!	no	?	yes	YES!	30
Because I have a loud voice I can easily break into a conversation.	NO!	no	?	yes	YES!	31
Often I physically and vocally act out what I want to communicate.	NO!	no	?	yes	YES!	32
I have an assertive voice.	NO!	no	?	yes	YES!	33
I readily reveal personal things about myself.	NO!	no	?	yes	YES!	34
I am dominant in social situations.	NO!	no	?	yes	YES!	35
I am very argumentative.	NO!	no	?	yes	YES!	36
Once I get wound up in a heated discussion I have a hard time stopping myself.	NO!	no	?	yes	YES!	37
I am always an *extremely* friendly communicator.	NO!	no	?	yes	YES!	38

| I really *like* to listen very carefully to people. | NO! | no | ? | yes | YES! | 39 |

I really *like* to listen
very carefully to people.   NO!   no   ?   yes   YES!   39

Very often I insist that other
people document or present
some kind of proof for what
they are arguing.   NO!   no   ?   yes   YES!   40

I try to take charge of things
when I am with people.   NO!   no   ?   yes   YES!   41

It bothers me to drop an
argument that is not resolved.   NO!   no   ?   yes   YES!   42

In most social situations I tend
to come on strong.   NO!   no   ?   yes   YES!   43

I am very expressive nonverbally
in social situations.   NO!   no   ?   yes   YES!   44

The *way* I say something
usually leaves an impression
on people.   NO!   no   ?   yes   YES!   45

Whenever I communicate, I
tend to ve very encouraging
to people.   NO!   no   ?   yes   YES!   46

I actively use *a lot* of facial
expressions when I communicate.   NO!   no   ?   yes   YES!   47

I *very frequently* verbally
exaggerate to emphasize a
point.   NO!   no   ?   yes   YES!   48

I am an *extremely attentive*
communicator.   NO!   no   ?   yes   YES!   49

As a rule, I openly express my
feelings and emotions.   NO!   no   ?   yes   YES!   50

Out of a random group of six people, including myself, I would probably have a better communicator style than (circle one choice)

| 5 of them | 4 of them | 3 of them | 2 of them | 1 of them | None of them | 51 |

KEY TO SCORING THE
COMMUNICATOR STYLE INSTRUMENT

1. Only 45 items are scored. Ten subconstructs with four items per subconstruct can be treated as independent variables. One subconstruct, communicator image, can be treated as a a dependent variable. Items 1, 2, 12, 25, 31, and 33 are filler items and should be ignored.

2. It is advisable, although not necessary, to convert all scores for the respective items to z scores and then average them for the subconstruct.

3. Use the following weights for the responses: YES! = 5; yes = 4; ? = 3; no = 2; NO! = 1.

4. Be sure to attend to missing data. It can be treated several ways depending upon the reasonable argument. One way would be to substitute the mean score for the respective item for the missing value. A second way would be to replace the missing value with 3, the expected mean. The former option is advised.

5. Before averaging the items, **reverse** the score where indicated in the key. If the person got a 5 for that item, give it a 1. If a person got a 4 for that item, give it a 2. If a person got a 2 for that item, give it a 4. If a person got a 1 for that item, give it a 5. The items that should be reversed are indicated by R.

Friendly	3	6	38	46	
Impression Leaving	4	5	14	45	
Relaxed	8R	9	15R	16	
Contentious/Argumentative	10	36	37	42	
Attentive	11	20	39	49	
Precise	13	27	30	40	
Animated/Expressive	17	23	44	47	
Dramatic	18	22	32	48	
Open	21R	24	34	50	
Dominant	28	35	41	43	
Communicator Image	7	19	26	29	51

DRAMATIC COMMUNICATOR STYLE

There are many kinds of dramatic styles of communicating. There is no such thing as a good dramatic style or a bad dramatic style—there are only different styles.

Of course, the way you show your style varies greatly. The various *dramatic styles* are hard to identify. The questions below concern different components of the dramatic styles. Many of the questions are similar but get at slightly different aspects. Please read each item carefully and try to answer it as honestly as possible.

Use the following guide for the items:

YES! = *strong* agreement with the statement
yes = agreement with the statement
? = neither agree nor disagree with the statement
no = disagreement with the statement
NO! = *strong* disagreement with the statement

For example, if you agree with the following statement, you should circle yes.

Winters are too cold.	NO!	no	?	(yes)	YES!

I am a perfectionist.	NO!	no	?	yes	YES!	1
I get along with all kinds of people.	NO!	no	?	yes	YES!	2
I am very good at making puns.	NO!	no	?	yes	YES!	3
I know how to build tension when I am telling a story.	NO!	no	?	yes	YES!	4
I am very witty.	NO!	no	?	yes	YES!	5
I often poke fun at people.	NO!	no	?	yes	YES!	6
I am a good performer.	NO!	no	?	yes	YES!	7
I am very fast *in reacting* to what others say.	NO!	no	?	yes	YES!	8
Sometimes I swear to create an effect.	NO!	no	?	yes	YES!	9
Often I deliberately use my laughter to create a dramatic effect.	NO!	no	?	yes	YES!	10
Very frequently I gently tease my friends.	NO!	no	?	yes	YES!	11
I think of myself as entertaining.	NO!	no	?	yes	YES!	12
I am a dramatic communicator.	NO!	no	?	yes	YES!	13
It is easy for me to make a large group of strangers laugh.	NO!	no	?	yes	YES!	14
I often use gossip to keep people entertained.	NO!	no	?	yes	YES!	15
I frequently tell jokes to people.	NO!	no	?	yes	YES!	16
I dramatize a lot.	NO!	no	?	yes	YES!	17
Often I verbally clown around.	NO!	no	?	yes	YES!	18

I am *conscious of deliberately* using my laughter for an effect.	NO!	no	?	yes	YES!	19
I know how to mimic people.	NO!	no	?	yes	YES!	20
I can easily insult a person if I wanted to.	NO!	no	?	yes	YES!	21
I know how to tell a good story.	NO!	no	?	yes	YES!	22
My speech tends to be very picturesque.	NO!	no	?	yes	YES!	23
Sometimes I deliberately pretend to be embarrassed to create an effect.	NO!	no	?	yes	YES!	24
When I am excited about something, I know how to get others excited also.	NO!	no	?	yes	YES!	25
I am very humorous.	NO!	no	?	yes	YES!	26
Sometimes I act out a communication physically as well as vocally.	NO!	no	?	yes	YES!	27
I have very good timing when I tell jokes or stories	NO!	no	?	yes	YES!	28
Often I use *different voices* to create a dramatic effect.	NO!	no	?	yes	YES!	29
I use a lot of colorful words.	NO!	no	?	yes	YES!	30
I often use a *pause* to create a dramatic effect.	NO!	no	?	yes	YES!	31
I provide other people with a lot of feedback by my laughter.	NO!	no	?	yes	YES!	32
I often exaggerate for emphasis.	NO!	no	?	yes	YES!	33
Sometimes I shade or tone my voice to create a dramatic effect.	NO!	no	?	yes	YES!	34
Frequently I deliberately act silly.	NO!	no	?	yes	YES!	35
Often I am sarcastic.	NO!	no	?	yes	YES!	36
I often plan the stories or topics I am going to talk about with people.	NO!	no	?	yes	YES!	37
My laughter is loud.	NO!	no	?	yes	YES!	38
Often I deliberately try to create specific emotional feelings when I communicate.	NO!	no	?	yes	YES!	39
I am very good at responding to an insult when I need to.	NO!	no	?	yes	YES!	40
I like to report unusual news events to people.	NO!	no	?	yes	YES!	41

I am quite good at acting when I want to.	NO!	no	?	yes	YES!	42
I often use my laughter to get the other person to keep talking.	NO!	no	?	yes	YES!	43
I know how to catch the imagination of others.	NO!	no	?	yes	YES!	44
Often I deliberately use my laughter to create a dramatic effect.	NO!	no	?	yes	YES!	45
I like saying things in such a way that people see multiple meanings in my communication.	NO!	no	?	yes	YES!	46
I have several *different kinds of laughter* that I use to create a dramatic effect.	NO!	no	?	yes	YES!	47
When I talk to people I know how to catch their attention.	NO!	no	?	yes	YES!	48
I get excited easily.	NO!	no	?	yes	YES!	49
I know how to get people to feel very sympathetic for others.	NO!	no	?	yes	YES!	50
I know how to tell a joke.	NO!	no	?	yes	YES!	51
I often fantasize to others.	NO!	no	?	yes	YES!	52
I have a set of good stories which I use to create a dramatic effect.	NO!	no	?	yes	YES!	53
I am very good at manipulating the mood of other people by the way I say things.	NO!	no	?	yes	YES!	54
I can always think of a story to tell people.	NO!	no	?	yes	YES!	55
I often use my laughter to indicate that I have negative feelings about what is said.	NO!	no	?	yes	YES!	56
Frequently I tell people my dreams.	NO!	no	?	yes	YES!	57
I know how to get other people fantasizing.	NO!	no	?	yes	YES!	58
I can catch a person up in my stories.	NO!	no	?	yes	YES!	59
I like to emotionally color what I am saying.	NO!	no	?	yes	YES!	60
I am quite an outgoing person.	NO!	no	?	yes	YES!	61
I like to get people laughing.	NO!	no	?	yes	YES!	62
I use a lot of energy communicating.	NO!	no	?	yes	YES!	63

I go to excess to maintain attention.   NO!   no   ?   yes   YES!   64

Out of a random group of seven people, including myself, I probably am more *dramatic* in a general, one-to-one situation than (circle one)

All of them	5 of them	4 of them	3 of them	2 of them	1 of them	None of them	
							65

Your dramatic style probably is affected by the situation in which you communicate. For the following situations, please indicate the amount of dramatizing you are likely to do.

With a close friend	*A little*	1	2	3	4	5	6	7	*A lot*	66
With a large group of strangers	*A little*	1	2	3	4	5	6	7	*A lot*	67
With a superior	*A little*	1	2	3	4	5	6	7	*A lot*	68
With a small group of friends	*A little*	1	2	3	4	5	6	7	*A lot*	69
With a stranger	*A little*	1	2	3	4	5	6	7	*A lot*	70

Are you a good communicator in general?   NO!   no   ?   yes   YES!   71

The following section contains a checklist of attributes which may describe your general *nonverbal* behavior. For each of the attributes, circle the position which best describes the particular behavior. Answer all questions. Assume that the communication is a general one-to-one situation.

YOUR EYE BEHAVIOR   72

	1	2	3	4	5	
Tends to be Dramatic	Above Average	Slightly Above Average	Average	Slightly Below Average	Below Average	**Tends to be Not Dramatic**

YOUR FACIAL BEHAVIOR   73

	1	2	3	4	5	
Tends to be Dramatic	Above Average	Slightly Above Average	Average	Slightly Below Average	Below Average	**Tends to be Not Dramatic**

YOUR VERBAL BEHAVIOR   74

	1	2	3	4	5	
Tends to be Dramatic	Above Average	Slightly Above Average	Average	Slightly Below Average	Below Average	**Tends to be Not Dramatic**

YOUR POSTURE   75

	1	2	3	4	5	
Tends to be	Above	Slightly	Average	Slightly	Below	**Tends to be**
Dramatic	Average	Above		Below	Average	**Not Dramatic**
		Average		Average		

YOUR OVERALL BEHAVIOR   76

	1	2	3	4	5	
Tends to be	Above	Slightly	Average	Slightly	Below	**Tends to be**
Dramatic	Average	Above		Below	Average	**Not Dramatic**
		Average		Average		

KEY TO THE DRAMATIC STYLE MEASURE

1. Ignore items 1 and 2. They are fillers.

2. It is advisable to convert all scores to z scores.

3. A total dramatic score can be created by summing the z score values from item 3 to item 64 and dividing by 62.

4. Use item 65 as a dependent variable.

5. Use items 66 through 70 in a one-way analysis of variance design where the total dramatic score created in step 3 is used as cell values.

6. Use item 71 as a dependent variable.

7. Use the total dramatic score created in step 3 as a dependent variable and items 72 through 76 as predictor variables in a regression analysis.

OPEN STYLE MEASURE

(Developed by Robert Norton and Barbara Montgomery)

An open style signals that what someone is communicating reflects the person's true feelings and beliefs. It consists of both verbal and nonverbal clues. People exhibit many different kinds of open style. No one style is better than the others.

Of course, the way you show your style varies greatly. The various *open styles* are difficult to identify. The statements below represent different components of open styles. Mnay of the items are similar but get at slightly different aspects. Please read each item carefully and try to answer it is as honestly as possible.

Use the following guide for the first set of items:

YES = *very strong agreement* with the item
yes = strong agreement with the item
? = neither agreement nor disagreement with the item
no = strong disagreement with the item
NO = *very strong disagreement* with the item

1. lau :gh easily.	NO	no	?	yes	YES
2. I get along with all kinds of people.	NO	no	?	yes	YES
3. I openly show my disagreement with people.	NO	no	?	yes	YES
4. When I strongly feel an emotion, I show it.	NO	no	?	yes	YES
5. People always seem to know my moods from my nonverbal behavior.	NO	no	?	yes	YES
6. People can easily read my emotional state from my facial expressions.	NO	no	?	yes	YES
7. I send a lot of nonverbal signals to show that I am an open communicator.	NO	no	?	yes	YES
8. I can talk about any intimate subject about myself with most people.	NO	no	?	yes	YES
9. My facial expressions reflect my concern for other people.	NO	no	?	yes	YES
10. I tell people when I really do not like them.	NO	no	?	yes	YES
11. When I disagree with a person in authority, I express my disagreement.	NO	no	?	yes	YES
12. I have no trouble expressing strong positive feelings to people.	NO	no	?	yes	YES
13. I have told people that they can talk to me about their personal problems.	NO	no	?	yes	YES
14. I usually signal to people that they can openly communicate with me.	NO	no	?	yes	YES

15. I have no trouble expressing strong
negative feelings to people. NO no ? yes YES

16. I readily reveal personal things
about myself. NO no ? yes YES

17. I am an *extremely* open communicator. NO no ? yes YES

18. Usually I do not tell people very
much about myself until I get to
know them *quite* well. NO no ? yes YES

19. As a rule, I *openly* express my
feelings or emotions. NO no ? yes YES

20. I am a good communicator in
general. NO no ? yes YES

Topics also affect your openness. How open are you—that is, letting people know the "real" you—in your discussion of each of the following topics?

Your physical health	*Not open*	1	2	3	4	5	*Very open*
Your religious beliefs	*Not open*	1	2	3	4	5	*Very open*
Your attitudes toward stealing or cheating	*Not open*	1	2	3	4	5	*Very open*
Your body	*Not open*	1	2	3	4	5	*Very open*
Your attitudes about death and life after death	*Not open*	1	2	3	4	5	*Very open*
Your sexual behavior	*Not open*	1	2	3	4	5	*Very open*
Your failures	*Not open*	1	2	3	4	5	*Very open*
Your extreme negative behaviors	*Not open*	1	2	3	4	5	*Very open*
Your personal mental health	*Not open*	1	2	3	4	5	*Very open*
Your fears	*Not open*	1	2	3	4	5	*Very open*

Your openness probably is affected by the situation in which you communicate. For the following situations, please indicate the amount of openness you would show.

With a close friend of the same sex	*A little*	1	2	3	4	5	*A lot*
With a stranger	*A little*	1	2	3	4	5	*A lot*
With somebody in authority	*A little*	1	2	3	4	5	*A lot*
With a close friend of the opposite sex	*A little*	1	2	3	4	5	*A lot*

Out of the random group of seven people, I probably would have a more open style of communicating than (circle one)

All of them	6 of them	5 of them	4 of them	3 of them	2 of them	1 of them	None of them

Out of a random group of seven people, I probably would be willing to disclose personally private information more readily than (circle one)

All of them	6 of them	5 of them	4 of them	3 of them	2 of them	1 of them	None of them

---

This section contains a list of attributes which may describe your general *nonverbal* behavior relating to an open style of communicating. For each attribute, circle the position which best describes your particular behavior. Answer all questions. Assume that the communication is a general one-to-one situation.

Your eye behavior	*Tends to not signal openness*	1	2	3	4	5	*Tends to signal openness*
Your facial behavior	*Tends to not signal openness*	1	2	3	4	5	*Tends to signal openness*
Your gestures	*Tends to not signal openness*	1	2	3	4	5	*Tends to signal openness*
Your posture	*Tends to not signal openness*	1	2	3	4	5	*Tends to signal openness*
Your vocal cues	*Tends to not signal openness*	1	2	3	4	5	*Tends to signal openness*
Your interpersonal space with others	*Tends to not signal openness*	1	2	3	4	5	*Tends to signal openness*
Your general non-verbal behavior	*Tends to not signal openness*	1	2	3	4	5	*Tends to signal openness*

One of the most difficult things about defining open styles is that a person can signal openness but, in fact, not be a disclosing person. Of the four combinations at the right, which combination best characterizes your behavior? (circle one box)

I signal openness and amd a high discloser.	I do not signal openness but am a high discloser.
I signal openness, but am not a high discloser	I do not signal openess and am not a high discloser.

ATTENTIVE STYLE MEASURE

An attentive style consists both verbal and nonverbal clues. People exhibit many different kinds of attentive style. No one style is better than the others.

Of course, the way you show your style varies greatly. The various attentive styles are difficult to identify. The statements below represent different components of attentive styles. Many of the items are similar but get at slightly different aspects. Please read each item carefully and try to answer it as honestly as possible.

Use the following guide for the set of items:

YES = very strong agreement with the item
yes = strong agreement with the item
  ? = neither agreement nor disagreement with the item
no = strong disagreement with the item
NO = very strong disagreement with the item

---

1. I have a habit of encouraging the other person to continue talking by frequently smiling during the conversation.   YES   yes ? no NO

2. I have a habit of encouraging the other person to continue talking by frequently nodding my head during the conversation.   YES   yes ? no NO

3. Usually, I deliberately react in such a way that people know that I am listening to them.   YES   yes ? no NO

4. I am very good at knowing the exact feelings of other people.   YES   yes ? no NO

5. Usually I can read another person "like a book."   YES   yes ? no NO

6. When I communicate in a general one-to-one situation, I always am a very careful listener.   YES   yes ? no NO

7. I am an extremely attentive communicator.   YES   yes ? no NO

8. I really like to listen very carefully to people.   YES   yes ? no NO

9. When I communicate in a general one-to-one situation, I always am very sensitive.   YES   yes ? no NO

REFERENCES

Alberti, R., & Emmons, M. *Your perfect right.* San Luis Obispo, CA: Impact, 1974.

Allen, K., Hart, B., Buell, J., Harris, F., & Wolf, M. Effects of social reinforcement on isolated behavior of a nursery school child. *Child Development,* 1964, *35,* 511.

Altman, I., & Taylor, D. *Social penetration: The development of interpersonal relationships.* New York: Holt, Rinehart & Winston, 1973.

Andrews, F., Morgan, J., Sonquist, J., & Klem, L. *Multiple classification analysis: A report on a computer program.* Ann Arbor: Institute for Social Research, University of Michigan, 1973.

Argyle, M., & Dean, J. Eye contact, distance and affiliation. *Sociometry,* 1965, *28,* 289-304.

Ausubel, D. How reversible are cognitive and motivational effects of cultural deprivation? Implications for teaching the culturally deprived child. *Urban Education,* 1964, *1,* 16-38.

Baken, P. (Ed.). *Attention: An enduring problem in psychology.* Princeton, NJ; Van Nostrand, 1966.

Bales, R. *Interaction process analysis: A method for the study of small groups.* Reading, MA: Addison-Wesley, 1950.

Bales, R. Talk status and likeability as a function of talking and listening in decision-making groups. In L. White (Ed.), *The state of the social sciences.* Chicago: University of Chicago Press, 1956.

Bales, R. *Personality and interpersonal behavior.* New York: Holt, Rinehart & Winston, 1970.

Bales, R., & Hare, P. Diagnostic use of the Interaction Profile. *Journal of Social Psychology,* 1965, *74,* 239-258.

Bandler, R., & Grinder, J. *Patterns of the hypnotic techniques of Milton H. Erickson, M.D.* (Vol. 1). Cupertino, CA: Meta, 1975. (a)

Bandler, R., & Grinder, J. *The structure of magic, I: A book about language and therapy.* Palo Alto, CA: Science and Behavior, 1975. (b)

Bateson, G. *Steps to an ecology of mind.* New York: Ballantine, 1972. (a)

Bateson, G. A theory of play and fantasy. In G. Bateson, *Steps to an ecology of mind.* New York: Ballantine, 1972. (b)

Bauby, C. *Between consenting adults: Dialogue for intimate living.* New York: Macmillan, 1974.

Bayes, M. Behavioral cues of interpersonal warmth. *Journal of Consulting and Clinical Psychology,* 1972, *39,* 333-339.

Becker, J. F., & Munz, D. C. Extraversion and reciprocation of interview disclosures. *Journal of Consulting and Clinical Psychology,* 1975, *43,* 593.

Berger, C. R., & Calabrese, R. J. Some explorations in initial interaction and beyond: Toward a development theory of interpersonal communication. *Human Communication Research,* 1975, *1,* 99-112.

Bloom, L., & Coburn, K. *Assertive women.* New York: Delacorte, 1975.

Bormann, E. *Discussion and group methods: Theory and practice.* New York: Harper & Row, 1975.

Breed, G., Christiansen, E., & Larson, D. Effect of a lecturer's gaze direction upon teaching effectiveness. *Catalog of Selected Documents in Psychology,* 1972, *2,* 115.

Brown, G. *Laws of form.* New York: Bantam, 1973.

Brown, R. *Social psychology.* New York: Macmillan, 1965.

Buber, M. Distance and relation. *Psychiatry,* 1957, *20,* 101-102.

Bundza, K. A., & Simonson, N. R. Therapist self-disclosure: Its effect on impressions of therapist and willingness to disclose. *Psychotherapy: Theory, Research and Practice,* 1973, *10,* 215-217.

Bushard, B. Methodology of the study. In K. Artis (Ed.), *The symptom as communication in schizophrenia.* New York: Grune & Stratton, 1959.

Byrne, D. Attitudes and attraction. In L. Berkowitz (Ed.), *Advances in experimental social psychology.* New York: Academic, 1969. (a)

Byrne, D. Similarity and awareness of similarity of personality characteristics as determinants of attraction. *Journal of Experimental Research in Personality,* 1969, *3,* 179-186. (b)

Byrne, D. *The attraction paradigm.* New York: Academic, 1971.

Byrne, D., Clore, G., & Worchel, P. The effect of economic similarity on interpersonal attraction. *Journal of Personality and Social Psychology,* 1966, *14,* 220-224.

Byrne, D., Ervin, C., & Lambert, J. Continuity between the experimental study of attraction and real-life computer dating. *Journal of Personality and Social Psychology,* 1970, *16,* 157-165.

Byrne, D., & Griffitt, W. Interpersonal attraction. *Annual Review of Psychology,* 1973, *11,* 317-336.

Byrne, D., London, O., & Reeves, K. The effects of physical attractiveness, sex, and attitude similarity on interpersonal attraction. *Journal of Personality,* 1968, *36,* 259-271.

Carkhuff, R. R. Counseling research theory and practice: 1965. *Journal of Counseling Psychology,* 1966, *13,* 467-480.

Carson, R. C. *Interaction concepts of personality.* Chicago: Aldine, 1969.

Cash, D., & Soloway, D. Self-disclosure correlates of physical attractiveness: An exploratory study. *Psychological Reports,* 1975, *36,* 579-586.

Cattell, R., & Scheier, I. The nature of anxiety: A review of thirteen multivariate analyses comprising 814 variables. *Psychological Reports,* 1958, *4,* 351-388.

Centra, J. Effectiveness of student feedback in modifying college instruction. *Journal of Educational Psychology,* 1973, *65,* 395-401.

Chaikin, A., & Derlega, V. Variables affecting the appropriateness of self-disclosure. *Journal of Consulting and Clinical Psychology,* 1974, *42,* 558-593.

Chaikin, A., Derlega, V., & Shaw, J. Neuroticism and disclosure reciprocity. *Journal of Consulting and Clinical Psychology,* 1975, *43,* 13-19.

Chapman, A., & Foot, H. (Eds.). *Humour and laughter: Theory, research and applications.* New York: John Wiley, 1976.

Chelune, G. Sex differences, repression-sensitization, and self-disclosure: A behavioral look. *Psychology,* 1977, *40,* 667-670.

Clark, H., & Marshall, C. Definite reference and mutual knowledge. In A. Joshi, I. Sag, & B. Webber (Eds.), *Elements of discourse understanding.* Cambridge: Cambridge University Press, 1981.

Cook, J. Silence in psychotherapy. *Journal of Counseling Psychology,* 1964, *11,* 42-46.

Cooley, W., & Lohnes, P. *Multivariate data analysis.* New York: John Wiley, 1971.

Coppernoll, P., & Davies, D. Goal-oriented evaluation of teaching methods by medical students and faculty. *Journal of Medical Education*, 1974, *49*, 424-430.

Coser, R. Some social functions of laughter. *Human Relations*, 1959, *12*, 171-182.

Costin, F., Greenough, W., & Menges, T. Student ratings of college teaching: Reliability, validity, and usefulness. *Review of Educational Research*, 1971, *41*, 511-535.

Culbert, S. *Interpersonal process of self-disclosure: It takes two to see one.* Washington, DC: Institute for Applied Behavioral Sciences, 1967.

Darwin, C. *The expression of emotions in man and animals.* London: Murray, 1872.

d'Augelli, A. Interpersonal skill training for dating couples: An evaluation of an educational mental health service. *Journal of Counseling Psychology*, 1975, *21*, 385-389.

Davis, J. Effects of communication about interpersonal process on the evolution of self-disclosure in dyads. *Journal of Personality and Social Psychology*, 1977, *35*, 31-37.

Davis, J., & Skinner, A. Reciprocity of self-disclosure in interviews: Modeling or social exchange. *Journal of Experimental Social Psychology*, 1974, *29*, 779-784.

Deaux, K. Sex differences in social behavior. In T. Blass (Ed.), *Personality variables in social behavior.* Hillsdale, NJ: Erlbaum, 1977.

Deethardt, J., & McLaughlin, M. *A pilot study of communicator types and styles.* Paper presented at the meeting of the International Communication Association, Berlin, Germany, 1976.

Deher, D., & Banikotes, A. Measurement of self-disclosure: Note on format and the deviant. *Journal of Experimental Psychology*, 1976, *9*, 277-284.

De Rivera, J. *A structural theory of the emotions.* New York: International Universities Press, 1977.

Derlega, V., Harris, M., & Chaiken, A. Self-disclosure reciprocity, liking and the deviant. *Journal of Experimental Social Psychology*, 1973, *9*, 277-284.

Derogatis, L., Lipman, R., Rickels, K., Uhlenhuth, E., & Covi, L. *Behavioral Science*, 1974, 1-15.

de Unamuno y Jugo, M. *Abel Sanchez.* Reprinted in L. Hamalian & E. Volpe (Eds.), *Ten modern short novels.* New York: Putnam, 1958.

Deutsch, J., & Deutsch, D. Attention: Some theoretical considerations. *Psychological Review*, 1963, *70*, 8-90.

Dion, K., & Berscheid, E. Physical attractiveness and peer perception among children. *Sociometry*, 1974, *37*, 1-12.

Dion, K., & Walster, E. What is beautiful is good. *Journal of Personality and Social Psychology*, 1972, *24*, 285-290.

Dittman, A. The relationship between body movements and moods in interviews. *Journal of Consulting Psychology*, 1962, *26*, 480.

Dittman, A., & Llewellyn, L. Relationship between vocalizations and head nods as listener responses. *Journal of Personality and Social Psychology*, 1968, *9*, 79-84.

Draper, N., & Smith, H. *Applied regression analysis.* New York: John Wiley, 1966.

Duncan, S. Some signals and rules for taking turns in conversations. *Journal of Personality and Social Psychology*, 1972, *23*, 283-292.

Duncan, S. On the structure of speaker-auditor interaction during speaking turns. *Language in Society*, 1974, *2*, 161-180.

Ehrentheil, O., Chase, S., & Hyde, M. Revealing and body display. *Archives of General Psychiatry*, 1973, *29*, 363-367.

Eisler, R., Miller, P., & Hersen, M. Components of assertive behavior. *Journal of Clinical Psychology*, 1973, *29*, 295-299.

Ekman, P., & Friesen, W. *Unmasking the face: A guide to recognizing emotions from facial expressions.* Englewood Cliffs, NJ: Prentice-Hall, 1976.

Elizur, D. *Adapting to innovation.* Jerusalem: Jerusalem Academic Press, 1970.

Ellsworth, P., & Carlsmith, J. Effects of eye contact and verbal content on affective responses to a dyadic interaction. *Journal of Personality and Social Psychology,* 1968, *3,* 105-120.

Ellsworth, P., Carlsmith, J., & Henson, A. The stare as a stimulus to flight in human subjects: A series of field experiments. *Journal of Personality and Social Psychology,* 1972, *21,* 302-311.

Ellison, C., & Firestone, I. Development of interpersonal trust as a function of self-esteem, target status, and target style. *Journal of Personality and Social Psychology,* 1974, *29,* 655-663.

Emener, W., & Rye, D. Counselor education applied to industry. *Counselor Education and Supervision,* 1975, *15,* 72-76.

Endler, N., & Okada, M. *A S-R inventory of general trait anxiousness* (Department of Psychology Report 1). Toronto: York University, 1974.

Endler, N., & Okada, M. A multidimensional measure of trait anxiety: The S-R inventory of general trait anxiousness. *Journal of Consulting and Clinical Psychology,* 1975, *43,* 319-329.

Erickson, M., & Rossi, E. *Experiencing hypnosis: Therapeutic approaches to altered states.* New York: Irvington, 1981.

Exline, R. The glances of power and preference. In J. Cole (Ed.), *Nebraska Symposium on Motivation* (Vol. 19). Lincoln: University of Nebraska Press, 1971.

Farrelly, F., & Brandsma, J. *Provocative therapy.* Fort Collins, CO: Shields, 1974.

Feffer, M., & Suchotliff, L. Decentering implications of social interactions. *Journal of Personality and Social Psychology,* 1966, *4,* 415-422.

Fensterheim, H., & Baer, J. *Don't say yes when you want to say no! How assertiveness training can change your life.* New York: David McKay, 1975.

Festinger, L. *A theory of cognitive dissonance.* Evanston, IL: Row, Peterson, 1957.

Fiedler, L. *Freaks, myths and images of the secret self.* New York: Simon & Schuster, 1978.

Finkbeinder, C., Lathrop, Jr., & Schuerger, J. Course and instructor evaluation: Some dimensions of a questionnaire. *Journal of Educational Psychology,* 1973, *64,* 159-163.

Fisher, M., & Apostal, R. Selected vocal cues and counselor's perceptions of genuineness, self-disclosure, and anxiety. *Journal of Counseling Psychology,* 1975, *22,* 92-96.

Flanders, N. Basic teaching skills derived from a model of speaking and listening. *Journal of Teacher Education,* 1973, *24,* 24-37.

Freud, S. *Jokes and their relation to the unconscious.* Toronto: Hogarth, 1905.

Freud, S. *New introductory lectures on psycho-analysis* (Vol. 22). New York: Norton, 1933.

Freud, S. *The psychopathology of everyday life* (Vol. 6; A. Tyson, trans.). New York: Norton, 1965.

Frey, P. Student ratings of teaching: Validity of several rating factors. *Science,* 1973, *182,* 83-85.

Fromme, D., & Beam, D. Dominance and sex differences in nonverbal responses to differential eye contact. *Journal of Research in Personality,* 1974, *8,* 76-87.

Gage, N. *Teacher effectiveness and teacher education: The search for a scientific basis.* Palo Alto, CA: Pacific, 1972.

Garcia Marquez, G. *One hundred years of solitude.* New York: Harper & Row, 1971.

Gessner, P. Evaluation of instruction. *Science,* 1973, *180,* 566-570.

Giffin, K. The contribution of studies of source credibility to a theory of interpersonal trust in the communication process. *Psychological Bulletin,* 1967, *68,* 102-120.

Giffin, K., & Patton, B. *Interpersonal communication: Basic text and readings.* New York: Harper & Row, 1974.

Gilbert, S. Empirical and theoretical extensions of self-disclosure. In G.R. Miller (Ed.), *Explorations in interpersonal communication.* Beverly Hills, CA: Sage, 1976.

Giles, H., & Powesland, P. *Speech style and social evaluation.* New York: Academic, 1975.

Glassi, J., Glassi, M., & Bastien, S. The college self-expression scale: A measure of assertiveness. *Behavior Therapy,* 1974, *5,* 165-171.

Goffman, E. *Encounters: Two studies in the sociology of interaction.* Indianapolis: Bobbs-Merrill, 1961.

Goffman, E. *Frame analysis: An essay on the organization of experience.* Cambridge, MA: Harvard University Press, 1974.

Goldstein, A., Martens, J., Hubben, J., Van Belle, H., Shaaf, W., Wiersman, H., & Goedhart, A. The use of modeling to increase independent behaviour. *Behaviour Research and Therapy,* 1973, *11,* 31-42.

Goodchilds, J., & Smith, E. The wit and his group. *Human Relations,* 1964, *17,* 23-32.

Gordon, D. *Therapeutic metaphors.* Cupertino, CA: Meta, 1978.

Gordon, G. *The language of communication.* New York: Hastings House, 1970.

Goslin, D. Accuracy of self perception and social acceptance. *Sociometry,* 1962, *25,* 283-290.

Gratch, M. *Twenty-five years of social research in Israel: A review of the work of the Israel Institute of Applied Social Research.* Jerusalem: Jerusalem Academic Press, 1973.

Greenwood, G., Bridges, C., Ware, W., & McLean, J. Student evaluation of college teaching behaviors instrument: A factor analysis. *Journal of Higher Education,* 1973, *44,* 596-604.

Grice, H. Logic and conversation. In P. Cole & J. Morgan (Eds.), *Syntax and semantics: Speech acts* (Vol. 3). New York: Academic, 1975.

Griffitt, W. Interpersonal attraction as a function of self-concept and personality similarity-dissimilarity. *Journal of Personality and Social Psychology,* 1966, *4,* 581-584.

Griffitt, W. Personality similarity and self-concept as determinants of interpersonal attraction. *Journal of Social Psychology,* 1969, *78,* 137-146.

Grinder, J., & Bandler, R. *The structure of magic, II: A book about communication and change.* Palo Alto, CA: Science and Behavior, 1976.

Gullahorn, J. Distance and friendship as factors in the gross interaction matrix. *Sociometry,* 1952, *15,* 123-134.

Guttman, L. A general nonmetric technique for finding the smallest coordinate space for a configuration of points. *Psychometrika,* 1968, *33,* 369-506.

Guttman, L. Facet theory, smallest space analysis, and factor analysis. *Conceptual Motor Skills,* 1982, *54,* 487-493.

Haase, R., & Tepper, D. Nonverbal components of empathic communication. *Journal of Counseling Psychology,* 1972, *19,* 417-424.

Hackney, H. Facial gestures and subject expression of feelings. *Journal of Counseling Psychology,* 1974, *21,* 173-178.

Haley, J. *Uncommon therapy: The psychiatric techniques of Milton H. Erickson, M.D.* New York: Norton, 1973.

Haley, J. *Problem-solving therapy.* San Francisco: Jossey-Bass, 1978.

Hayes, D., & Meltzer, L. Interpersonal judgments based on talkativeness: Fact or artifact? *Sociometry,* 1972, *35,* 338-561.

Heilbrun, A. A history of self-disclosure in females and early defection from psychotherapy. *Journal of Counseling Psychology,* 1973, *20,* 250-257.

Hersen, M., Eisler, R., Miller, P., Johnson, M., & Pinkston, S. Effects of practice instructions and modeling on components of assertive behavior. *Behaviour Research and Therapy,* 1973, *11,* 443-451.

Hind, R., Dornbusch, S., & Scott, W. A theory of evaluation applied to a university faculty. *Sociology of Education,* 1974, *47,* 114-128.

Hogan, R. Empathy: A conceptual and psychometric analysis. *Counseling Psychologist,* 1975, *5,* 14-18.

Holstein, C., Goldstein, J., & Bem, D. The importance of expressive behaviors, involvement, sex, and need-approval in inducing liking. *Journal of Experimental Psychology,* 1971, *7,* 534-544.

Huber, E. *Evolution of facial musculature and facial expression.* Baltimore: Johns Hopkins University Press, 1931.

Iannotti, R. The nature and measurement of empathy in children. *Counseling Psychologist,* 1975, *5,* 21-25.

Isaacson, R., McKeachie, W., Milholland, J., Lin, Y., Hofeller, M., Baerwaldt, J., & Zinn, K. Dimensions of student evaluations of teaching. *Journal of Educational Psychology,* 1964, *55,* 344-351.

Ivey, A. *Microcounseling: Innovations in interviewing training.* Springfield, IL: Charles C Thomas, 1971.

Izard, C. Personality similarity and friendship. *Journal of Abnormal Psychology,* 1961, *61,* 47-51.

Jakubowski-Spector, P. Facilitating the growth of women through assertive training. *Counseling Psychologist,* 1973, *4,* 75-86.

Jamison, R., & Johnson, J. Empathy and therapeutic orientation in paid and volunteer crisis phone workers, professional therapists, and undergraduate college students. *Journal of Community Psychology,* 1975, *3,* 269-274.

Janov, A. *The primal scream.* New York: Dell, 1970.

Johnson, D., & Noonan, P. Effects of acceptance and reciprocation of self-disclosures on the development of trust. *Journal of Counseling Psychology,* 1973, *19,* 411-416.

Jourard, S. *Self-disclosure: An experimental analysis of the transparent self.* New York: John Wiley, 1971.

Jourard, S., & Jaffee, P. Influence of an interviewer's disclosure on the self-disclosing behavior of interviewers. *Journal of Counseling Psychology,* 1970, *17,* 252-257.

Jourard, S., & Lasakow, P. Some factors in self-disclosure. *Journal of Abnormal and Social Psychology,* 1958, *50,* 91-98.

Kauffman, J., Hallahan, D., Payne, J., & Ball, D. Teaching/learning: Quantitative and functional analysis of educational performance: *Journal of Special Education,* 1973, *7,* 261-268.

Kazdin, A. Effects of covert modeling and model reinforcement on assertive behavior. *Abnormal Psychology,* 1974, *83,* 246-252.

Kelly, B. Concerned confrontation: The art of counseling. *Southern Journal of Educational Research,* 1975, *9,* 110-122.

Kendon, A. Some functions of gaze direction in social interaction. *Acta Psychologica,* 1967, *26,* 22-63.

Kennedy, J., & Zimmer, J. A comparison of the reinforcing value of five stimuli conditions and the production of self-reference statements in a quasi-counseling situation. *Journal of Counseling Psychology*, 1968, *15*, 357-362.

Kent, G., Davis, J., & Shapiro, D. Resources required in the construction and reconstruction of conversations. *Journal of Personality and Social Psychology*, 1978, *36*, 13-22.

Kleinke, C. Interpersonal attraction as it relates to gaze and distance between people. *Representative Research in Social Psychology*, 1972, *3*, 105-120.

Kleinke, C., Bustos, A., Meeker, F., & Staneski, R. Effects of self-attributed and other-attributed gaze on interpersonal evaluations between males and females. *Journal of Experimental Social Psychology*, 1973, *9*, 154-163.

Kleinke, C., Staneski, R., & Berger, D. Evaluation of an interviewer as a function of interviewer gaze, reinforcement of subject gaze, and interviewer attractiveness. *Journal of Personality and Social Psychology*, 1975, *31*, 115-122.

Knapp, M., Hart, R., & Dennis, H. An exploration of deception as a communication. *Human Communication Research*, 1974, *1*, 15-29.

Knott, P., & Drost, B. A measure of interpersonal dominance. *Behavioral Research Methods and Instruments*, 1965, *1*, 139-140.

Kogan, N., & Wallack, A. Risk-taking as a function of the situation, the person, and the group. In G. Mandler, P. Mussen, N. Kogan, & M. Wallach (Eds.), *New directions in psychology III*. New York: Holt, Rinehart & Winston, 1967.

Kohen, J. The development of reciprocal self-disclosure in opposite sex interaction. *Journal of Counseling Psychology*, 1975, *22*, 404-410.

Krauss, R., & Bricker, P. Effects of transmission delay and access delay on the efficiency of communication. *Journal of the Acoustical Society of America*, 1967, *41*, 286-292.

Krauss, R., Garlock, C., Bricker, P., & McMahon, L. The role of audible and visible back-channel responses in interpersonal communication. *Journal of Personality and Social Psychology*, 1977, *35*, 523-529.

Krauss, R., & Glucksberg, S. Social and nonsocial speech. *Scientific American*, 1977, *35*, 523-529.

Krauss, R., & Weinheimer, S. Concurrent feedback, confirmation, and the encoding of referents in verbal interaction. *Journal of Personality and Social Psychology*, 1966, *4*, 342-346.

Kraut, R., Lewis, S., & Swezey, L. Listener responsiveness and the coordination of conversation. *Journal of Personality and Social Psychology*, 1982, *43*, 718-731.

L'Abate, L. Intimacy is sharing hurt feelings: A reply to David Mace. *Journal of Marriage and Family Counseling*, 1978, *3*, 13-16.

Lalljee, M., & Cook, M. Uncertainty in the first encounters. *Journal of Personality and Social Psychology*, 1973, *26*, 137-141.

Leary, T. *Interpersonal diagnosis of personality*. New York: Ronald, 1957.

Leathers, D. The information potential of the nonverbal and verbal components of feedback responses. *Southern Speech Communication Journal*, 1979, *44*, 331-354.

Leginski, W., & Izzett, R. Linguistic style as indices of interpersonal distance. *Journal of Social Psychology*, 1973, *91*, 291-304.

Levinger, G., & Senn, D. Disclosure of feelings in marriage. *Merrill-Palmer Quarterly*, 1967, *13*, 237-249.

Levy, S. *Political involvement and attitude* (Pub. SL/550/E). Jerusalem: Israel Institute of Applied Social Research, 1975.

Lieberman, M., Yalom, I., & Miles, M. *Encounter groups: First facts*. New York: Basic Books, 1973.

Lingoes, J. *The Guttman-Lingoes nonmetric program series*. Ann Arbor, MI: Mathesis, 1973.

Lingoes, J., Guttman, L., & Roskam, E. *Geometric representation of relational data*. Ann Arbor, MI: Mathesis, 1977.

Lomranz, J., & Shapira, A. Communicative patterns of self-disclosure and touching behavior. *Journal of Psychology*, 1974, *88*, 223-227.

Lonber, N. The group as a medium for change. *Psychology*, 1975, *13*, 30-32.

Lore, R., & Flannelly, K. Rat societies. *Scientific American*, 1978, *36*, 106-116.

Lorenz, K. Der Kumpan in der Umwelt des Vogels. *Journal of Ornithology*, 1935, *83*, 137-215, 289-413.

Lowe, C., & Goldstein, J. Reciprocal liking and attributions of ability: Mediating effects of perceived intent and personal involvement. *Journal of Personality and Social Psychology*, 1970, *16*, 291-297.

Lundbert, C. Person-focused joking: Pattern and function. *Human Organization*, 1969, *28*, 22-28.

MacDonald, A., Games, R., & Mink, O. Film-mediated facilitation of self-disclosure and attraction to sensitivity training. *Psychological Reports*, 1972, *30*, 847-857.

Makworth, J. *Vigilance and attention*. Middlesex, England: Penguin, 1970.

Mann, R., Gibbard, G., & Hartman, J. *Interpersonal styles and group development*. New York: John Wiley, 1967.

Marlatt, G. A comparison of vicarious and direct reinforcement control of verbal behavior in an interview setting. *Journal of Personality and Social Psychology*, 1977, *16*, 695-703.

Marsh, H., & Ware, J. Effects of expressiveness, content coverage, and incentive on multidimensional student rating scales: New interpretations of the Dr. Fox effect. *Journal of Educational Psychology*, 1982, *74*, 126-134.

Mastin, V. Teacher enthusiasm. *Journal of Educational Research*, 1963, *56*, 385-386.

McAllister, A., & Kiesler, D. Interviewee disclosure as a function of interpersonal trust, task modeling, and interviewer self-disclosure. *Journal of Consulting and Clinical Psychology*, 1975, *43*, 428.

McCall, W. *How to experiment in education*. New York: Macmillan, 1923.

McCroskey, J., Daly, J., Richmond, V., & Falcione, R. Studies of the relationship between communication apprehension and self-esteem. *Human Communication Research*, 1977, *3*, 369-373.

McDaniels, J., Yarbrough, E., Kuszmaul, C., & Giffin, K. *Openness: Personalized expression in interpersonal communication*. Paper presented at the meeting of the International Communication Association, Phoenix, 1971.

McFall, R., & Lillesand, D. Behavior rehearsal with modeling and coaching in assertion training. *Journal of Abnormal Psychology*, 1971, *77*, 313-323.

McQuitty, L. Elementary linkage analysis for isolating orthogonal and oblique types and typal relevancies. *Educational and Psychological Measurement*, 1957, *17*, 207-229.

McQuitty, L., & Clark, J. Clusters from interactive, intercolumnar correlational analysis. *Educational and Psychological Measurement*, 1968, *31*, 321-346.

Mehrabian, A. Inference of attitudes from the posture, orientation, and distance of a communicator. *Journal of Consulting and Clinical Psychology*, 1968, *32*, 296-308.

Mehrabian, A. Significance of posture and position in the communication of attitudes and status relationships. *Psychological Bulletin*, 1969, *71*, 359-372.

Meier, R., & Feldhusen, J. Another look at Dr. Fox: Effect of stated purpose for evaluation, lecturer expressiveness, and density of lecture content on student ratings. *Journal of Educational Psychology*, 1979, *71*, 339-345.

Meredith, G. Structure of student-based evaluation ratings. *Journal of Psychology*, 1975, *91*, 3-9.

Millar, F. E., & Rogers, L. E. A relational approach to interpersonal communication. In G. R. Miller (Ed.), *Explorations in interpersonal communication*. Beverly Hills, CA: Sage, 1976.

Miller, L. *Perceptual accuracy as a function of communicator style in dyads.* Unpublished doctoral dissertation, University of Michigan, 1975.

Miller, L. Dyadic perception of communicator style: Replication and confirmation *Communication Research*, 1977, *4*, 87-112.

Miller, L. Correspondence between self and other perceptions of communication dominance. *Western Journal of Speech Communication*, 1980, *44*, 120-131.

Miller, S., Corraltes, R., & Wackman, D. Recent progress in understanding and facilitating marital communication. *Family Coordinator*, 1975, *24*, 143-152.

Millinger, G. Interpersonal trust as a factor in communication. *Journal of Abnormal and Social Psychology*, 1956, *52*, 304-309.

Mims, P., Harnett, J., & Nay, R. Interpersonal attraction and help volunteering as a function of physical attractiveness. *Journal of Psychology*, 1975, *89*, 125-131.

Montgomery, B. *Reliability and validity of self, spouse, and observer assessments.* Unpublished doctoral dissertation, Purdue University, 1980.

Montgomery, B. M., & Norton, R. Sex differences and similarities in communicator style. *Communication Monographs*, 1981, *48*, 121-132.

Morgan, J., & Messenger, R. *THAID: A sequential analysis program for the analysis of nominal scale dependent variables.* Ann Arbor: Institute for Social Research, University of Michigan, 1973.

Mortensen, D. *A report on the construct of speech intensity.* Paper presented at the meeting of the Speech Communication Association, Chicago, December 1972.

Mortensen, D., & Arntson, P. The effects of predispositions toward verbal behavior on interaction patterns in dyads. *Quarterly Journal of Speech*, 1974, *61*, 421-430.

Mosteller, F., & Tukey, J. *Data analysis and regression*. Reading, MA: Addison-Wesley, 1977.

Mulaik, S. *The foundations of factor analysis.* New York: McGraw-Hill, 1972.

Naftulin, D., Ware, J., & Donnelly, F. The Dr. Fox lecture: A paradigm of educational seduction. *Journal of Medical Education*, 1973, *48*, 630-635.

Naiman, T., & Breed, G. Gaze duration as a cue for judging conversational tone. *Representative Research in Social Psychology*, 1974, *5*, 115-122.

Nel, B. The role of sensitivity in pedagogical observation and discourse. *Interpersonal Development*, 1975, *4*, 190-196.

Newcomb, T. *The acquaintance process*. New York: Holt, Rinehart & Winston, 1961.

Nichols, K., & Champness, B. Eye gaze and the GSR. *Journal of Experimental Psychology*, 1971, *7*, 623-626.

Nichols, R. *Are you listening?* New York: McGraw-Hill, 1957.

Norman, D. *Memory and attention.* New York: John Wiley, 1976.

Norton, R. Measurement of ambiguity tolerance. *Journal of Personality Assessment*, 1975, *39*, 607-613.

Norton, R. Teacher effectiveness as a function of communicator style. In B. Ruben (Ed.), *Communication yearbook 1.* New Brunswick, NJ: Transaction, 1977.

Norton, R. Foundation of a communicator style construct. *Human Communication Research,* 1978, *4,* 99-112.

Norton, R. Nonmetric multidimensional scaling in communication research: Smallest space analysis. In P. Monge & J. Cappella (Eds.), *Multivariate techniques in human communication research.* New York: Academic, 1980. (a)

Norton, R. *Style profiles of the ineffective teacher: Research directions on the communicator style variable in instruction.* Paper presented at the meeting of the speech Communication Association, New York, 1980. (b)

Norton, R., Andersen, J., & Nussbaum, J. Three investigations exploring relationships among perceived communication style, perceived teacher immediacy, teaching effectiveness, and student learning. *Communication Education,* 1981, *30,* 377-392.

Norton, R., Baker, N., Bednar, D., Salyer, R., & McGough, T. *Impressions of interpersonal dramatic style.* Paper presented at the meeting of the Speech Communication Association, Minneapolis, 1978.

Norton, R., Feldman, C., & Tafoya, D. Risk parameters across types of secrets. *Journal of Counseling Psychology,* 1974, *21,* 450-454.

Norton, R., & Holladay, S. *Dramatic behaviors of the effective teacher.* Paper presented at the meeting of the International Communication Association, Dalas, 1983.

Norton, R., & Miller, L. Dyadic perception of communicator style. *Communication Research,* 1975, *2,* 50-67.

Norton, R., & Montgomery, B.M. Style, content, and target components of openness. *Communication Research,* 1982, *9,* 399-431.

Norton, R., Moore, K., Williams, B., & Montgomery, B. *Structural analysis of types of risky self-disclosure.* Paper presented at the meeting of the Central States Speech Association, Chicago, 1978.

Norton, R., Mulligan, M., & Petronio, S. *Strategies to elicit self disclosure.* Paper presented at the meeting of the International Communication Association, Chicago, 1975.

Norton, R., Murray, E., & Arntson, P. *Communicative links to health: Dramatic style covariates of health perceptions.* Paper presented to the Health Communication Division at the meeting of the International Communication Association, Boston, 1982.

Norton, R., & Nussbaum, J. Dramatic behaviors of the effective teacher. In B. Ruben (Ed.), *Communication yearbook 4.* New Brunswick, NJ: Transaction, 1980.

Norton, R., & Pettegrew, L. Communicator style as an effect determinant of attraction. *Communication Research,* 1977, *4,* 257-282.

Norton, R., & Pettegrew, L. Attentiveness as a style variable. *Communication Monographs,* 1979, *46,* 12-27.

Norton, R., Petronio, R., & Leenhouts, T. *Units of self-disclosure: A basic problem of intimacy research.* Paper presented at the meeting of the Speech Communication Association, Houston, 1975.

Norton, R., & Robinson, D. *Communicator style in career decisions.* Paper presented at the meeting of the Speech Communication Association, New York, 1980.

Norton, R., Schroeder, A., & Webb, J. Communicator style as a predictor of effectiveness and attractiveness: A developmental study. *Michigan Speech Association Journal,* 1979, *14,* 12-27.

Norton, R., Sypher, H., & Bradey, R. *The dramatic style.* Paper presented at the meeting of the International Communication Association, Chicago, 1978.

Norton, R., Sypher, H., Clarke, C., & Bradey, R. *Dimensions of a dramatic communicator style.* Paper presented at the meeting of the Speech Communication Association, Washington, DC, 1977.

Norton, R., & Warnick, B. Evaluation of assertiveness as a communication construct. *Human Communication Research,* 1976, *1,* 62-66.

Norton, R., Wartman, M., Gaine, E., Ellis, D., & Schuster, J. *Open style differences in high risk self disclosure communication.* Paper presented at the meeting of the Speech Communication Association, San Antonio, Texas, 1980.

Null, E., & Walter, J. Values of students and their ratings of a university professor. *College Student Journal,* 1972, *6,* 46-51.

Nunnally, J. *Pschometric theory.* New York: McGraw-Hill, 1967.

O'Brien, M. *Communications and relationships in nursing.* Saint Louis: Mosby, 1974.

O'Connel, W. Creativity in humor. *Journal of Social Psychology,* 1969, *78,* 237-241.

O'Connor, G., & Alderson, J. Human relations groups for human services practitioners. *Small Group Behavior,* 1974, *5,* 495-505.

Osborn, S., & Harris, G. *Assertive training for women.* Springfield, IL: Charles C Thomas, 1975.

Overall, J., & Klett, C. *Applied multivariate analysis.* New York: McGraw-Hill, 1972.

Paisley, W. Communication theory and the arts: Confrontation and dialogue. In M. Knapp (Ed.), *Proceedings of the first Symposium on Communication Theory and the Arts.* Milwaukee: University of Wisconsin, n.d.

Pearce, G., & Sharp, M. Self-disclosing communication. *Journal of Communication,* 1973, *23,* 409-425.

Peckham, P., Glass, G., & Hopkins, K. The experimental unit in statistical analysis. *Journal of Special Education,* 1969, *3,* 337-349.

Pedersen, D. Self-disclosure, body-accessibility, and personal space. *Psychological Reports,* 1973, *33,* 975-980.

Pedersen, D., & Higbee, K. Personality correlates of self-disclosure. *Journal of Social Psychology,* 1969, *78,* 81-89.

Peiper, A. *Cerebral function in infancy and childhood.* New York: Consultants Bureau, 1963.

Perls, F., Hefferline, R., & Goodman, P. *Gestalt therapy.* New York: Dell, 1965.

Pettegrew, L. *An Investigation of communicator style in therapeutic relationships.* Unpublished doctoral dissertation, University of Michigan, 1977. (a)

Pettegrew, L. An investigation of therapeutic communicator style. In B. Ruben (Ed.), *Communication yearbook 1.* New Brunswick, NJ: Transaction, 1977. (b)

Piderit, T. *Mimik und Physiognomik.* Munich: Detmold, 1925. (Originally published in 1867.)

Regula, R. Marriage Encounter: What makes it work? *Family Coordinator,* 1975, *24,* 153-159.

Reich, W. *Character analysis.* New York: Farrar, Straus & Giroux, 1972.

Reis, H., Wheeler, L., Spiegel, N., Kernis, M., Nezlek, J., & Perri, M. Physical attractiveness in social interaction, II: Why does appearance affect social experience? *Journal of Personality and Social Psychology,* 1982, *43,* 979-996.

Reusch, J. *Disturbed communication.* New York: Norton, 1957.

Reusch, J. *Therapeutic communication.* New York: Norton, 1961.

Rico, G. College students' perception of teacher effectiveness along given postualted dimensions. *St. Louis University Research Journal,* 1971, *2,* 363-438.

Rippey, R. Student evaluations of professors: Are they of value? *Journal of Medical Education*, 1971, 22, 469-473.

Roberson, E. Teacher self-appraisal: A way to improve instruction. *Journal of Teacher Education*, 1971, 22, 469-473.

Rodin, M., & Rodin, B. Student evaluations of teachers. *Science*, 1972, 177, 1164-1166.

Roger, L. The great response style myth. *Psychological Bulletin*, 1965, 63, 129-156.

Rogers, C. *Client-centered therapy.* Boston: Houghton Mifflin, 1951.

Rogers, C. Empathic: An unappreciated way of being. *Counseling Psychologist*, 1975, 5, 2-10.

Rorer, L. The great response-style myth. *Psychological Bulletin*, 1965, 63, 129-156.

Rosen, S. *My voice will go with you: The teaching tales of Milton Erickson.* New York: Norton, 1982.

Rosenfeld, H. Instrumental affiliative functions of facial and gestural expressions. *Journal of Personality and Social Psychology*, 1966, 4, 65-72.

Rosenfeld, H. Nonverbal reciprocation of approval: An experimental analysis. *Journal of Experimental Social Psychology*, 1967, 3, 102-111.

Rosenfeld, H. Conversational control functions of nonverbal behavior. In A. Seigman & A. Feldstein (Eds), *Nonverbal behavior and communication*. Hillsdale, NJ; Erlbaum, 1978.

Rosenshine, B. Enthusiastic teaching. *School Review*, 1970, 499-514.

Ross, S. *Persuasion: Communication and interpersonal relations.* Englewood Cliffs, NJ: Prentice-Hall, 1974.

Rubin, Z. Disclosing oneself to a stranger: Reciprocity and its limits. *Journal of Experimental Social Psychology*, 1975, 11, 233-260.

Rummel, R. *Applied factor analysis.* Evanston, IL: Northwestern University Press, 1970.

Ryle, G. *The concept of mind.* New York: Academic, 1949.

Sainesbury, P. Gestural movement during psychiatric interviews. *Psychosomatic Medicine*, 1955, 17, 458-469.

Sandell, R. *Linguistic style and persuasion.* New York: Academic, 1977.

Savicki, V. Outcomes of nonreciprocal self-discosure strategies. *Journal of Personality and Social Psychology*, 1973, 23, 271-276.

Scheflen, A. Quasi-courtship behavior in psychotherapy. *Psychiatry*, 1965, 28, 245-257.

Scheidel, T. *Persuasive speaking.* Glenview, IL: Scott, Foresman, 1967.

Schereer, K., London, H., & Wolf, J. The voice of confidence: Paralinguistic cues and audience evaluation. *Journal of Research in Personality*, 1973, 7, 31-44.

Scherwitz, L., & Helmrich, R. Interactive effects of eye contact and verbal content on interpersonal attraction in dyads. *Journal of Personality and Social Psychology*, 1973, 25, 6-14.

Schutz, W. *FIRO: A three-dimensional theory of interpersonal behavior.* New York: Holt, Rinehart & Winston, 1958.

Scriven, M. The evaluation of teachers and teaching. *California Journal of Educational Research*, 1974, 25, 109-115.

Serber, M. Teaching the nonverbal components of assertive training. *Journal of Behavior Therapy and Experimental Psychiatry*, 1972, 3, 179-183.

Shantz, C. Empathy in relation to social cognitive development. *Counseling Psychologist*, 1975, 5, 18-21.

Shapiro, A., & Swenson, C. Self-disclosure as a function of self-concept and sex. *Journal of Personality Assessment*, 1977, 41, 144-149.

Shapiro, D. *Neurotic styles.* New York: Basic Books, 1965.

Shapiro, J., Krauss, H., & Truax, C. Therapeutic conditions and disclosure beyond the therapeutic encounter. *Journal of Counseling Psychology,* 1969, *16,* 290-294.

Shave, D. *The therapeutic listener.* Huntington, NY: Robert Krieger, 1974.

Shave, D. *Communication breakdown: Cause and cure.* St. Louis: Warren H. Green, 1975.

Simons, H. *Persuasion: Understanding, practice and analysis.* Reading, MA: Addison-Wesley, 1976.

Simonson, N., & Bahr, S. Self-disclosure by the professional and para-professional. *Journal of Consulting and Clinical Psychology,* 1974, *42,* 359-363.

Skinner, B. F. *Science and human behavior.* New York: Macmillan, 1953.

Smith, A. *Communication and culture: Readings in the codes of human interaction.* New York: Holt, Rinehart & Winston, 1966.

Smith, M. *When I say no I feel guilty.* New York: Bantam, 1975.

Sneath, P., & Sokal, R. *Numerical taxonomy.* San Francisco: Freeman, 1973.

Solomon, D. Teacher behavior dimensions, course characteristics, and student evaluation of teachers. *American Educational Research Journal,* 1966, *3,* 35-47.

Speilberger, C. Trait state anxiety and motor behavior. *Journal of Motor Behavior,* 1972, *3,* 265-279.

Stanley, J., & Campbell, J. *Experimental and quasi-experimental designs for research.* Chicago: Rand McNally, 1963.

Steiner, C. *Scripts people live: Transactional analysis of lifescripts.* New York: Grove, 1974.

Stephens, J. *The process of schooling: A psychological examination.* New York: Holt, Rinehart & Winston, 1967.

Stoebe, W., Inski, C., Thompson, V., & Layton, B. Effects of physical attraciveness, sex, and attitude similarity on interpersonal attraction. *Journal of Personality and Social Psychology,* 1971, *18,* 77-91.

Stohl, C. Perceptions of social attractiveness and communicator style: A developmental study of preschool children. *Communication Education,* 1981, *30,* 367-376.

Strahan, R. Situational dimension of self-reported nervousness. *Journal of Personality Assessment,* 1974, *38,* 341-352.

Sudnow, D. *The ways of the hand.* New York: Bantam, 1978.

Sullivan, H. *The interpersonal theory of psychiatry.* New York: Norton, 1953.

Sullivan, H. *Personal psychopathy.* New York: Norton, 1972.

Taylor, D., & Altman, I. Intimacy-scaled stimuli for use in studies of interpersonal relations. *Psychological Reports,* 1966, *19,* 729-730.

Thase, M., & Page, R. Modeling of self-disclosure in laboratory and nonlaboratory settings. *Journal of Counseling Psychology,* 1977, *24,* 35-40.

Thayer, S. The effect of interpersonal looking duration on dominance judgments. *Journal of Social Psychology,* 1969, *79,.* 285-286.

Thayer, S., & Schiff, W. Observer judgment of social interaction: Eye-contact and relationship inferences. *Journal of Personality and Social Psychology,* 1974, *30,* 110-114.

Thompson, W. *At the edge of history: Speculations on the transformation of culture.* New York: Harper & Row, 1971.

Truax, C., & Carkhuff, R. *Toward effective counseling and psychotherapy.* Chicago: Aldine, 1967.

Tukey, J. *Exploratory data analysis.* Reading, MA: Addison-Wesley, 1977.

Twain, M. *Roughing it.* New York: Harper & Row, 1871.

Van Zoost, B. Premarital communication skills education with university students. *Family Coordinator,* 1973, *22,* 187-191.

von Wright, G.H. *Explanation and understanding.* Ithaca, NY: Cornell University Press, 1971.

Wallen, N. *Relationships between teacher characteristics and student behavior* (Cooperation Research Project SAE OES-10-181). Washington, DC: Office of Education, 1966.

Ware, R., & Harvey, O. A cognitive determinant of impression formation. *Journal of Personality and Social Psychology,* 1967, *5,* 38-44.

Watzlawick, P. *The language of change: Elements of therapeutic communication.* New York: Basic Books, 1978.

Watzlawick, P., Beavin, J., & Jackson, D. *Pragmatics of human communication: A study of interactional patterns, pathologies, and paradoxes.* New York: Norton, 1967.

Weblin, J. Communication and schizophrenic behavior. *Family Process,* 1962, *1,* 5-14.

Weiner, M., & Mehrabian, A. *Language within language.* Englewood Cliffs, NJ: Prentice-Hall, 1968.

Wells, R. Training in facilitative skills. *Social Work,* 1975, *20,* 242-243.

West, L. Mapping the communication patterns of adolescents. *Canadian Counselor,* 1974, *8,* 54-65.

West, L., & Boutillien, R. Increasing concreteness of expression of counsellees through observation learning. *Canadian Journal of Behavioural Science,* 1972, *4,* 364-370.

Wheeless, L. A follow-up study of the relationships among trust, disclosure, and interpersonal solidarity. *Human Communication Research,* 1978, *4,* 143-157.

White, A. *Attention.* Oxford: Basil Blackwell, 1964.

Whitley, D., & Sulzer, B. Reducing disruptive behavior through consultation. *Personnel and Guidance Journal,* 1970, *48,* 836-841.

Wiggins, J. *Personality and prediction: Principles of personality assessment.* Reading, MA: Addison-Wesley, 1973.

Williams, B. Trust and self-disclosure among black college students. *Journal of Counseling Psychology,* 1974, *21,* 522-525.

Williams, E. Medium or message: Communication medium as a determinant of interpersonal evaluation. *Sociometry,* 1975, *38,* 119-130.

Williams, R., & Ware, J. An extended visit with Dr. Fox: Validity of student satisfaction with instruction ratings after repeated exposures to a lecture. *American Educational Research Journal,* 1977, *14,* 449-457.

Worthy, M., Gary, A., & Kahn, G. Self-disclosure as an exchange process. *Journal of Personality and Social Psychology,* 1969, *13,* 59-69.

Wundt, W. *Deutsche Rundschau,* 1877, *3,* 120.

Yngve, V. On getting a word in edgewise. In *Papers from the Sixth Regional Meeting, Chicago Linguistics Circle.* Chicago: Chicago Linguistics Circle, 1970.

INDEX

ABOUT THE AUTHOR

Robert Norton is an Associate Professor in the Communication Department at Purdue University. He received his B.A. in 1967 from Montana State University in English literature and his M.A. from the University of New Mexico in 1968 in communication. He received his Ph.D. in 1972 from the University of Wisconsin — Madison in communication. He has published articles in *Journal of Personality Assessment, Communication Research, Human Communication Research, Journal of Counseling Psychology, Communication Monographs, Journal of Marriage and the Family, Communication Education, Small Group Behavior, Simulation & Games,* and other journals. He has extensive interests in interpersonal, marital, and therapeutic communication.